T0196970

Balboa Press books may be ordered through booksellers or by contacting:

Balboa Press
A Division of Hay House
1663 Liberty Drive
Bloomington, IN 47403
www.balboapress.com
1 (877) 407-4847

Because of the dynamic nature of the Internet, any web addresses or links contained in this book may have changed since publication and may no longer be valid. The views expressed in this work are solely those of the author and do not necessarily reflect the views of the publisher, and the publisher hereby disclaims any responsibility for them.

The author of this book does not dispense medical advice or prescribe the use of any technique as a form of treatment for physical, emotional, or medical problems without the advice of a physician, either directly or indirectly. The intent of the author is only to offer information of a general nature to help you in your quest for emotional and spiritual well-being. In the event you use any of the information in this book for yourself, which is your constitutional right, the author and the publisher assume no responsibility for your actions.

Any people depicted in stock imagery provided by Thinkstock are models, and such images are being used for illustrative purposes only.
Certain stock imagery © Thinkstock.

Print information available on the last page.

ISBN: 978-1-5043-7127-8 (sc)
ISBN: 978-1-5043-7128-5 (hc)
ISBN: 978-1-5043-7140-7 (e)

Library of Congress Control Number: 2016920342

Balboa Press rev. date: 01/13/2017

BALBOA.
PRESS
A DIVISION OF HAY HOUSE

New Researches on the Quran

Why and how two versions of Islam entered the history of mankind

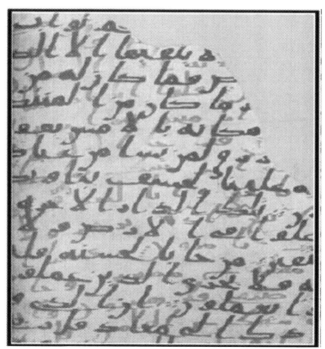

Figure 1 - Quran- In the Great Mosque of Sana'a in Yemen.
(649-715 AD. In Hijazi Script, written twice on each page)

Seyed Mostafa Azmayesh

Forwarded by Professor Peter Antes

Azmayesh, Seyed Mostafa
New Researches on the Quran:
Why and how two versions of Islam entered the history of mankind

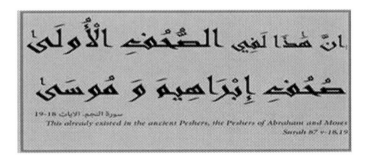

إِنَّ هَـٰذَا لَفِي الصُّحُفِ الْأُولَىٰ

صُحُفِ إِبْرَاهِيمَ وَ مُوسَىٰ

سورة النجم. الآيات 18-19
This already existed in the ancient Psalters, the Psalters of Abraham and Moses
Surah 87 v-18,19

Contents

Forward

In my opinion it is highly relevant, to make a distinction regarding the Medinensic time as adduced by Dr. Azmayesh and become aware of the fact that, two different versions of Islam evolved in the period of Medina. In fact, this period, usually, in political views is interpreted as being homogenic and is not considered as a time of internal opposition within the Muslim community. Hence, the approach of Dr Azmayesh is highly interesting and allows us to have a new understanding of the complete history of Islam from its origin until today.

How could the theses in this book help to provide an answer to Islamic extremism? From my point of view, this perspective is extremely helpful in the understanding that most of the information on Islam, in accordance with the findings of Dr. Azmayesh, is misleading and based on false interpretations of Islam made by Muslims. It will take a great amount of effort to bring this into the public observation and under discussion, as the general public debates focus largely on militant definitions. Extremism is a very attractive subject for the media, and much more interesting than the reconciling work of Dr Azmayesh. For this reason it is very important to spread these theses publicly and to discuss them as widely as possible.

Prof. Dr. theol. Dr. phil. Peter Antes, Emeritus of
Department of Theology and the Study of
Religions at the Leibniz, University of Hannover,
Germany.

Book Review

From Frankfurter Allgemeine Zeitung

What Muslim believers regard as Islam is quite a vast field. From one side, Abdullah al Muhadjir, an ideologue of Daesh, deduces from the foundations of Islam, the obligation to kill every "non-believer" as put forward in his book "The justification for killing". From the other side, the Iranian born Juristic scholar, human rights activist and Quran expert Mostafa Azmayesh explains the Quran in a spiritual manner. (Seyed Mostafa Azmayesh: "New Researches on the Quran -Why and How Two Versions of Islam Entered the History of Mankind". Mehraby Publishing House, London, Karamat, Hannover, 2016). He deduces from the Quran the task and mission to establish justice in society and empower individuals to lead a dignified life. Azmayesh was born in 1952 in Tehran and moved to Paris in 1976 for a life in exile. He is a master of the Nematollah Gonabadi Sufi order.

In his Monograph "New Researches on the Quran" he outlines how during Muhammad's life time (he died in 632) two versions of Islam had already come into existence and how they affect our life today. Azmayesh traces back the ideology of Daesh to that period when Muhammad lived in Medina (he went there in 622 AD) where two versions, a thesis and antithesis, of Islam arose. The line of argumentation of Azmayesh is this: Muhammad was one of many who had warned of the coming Last

Judgement. The revelations of the Quran intended to create a civilisation based on mutual respect and human rights for each individual.

According to the author, the residents of Mecca who joined Muhammad's community towards the end of his life formally became 'Muslims', but they kept their traditional Bedouin values and practices, which were antagonistic to the original teachings of the Quran. After Muhammad's death they took the power of the newly established community into their hands and exported their own interpretation of Islam - which is an Islam of state, power and violence - into the world.

First, Azmayesh retraces the spiritual context of the time in which Mohammed was born (570 AD) and the experiences that influenced him. In a time with little mobility in the Near East and on the Peninsula of Arabia many religious teachings could co-exist. One of the preachers and messengers in the tradition of Abraham (and thus of Monotheism) was a close relative of Muhammad named Waraqa bin Naufal, who might have been a Christian but later became one of the first adherents of the new teachings of Muhammad. The author claims that Muhammad with his help gained contact with the monastery of the Syrian city Bosra, to which the family of Muhammad was already connected a long time ago. Muhammad's family might have run a spiritual school in Mecca, which translated books into Arabic. Muhammad presumably recited many stories from the Old Testament, and from earlier civilisations, in Arabic thus making them accessible to the Arab speaking population.

Azmayesh regards the flight of Muhammad and his first adherents from their aggressive adversaries into Medina in 622 as a breach. First

Muhammad founded an Islamic civilisation there based on spiritual principles. Azmayesh stresses that the community in Medina was not a state but a social contract. His familial adversaries from Mecca meanwhile continued attacking and fighting their insubordinate son and his new teachings. Even those who, after Mecca fell to the victorious Medinasians in 628, converted to Islam, only paid lip-service: "They remained strongly attached to their tribal traditions." Azmayesh accuses these "hypocrites" - as the Quran names them - that they "falsified" the meaning of the Quran according to their tribal traditions following the goal of "leading the new community towards their own opinions." Thus an Anti-Islam arose under the name of Islam that established itself during the first two Islamic caliphates of the Omajjad (661 to 750) and Abbasid (750 to 1258) dynasties. One of their main means of doing this, according to Azmayesh, was through the sayings and deeds of Muhammad that were created long after his death and that were placed next to the Quran as the second source of Islam in the form of hadiths.

The author thinks that most of the hadiths are forged. He claims that they were invented in order to interpret the Quran in a misleading manor. Thus a religion that postulates tolerance, equality of human beings and justice became a social system that is based on "violence, religious power and harshness towards its population" - including forced veiling of women and brutal punishments. This was continued by states and enforced by these states with violence. Azmayesh deplores that there is hardly anything left of Muhammad's spiritual quest. The author doesn't accept the objection that the Quran appeals towards violence. Only 3 percent of 6437 verses of the Quran concern violence and they regard the case of Muhammad being

11

attacked in Medina. The survey of Azmayesh is important as it shows how different Muslims view their religion - and that a peaceful Islam is possible.

Rainer Hermann,

FAZ (Frankfurter Allgemeine Zeitung Newspaper),

19th October, 2016.

Preface

The world's oldest Quran manuscript was recently discovered at the University of Birmingham. The manuscript is part of the University's Mingana Collection of Middle Eastern manuscripts, held in the Cadbury Research Library, which was founded by Quaker philanthropist Edward Cadbury. Through the use of modern scientific methods, such as radiocarbon analysis, which were carried out at the University of Oxford, the parchment on which the text is written has been dated to the period between AD 568 and 645, which coincides with the lifetime of Prophet Mohammad (570 to 632 AD).[1]

Figure 2 - Quran –The University of Birmingham
(570-632 AD. In Hijazi Script)

---

[1] Before this discovery the example of the Quran in Tübingen was considered to be the oldest manuscript of the Quran, written between twenty to forty years after the death of Prophet Mohammad (652 AD to 672AD).

Susan Worrall, Director of Special Collections (Cadbury Research Library), at the University of Birmingham, said: 'The radiocarbon dating has delivered an exciting result, which contributes significantly to our understanding of the earliest written copies of the Quran'. The Quran manuscript consists of two parchment leaves and contains parts of Surahs (chapters) 18 to 20, written with ink in an early form of Arabic script known as Hijazi script[2].

---

[2] http://www.birmingham.ac.uk/news/latest/2015/07/quran-manuscript-22-07-15.aspx

http://www.uni-tuebingen.de/en/13002?tx_ttnews%5Btt_news%5D=23132

'A Quran fragment from the University of Tübingen Library has been dated to the 7th century – the earliest phase of Islam – making it at least a century older than previously thought. Expert analysis of three samples of the manuscript parchment concluded that it was more than 95 percent likely to have originated in the period 649-675 AD – 20 to 40 years after the death of the Prophet Mohammed. Such scientific dating of early Quran manuscripts is rare. The Tübingen fragment was tested by the Coranica project, a collaboration between the Académie des Inscriptions et Belles-Lettres Paris and the Berlin-Brandenburgischen Academy of the Sciences and Humanities, sponsored by the German Research Foundation (DFG) and France's Agence Nationale de la Recherche (ANR). The project investigates the Quran in the context of its historical background using documents such as manuscripts and information derived from archaeological excavations.

The project carries out palaeographic analyses to determine the age of a text via its special characteristics. The carbon-14 analysis of the Tübingen fragment was carried out by the Ion Beam Physics Laboratory at ETH Zürich. The fragment in question is one of more than 20 in the University Library Collection written in Kufic script, one of the oldest forms of Arabic writing. The manuscript came to the University in 1864 as part of the collection of the Prussian consul Johann Gottfried Wetzstein. You can view it online at:

http://idb.ub.uni-tuebingen.de/diglit/MaVI165'

BBC News http://www.bbc.co.uk/news/business-33436021

Figure 3 - Quran – Topkapi Palace in Istanbul
(An example of Othman Quran, Kufi Script)

Then do they not reflect upon the Quran? If it had been from [any] other than Allah, they would have found within it much contradiction.' Surah 4, v: 82 [3]

There was certainly in their stories قصص [4] *a lesson for those of understanding. The Quran was never an invented narration, but a confirmation of what was before it and a detailed explanation of all things, and guidance and mercy for the people who believe.* Surah 12, v: 111 [5]

---

^[3] ۳ـ افلا يتدبرون القرآن و لو كان من عند غيرالله لوجدوا فيه اختلافا كثيرا سورة النساء- الاية 82

^[4] Ghesas, قصص means tales, legends and stories. This word is used in the Quran six times in plural and eleven times in the form of a verb. The title of Surah 28 is Ghesas (tales).

^[5] ۵ـ سورة يوسف. الاية 111

لقدكان فى قصصهم عبرة لاولى الالباب .ماكان حديثا يُفترى ولكن تصديق الذى بين يديه و تفصيل كل شىء و هدى و رحمة لقوم يومنون

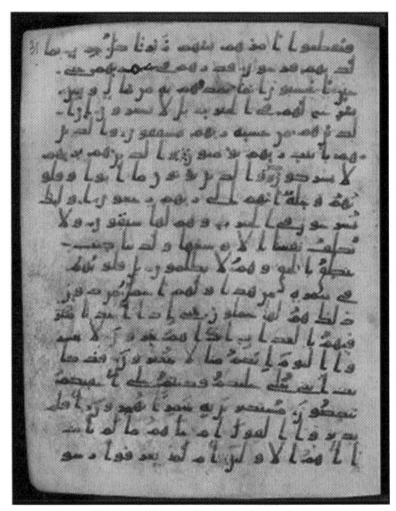

Figure 4 - Quran – Tuebingen University
(625-672 AD, in Hijazi Script)

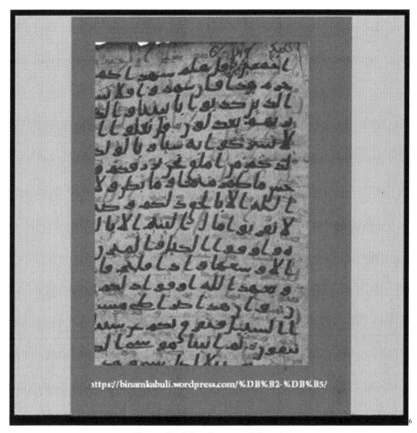

Figure 5 - The Quran of Sana'a.

Two versions are written on top of each other on each page. The final version is written by one of the companions of the Prophet Mohammad (maybe by Obayy ibn Ka'b) during the lifetime of the Prophet. The words are then washed and covered by the next text which corresponds to the usual official version of the Quran named the Othman version. Both texts are in Hijazi Script.

---

6 Radiocarbon dating of a Sana'a Quran parchment: the parchment has a 68% probability of belonging to 614 – 656 AD. It has a 95% probability of belonging to 578-669 AD (Behnam Sadeghi; Uwe Bergmann, "The Codex of a Companion of the Prophet and the Quran of the Prophet," Arabica, Volume 57, Number 4, 2010, p.348.)

Introduction

This book focuses on the time before the Quran and the emergence of Islam. The research delves into the origin of the Quran, using its verses alongside investigative works which support various new theories. The Quran is a written document which, according to recent discoveries[7], can be traced to the lifetime of Prophet Mohammad. Therefore, it is the main source of reference for this book. When relevant information about a related subject connected to the time, emergence, or importance of the Quran is not conveyed in the Quran itself, we occasionally resort in our research to other sources.

Nevertheless, the Quran is the main reference of this book and it will be investigated by employing a scientific phenomenological methodology. We will thus try to avoid any possible causes of confusion, in order to make the Quran more transparent to the reader. We will pay special attention to terms derived from the Quran and describe their meaning and their origin, in order to better understand their relevance and provide supporting evidence for our main hypotheses. This book focuses on the time preceding Islam and highlights the relationships that are pivotal for understanding the development of Islam. The danger posed by false interpretations of the Quran has become increasingly more serious from first appearance of Islam until today, the result of which we can see clearly in our current world.

---

[7] http://www.birmingham.ac.uk/news/latest/2015/07/quran-manuscript-22-07-15.aspx

http://www.uni-tuebingen.de/en/13002?tx_ttnews%5Btt_news%5D=23132

These are the documents that are the closest to the time of Mohammad and refer to Mohammad.

Hence the Quran itself is the most important document to be researched and studied for resolving the problems caused by its false interpretation.

The analysis in this book follows a clear methodology in order to gradually reach its conclusions, which often greatly differ from the many conclusions about the origin of the Quran that have been nurtured for centuries. Furthermore, all theses proposed in this research are backed up by evidence in the form of quotations from the Quran. We also include pictures of scriptures on rocks and other materials that have recently been discovered in Syria and the Arabian Peninsula, in order to support our conclusions.

Furthermore, this book views the Quran as a text that evolved during the life of Mohammad as the principle of evolution was also a driving principle in the life of Prophet Mohammad.

The following hypotheses and questions concerning the life of Mohammad and the Quran will be addressed in this book:

- The strikingly different language styles that are employed throughout the Quran;
- The refutation of the common notion that Mohammad was illiterate;
- The evidence revealing the mission of Mohammad, which was to spread the already established achievements and values by advanced civilisations to an environment that was tightly connected to its tribal traditions and ancestors;
- The notion that Mohammad was guided by an invisible source of inspiration;
- The fact that Mohammad was connected to a spiritual school in Bosra, Syria;
- The continuity of old scriptures and teachings that existed before the Quran, within the Quran;

- The importance of the methods of Prophet Abraham's education in the teachings of Prophet Mohammad;
- The continuity of the path of spiritual knighthood or chivalry;
- The Expectation for the apparition of a prophet predicted in the old scriptures, corresponding to the time of Prophet Mohammad's birth.

Many known facts and aspects concerning the Quran will be outlined and presented in a new way, and linked.

The reader will find two main points in this book. The first point will deal with the fundamental issue of how to encompass and explore the Quran. The second point deals with the life and mission of Mohammad and ends with a description of how Mohammad's mission was rejected by his main adversaries.

The approach of this book is constructed so that any reader with a general knowledge of the Quran can come to appreciate its research, whilst at the same time the experts will also come to understand why certain passages from the Quran have been covered in more detail than others. One should read this text with an open mind in order to understand the relevance of the Quran in the context of its time, and the reasons for the development of two opposing versions of Islam – a progressive one and a reactionary one.

The reader is advised to take note of the interdisciplinary approach of the research presented in this book. That is, in order to comprehend the origin of the Quran, various perspectives are taken into consideration such as the historical, social, and cultural factors that were present at the time of the development of the Quran, to name just a few.

Verses translated from the Quran have been derived from various online publications and scrutinized by the author and, where necessary, more clarification is presented about the subject of the passage concerned.

The Glossary introduces the Arabic transliteration to most of the terms used in this book and provides the Arabic script alongside an explanation.

Also any online reference, has been investigated to verify the main source of the author or the researcher.

The author would like to particularly thank Mrs F Salari and Dr Hans-Michael Haußig, Universität Potsdam, for the transliteration of Persian and Arabic terms. Furthermore the author thanks those who contributed to the accomplishment of this research.

Dr Seyed Mostafa Azmayesh

Paris, 30th October, 2015

Section One

Age determination of an old manuscript of the Quran

The discovery of the old manuscripts of the Quran and their age determination to around the lifetime[8] of Prophet Mohammad[9] sheds a very important light on the circumstances of the first appearance of Islam. In contrast to the opinion of those who believe that the teachings of Mohammad were in the category of verbal literature, the information that follows will show that a part of the Quran – called 'Sohof él Oulâ' الصحف الاولى – was taught by Mohammad from a book that existed before the Quran.

Scribes used different alphabets on the Arabian Peninsula from the first millenary BC. In the pre-Islamic period, in parallel with the illiterate inhabitants of Mecca and nomadic Bedouins of the deserts, Rab' رَبع, at least ten different alphabets were used by Arabic civilisations in the four corners of the Peninsula of Arabia – from Bosra-Petra-Negev (Syria-Jordan-Sinai in the north) to Saba and Najran (Yemen, in the south) and Madineh Saleh (in the centre) – alphabets such as Safaï, Aramaic, Phoenician, Nabatean, Greek, Syriac, Hebrew, Pahlavi, etc. for inscribing the books and carving on rocks and stones.

---

[8] http://www.birmingham.ac.uk/news/latest/2015/07/quran-manuscript-22-07-15.aspx

https://www.uni-tuebingen.de/aktuelles/pressemitteilungen/newsfullview-pressemitteilungen/article/raritaet-entdeckt-Quranhandschrift-stammt-aus-der-fruehzeit-des-islam.html

http://idb.ub.uni-tuebingen.de/diglit/MaVI165

[9] The author has a great respect towards Mohammad ibn Abdollah, the Prophet of the Muslim community, but for ease of readability, this book will refer to him as Mohammad.

These concrete discoveries bring irrefutable evidence of the existence of the Arabic alphabet in the first years of the sixth century AD, about hundred years before the first appearance of Islam and the revelation of the Quran.[10] By comparing all of the remaining old petroglyphs carved on the mountains in different regions of the Arabian peninsula – before or contemporary to the time of the appearance of Islam – we discover diverse styles of Arabic writing including Musnad المُسنَد.

Invention and evolution of the Arabic alphabet

The Quran contains advice for the people of faith to Islam, Mo'menoun المومنون, to write down their financial contracts in order to avoid all conflicts regarding properties:

'O you who have believed, when you contract a debt for a specified term, write it down. And let a scribe write it between you in justice. Let no scribe refuse to write as Allah has taught him. So let him write and let the one who has the obligation dictate. And let him out of respect for Allah, his Lord not leave anything out of it. But if the one who has the obligation is of limited understanding or weak or unable to dictate himself, then let his guardian dictate in justice... And do not be too weary to write it, whether it

---

[10] 'Until the sixth century AD, Arabic was a spoken language only, and used in the tribal kingdoms in Syria, Jordan and southern Iraq (Lakhmid Kingdom). The sole evidence of writing in the centuries before Islam are stone inscriptions written in a form of Aramaic script practiced by the Nabataeans, based at Petra (first century BC to first century AD). The revelation of Islam in the seventh century dramatically changed the role of the Arabic script. As now there was a pressing need to write down God's words to the Prophet Mohammad. Arabic quickly became the language and script of the administration of the Muslim empire. The Arabic script is extraordinarily flexible and can be written in many different ways. In order to write the Quran, the most beautiful scripts possible had to be employed. This led to the development of a constant stream of creativity by the calligraphers, who perfected, re-invented and developed new styles from the earliest Islamic times. These series of scripts in addition to copying the Quran, were also soon used to inscribe other objects, from gravestones to ceramics.'

Text written in relation to Arabic calligraphy in British Museum, London. Islamic department.

is small or large, for its specified term. That is more just in the sight of Allah and stronger as evidence and more likely to prevent doubt between you, except when it is an immediate transaction, which you conduct among yourselves. For then there is no blame upon you if you do not write it. And take witnesses when you conclude a contract. Let no scribe be harmed or any witness. For if you do so, indeed, it is grave disobedience in you. And be mindful of Allah. And Allah teaches you. And Allah is knowing of all things'. Surah 2, v: 282

These sentences expressing advice can be considered as evidence confirming the existence of a common alphabet for writing in Arabic, even though the major part of the nomadic tribes of that area were illiterate.[11]

Words used in the Quran such as sohof الصُحُف (written pages), kotob الكُتب (books), qàràtis القراطيس (scrolls), àsâtir الاساطير (written texts line by line), yastoroun يسطرون (writing texts line by line), yaktoboun يكتبون (redacting books, contracts and letters), yadressoun يدرسون (teaching and learning), qàlàm القلم (pen), noun النون (ink cup), lowh اللوح (the stone tablet, metal plate, timber panel, or clay tablet for writing), are convincing proofs of the existence of a system of education all around the Arabian peninsula, including Mecca.

---

[11]Maybe one of the big mistakes of certain researchers on the history of Islam was to misinterpret the existence of illiterate nomadic people and conclude that an Arabic alphabet for writing down the Arabic language had not existed in that time. The region of Taef was surrounded by diverse civilisations inhabiting the Arabian Peninsula and its surroundings: Lakhmid, Ghassanian, Sabian, Petra, Bosra, Najran, and so on. Many famous and capable Arab poets existed before Islam and the first appearance of the Quran. This testifies to the interest of the inhabitants of Mecca and Medina to the art of poetry. Even nowadays in different countries of the Middle East a quantity of nomadic tribes and Bedouins live according to their ancestral traditions. These tribal people don't stay in a permanent place but move constantly from region to region. In different parts of Arabia – the Sultanat of Oman, Yemen, Iraq, Jordan, Syria, Iran – diverse nomadic tribes are moving constantly and the majority of them are still illiterate. But it is not logical to conclude that the majority of the population in these lands are illiterate! The adversaries of Mohammad were uneducated people; they disagreed with Mohammad because of their ignorance resulting from their lack of educational background.

In all of these schools, the students and disciples were learning the art of recitation and narration of the sacred texts composed of diverse incantations and prayers. The teachers used to apply a particular method to teach the pupils how to read the texts, and to memorise them by heart: Hâfezoun الحافظون.

The Arabic alphabet called Hijazi الحجازى, which was used by a circle of literate people in Mecca, existed in parallel with another style of Arabic calligraphy employed in the Jewish schools by the literate scribes of the Jewish tribes such as Bànou Qorayzeh بنوقريظه, and the inhabitants of Khaybar الخيبر in Medina, who were speaking a particular Arabic dialect called Yahoudyyehالیهودیه rather than Hebrew.[12]

---

[12] The Arabic style of calligraphy called Kufi-alphabet is somehow the evolution of Yahoudyyeh style of writing. It is called Kufi style because of the relocation of the Jewish community of Medina to the new city of al-Kufah 640 AD. Kufah الكوفة al-Kūfah is a city in Iraq of today, about 170 kilometres south of Baghdad, and ten kilometres north-east of Najaf. It is located on the banks of the Euphrates River. The city was the final capital of Alī ibn Abī Talib, and it was founded in 622 AD by the second Rashidun Caliph Omar ibn Al-Khattab. The city of Hira (capital of the Lakhmid kingdom) was situated in the location of Kufah before Islam (see footnote 321).

After the migration of Mohammad and the Mohajeroun to Medina, a considerable number of Muslim children went to the Jewish school to learn the technique of calligraphy and inscribing. See article of Christian Julien Robin: 'Langues et écritures', published in p.127 «Routes d'Arabie. Archéologie et histoire du Royaume d' Arabie Saoudite". Edition Louvre, Paris 2010.

More analytical research about the ensemble of the linguistic treasure in Syria , Arabia, Iraq, and Yemen can be found in the article 'Roots of Modern Arabic Script: From Musnad to Jazm', published by Saad D. Abulhab (Baruch College, CUNY) at the following address:

http://arabetics.com/public/html/more/History%20of%20the%20Arabic%20Script_article.

Also the thorough investigations of DÉROCHE François, Louis, Claude in this matter such as: Les manuscrits du Coran: Aux origines de la calligraphie coranique (1985). Les manuscrits du Coran: Du Maghreb à l'Insulinde (1996). The Abbasid tradition, Qur'âns of the 8th to the 10th centuries (1996). Les manuscrits du Coran en caractères higâzî, Position du problème et éléments préliminaires pour une enquête (1998). Le manuscrit arabe 328 (a) de la Bibliothèque nationale de France (en coll.) (1999). Buchkunst zur Ehre Allâhs, Der PrachtQuran im Museum für Islamische Kunst (en coll.) (2000). Manuel de

The Arabic Hijazi used in the circle of the scribes of Mecca was generated from the Arabic Jazm, rooted in the Musnad style. The comparison between one of the oldest pre-Islamic scriptures[13] and an old Quran[14] inscribed in the Hijazi-Mâél alphabet رَسمُ الخَط الحجازى المائل confirms the continuity of this pre-Islamic Arabic style of calligraphy in the Islamic period.

The sentence of the Quran written in Hijazi style on the rocks in the region of Mecca, dated by its author ibn Emareh ابن عمارة forty-eight years after Hegira, the Quran of Birmingham (568 AD to 645 AD), the Quran of Tübingen (650 AD to 670 AD), and the Quran kept in the British Museum written one or two centuries after Hegira, confirm the activity of the calligraphic school of Mecca for many years after the official publication of the Quran of Othman (third Caliph) in Kufi style. This confirms the survival of the school of calligraphy of Mecca, in parallel with the flourishing school of Medina and Kufah. This is because the school of Mecca was rooted in the pre-Islamic period, which appeared at least around one century before the apparition of Islam. From the other hand the discovery of the written texts in Arabic language-alphabet, in a southern region of Syria confirms the relationship between the scribes of the circle of the educated people in Mecca and the schools in Syria.

---

codicologie des manuscrits en écriture arabe (en coll.) (2001). Le manuscrit Or. 2165 (f. 1 à 61) de la British Library (en coll.) (2004). Le livre manuscrit arabe, Préludes à une histoire (2006). Le Coran (2009). La transmission écrite du Coran dans les débuts d'Islam.

[13] From a Greek-Arabic bilingual inscription found in Ḥarrān, south of Damascus, Syria, dated 568 AD.

[14] This Quran from the 1st /2nd century of Hegira (8th/9th century AD) is kept in the British Museum, London.

The relationship of the scribes in Mecca to the schools in Syria

According to Ahmad abi Ya'ghoub ibn Vazeh Ya'ghoubi in his book the *History of Islam* Umru'ol Qays امرو القيس, King of Hira[15] composed long

---

[15] 'It was necessary to wait for the first years of the sixth century AD, before the Arabic language was written in its own alphabet. But this new-born alphabet is a new variety of the Aramaic scripture, inspired meanwhile by the scriptures of late-nabatean used by the Arabs between south of Syria and Hijaz (region surrounding Mecca), and the Syriac scripture. The recent discoveries confirm that the first usage of this scripture appears in Zabad – about sixty kilometres to the south-east of Aleppo in Syria. A short text containing diverse names of the individuals complete a long bilingual text – in Greek and Syriac – memorising the construction in 512 AD of a Christian sanctuary in honour of Holy Sergius. The second text – according to chronological order – is carved upon a rock of the mountain called "Jabal Usays, situated about 100 kilometres from Damascus." The author of this petroglyph text – a missionary of "Al- Härith the king" – mentions the date of his writing 528-529 AD. The third text is written in Arabic and in Greek alphabet to memorise the construction of a Christian sanctuary in honour of St John, in the region of Harran in Lajâ' in the South of Syria. This text is dated 568-569AD, whose author is an unknown Arab chief (phylarque in Greek language). Next to these three Arabic alphabets it is possible that a fourth alphabet existed as well – by employing the copy of the text introduced by two medieval Arab authors "al Bakri" and "Yagout". It is a text that reminds us of the foundation of Hind in al-Hira, the capital of the kingdom of the Lakhmid dynasty on the shore of the Euphrates in Iraq. These evidences confirm the fact that the Arabic alphabet appeared in the region of the south of Syria and Iraq, between the Christian communities, in order to teach in an easy way the religion of Christianity to the Arab Bedouins of the desert. This style of writing was rudimentary. Its particularity was to write down the vocals such as I and û and not write â and to write down fifteen consonants and to use them for writing the twenty-eight letters of the Arabic language.

Because of this practice, one letter can be read in two to five different ways. So it is no possible to make a distinction between râ and zâ, bâ-tâ- and thâ; etc… The first usage of this manner of putting Points appears in the time of the Caliphate Rashedoun الخلفاءالراشدون in Medina, around 22 H /643 AD. The Arabo-Muslim tradition signals that the Arabic alphabet maybe was invented in the valley of the Euphrates and elaborated in Hira. From the Kingdom of al- Hira this alphabet enters in diverse regions including Dumât ol Jandal and Mecca. When Mohammad was young this alphabet was used by at least seventeen men and a few women in Mecca according to al-Bàlâdhuri. This style of Arabic writing has been chosen by Mohammad as the Arabic alphabet in place of other styles used by the Arabs in Yemen and other regions of the Peninsula of Arabia.'

Article de Christian Julien Robin. Langues et écritures. Parue en p. 131 du livre intitulé *Routes d'Arabie. Archeologie et histoire du Royaume d'Arabie Saoudite.* Edition Louvre, Paris, 2010.

fascinating poetical compositions, القصائد, and the scribes of his court wrote down those poems in so they could be given to the missionaries of the kingdom, who carried them to diverse regions in order to publicize their king and the rich culture of their civilisation.[16] They travelled to many cities, gathering people around them in the markets and narrating the compositions.[17] One of the regions where the poetry of that period was propagated was Mecca, which shows that the Arabs gave a very important place to the art of poetry, instead of science and philosophy.

Ya'ghoubi dedicates a detailed chapter to the names of the most famous poets of that period, whose poetry was recited during the period of pilgrimage in Mecca. The poetry was written in Arabic calligraphy on scrolls, which were presented to the pilgrims by being suspended from the roof of the Kabah to the ground on the four walls of the house of Allah. People gathered and listened to those who recited and narrated this poetry and voted for the best. The presented Qasayed (long poetical compositions) were named Mo'alaghat. Ya'ghoubi mentioned the names of seven poets who were the authors of Mo'alaghat é Sab'eh (seven suspended poems) المعلقات السبعة and ten others who were the authors of Mo'alaghat é Ashreh (ten suspended poems). In the Period of Ignorance ('Asr ol Jaheliat' الجاهليه عصر) in the desert of the Peninsula of Arabia, the art of poetry and the poetic compositions of the famous composers, written in an Arabic language, were a matter of pride for the courageous Bedouin horsemen of the different tribes, who met each other at least once a year in Mecca. They greatly appreciated the art of poetry. This yearning to learn and memorise the poetry was one of the reasons for the quick evolution of the Arabic alphabet.

---

[16] Ahmad abi Ya'ghoub Ibn Vazeh Ya'ghoubi. *Tarikh é Ya'ghoubi*, Farsi translation, M.E. Ayati. Edition: Entesharaté Elmi va Farhanghi. Tehran 1366, vol. 1. pp. 342 to 349.

[17] Ya'ghoubi, Ibid. vol. 1, p.342.

There are two remaining pre-Islamic scriptures from the period of Umru'ol Qays written in two different alphabets: Nabataean and Musnad. This confirms that these two styles of scripture coexisted but they are not related to each other. Certain experts thought that the first seed of Arabic of scripture, called Musnad style, appeared in Hira, and could have been generated from Nabataean النبطى origin. But a simple comparison of the particularities of these two styles of alphabets disapproves this hypothesis. It is true that the Nabataean alphabet (a branch of the Syriac alphabet which is actually itself a branch of the Aramaic alphabet) was also used to write down the Arabic poetry and sentences by the scribes of certain regions of a large area of Arabia, but it was in parallel with the Musnad, and Jazm Arabic alphabet.

Figure 6 - Nabataean word of 'al-Qays' Figure 7 - Arabic Musnad word of 'al-Qays'

The report given by Ya'ghoubi points the researcher to the first trace of the Arabic alphabet. In his *Book of History*, (التاريخ يعقوبى) he remarks that the family of Monzar was from a Yemenit origin, and took the throne of the kingdom of Hira, and remained the best ally of the kings of the Sassanid dynasty. They spoke their maternal Arabic, but because of the close contact with the Persian administration, they also spoke the Persian language fluently, writing the texts both in Persian and Arabic alphabets. Ya'ghoubi declares that the kings of Hira had a deep respect for the poets. He confirms this in the following extract:

"It was a family of the tribe of "Bani Umra'ol Qays ibn Zeyd ibn Mànât ibn Tamim" (بنى امروالقيس ابن منات ابن تميم) very close to (منذر بن نعمان) Monzar, the King of Hira.   A Man from this family of "Umra'ol Qays" called "Odayy ibn Zeyd Ibadi" عُدَى ابن زید عبادى was a poet, preacher, and scribe who was able to inscribe both in Arabic and Persian Alphabets".

King Monzar sent his own son called "No'man" نعمان بن منذر to a milk-giver in the family of "Bani Umra'ol Qays" بنى امروالقیس. No'man stayed and grew up amongst them. Later on, the great Sassanid King Kasra (Khosrow) خسروپرویز ساسانى sent a letter to King Monzar and ordered him to send a native Arabic speaker to translate the letters from Arabic to Persian and vice-versa.

Therefore King Monzar sent "Odayy ibn Zeyd" عدى بن زید in company of his two brothers "Obayy" and Somayy" أبَىَّ - سُمَىَّ. These three brothers of "Umrau'ol Qays family" remained in the royal court of King Kasra and occupied the role of translator of the Arabic and Persian texts. After the death of King Monzar in Hira, the great King Kasra consulted "Odayy" about who would be the most qualified person to become the successor of Monzar. Odayy replied to King Kasra that Monzar had thirteen sons, all capable of replacing their father on the throne. Therefore, Kasra called all thirteen brothers to his royal court in Ctesiphon. He finally chose No'man as the successor of his father Monzar..."[18]

The above extract testifies to the importance of the existence of the Arabic alphabets for the usage of the royal Sassanid kings, in the pre-Islamic period. In other words, we know that Arabic alphabet in the pre-Islamic period existed, but this report does not talk about how this alphabet was invented in Hira (or perhaps elsewhere). However, for our purposes it is not really important to discover the first place in which the alphabet was

---

[18] Ahmad ibn Abi Ya'ghoub; àt-Tarikh Ya'ghoubi; Farsi translation by Mohammad Ibrahim Ayati. Entesharat Elmi-Farhangi. 5th publication; Tehran- 1987. vol-1. Pp. 261 to 267

invented, but where it evolved and was developed.[19] It is certain that an important colony of Christian people had been living in the kingdom of Hira. The Christians of this region, as well as the Christians of the south of Syria in the regions such as Bosra البُصرى and Harran الحرّان , had their own specific holy literature including scriptures and Gospels. They didn't believe in the crucifixion of Jesus, and rejected the principle of the Trinity التثليث.

These particularities bring the specific idea to mind that they were disciples of another path, such as Manichean, hiding themselves under the cover of the Christian faith. The alphabet mainly used by this community was a category of secret Syriac style in use for the sacred texts, and understandable by the brothers and sisters of their path. The Manichean people had been forced to live covertly because they were tolerated neither in Persia[20] nor in Byzance.[21] The agents of the state church or the state fire-temples arrested them and forced them to confess their real faith under intense torture, then condemned them to be burned or executed.[22] Hence, they hid their belief, and needed to write their books and scriptures with a new alphabet unknown by other people.

In other regions such as Bosra in the south of Syria, in Petra, in Hira, and even in different corners of the Arabian peninsula, these large groups of Manichean and new Manichean[23] were dispersed, particularly in Yemen and in the region of Sana'a. Meanwhile the ruler of Hira – from the local

---

[19] According to ibn Nadim the first seed of Arabic calligraphy appeared in the tribe of Hemyari in Yemen, and was exported to Syria-Hira. The calligraphy of Arabic script shows the existence of Arabic literature.

[20] The main priest of the early Sassanid time (AD third century) named Kartir had decreed that all Manicheans had to be persecuted and killed.

[21] Augustine released a decree against Manichaean, which was applied in the Byzantine Empire.

[22] The event of the companions of Okhdoud is explained in the Quran, in the Surah called Borouj. We will learn more about this in the coming chapters.

[23] It is possible to suppose that they were followers of Mazdak.

dynasty of Lakhmides who brought his help to Seyf ibn zi Yazan Hemyari and the Yemenit people – was a Mazdakite.[24]

The revolution of Mazdak ended in 528 AD (forty-two years before the birth of Mohammad), and the conquest of Yemen by the Mazdakite warriors occurred in 570 AD (the birth year of Mohammad).

Mazdak and new Manicheaism in Hira and Yemen, in the pre-Islamic period

Mazdak, son of Bamdadan مزدک بامدادان, was killed in 528 or 524 AD by the plot of the Zoroastrian priests موبدان. Mazdak was a new Manichean prophet, Iranian reformer and religious activist who gained influence under the reign of the Sassanid Shahanshah Kavadh I قباد اول. He claimed to be a prophet of Ahura Mazda, and established the concept of communal possessions and social welfare programmes.

Mazdak was the chief representative of a religious and philosophical teaching called Mazdakism, which he viewed as a reformed and purified version of Zoroastrianism, although it has been argued that his teaching displays influences from Manichaeism as well.[25] However the religion of the Prophet Mani Farghalitous was already not tolerated throughout the entire Sassanid kingdom, and Mazdak was seen as a new Manichean reformer, with a renewed version of Manichaeism. Therefore, Anoushiravan انوشیروان, the young Sassanian Prince, launched a campaign against the Mazdakites in 524AD or 528AD, culminating in a massacre that killed most

---

[24] Wherry, Rev. E. M. *A Comprehensive Commentary on the Quran comprising Sale's translation and Preliminary Discourse*, Boston: Houghton, Mifflin and Company; 1882, p. 66.

[25] Yarshater, Ehsan (1983). *Cambridge History of Iran, the Seleucid, Parthian and Sassanian Periods 2*, pp. 995–997.

of the adherents, including Mazdak himself, and restoring orthodox Zoroastrianism as state religion.[26]

A few Mazdakites survived, however, who were arrested and imprisoned. Later on the Ethiopian invaders, headed by a man called Masrough ibn Abraheh, occupied Yemen. A noble man from the tribe of Hemyar in Yemen called Seyf ibn zi Yazan سيف ابن ذى يزن left his land and went to Hira to inform (منذر بن نعمان بن منذر) Monzar ibn No'man ibn Monzar, the king of the Lakhmid dynasty, about the occupation of Yemen by the Ethiopian Army. After few months Seyf and Monzar travelled to Mada'en/Ctesiphon تيسفون المدائن (the Sassanid capital), to visit the great king of the Sassanid dynasty Kasra Anoushiravan خسرو انوشيروان 'الكسرى' – in order to request his help. Anoushiravan formed a small army of about 900 men from those jailed Mazdakites under the leadership of an old warrior called Vaharz وهرز الفارسى. He sent them by eight boats to Yemen to support Seyf ibn zi Yazan سيف ابن ذى يزن and to fight against the Ethiopian army headed by Masrough ibn Abraheh مسروق ابن ابرهة الحبشى. The Mazdakite group defeated the larger Ethiopian army and conquered that region.[27] From the moment the Mazdakite group took possession of the area, they started to spread their world vision of Manichaeism in the south of the Arabian Peninsula. They even wrote down sentences of the books of Mani Farghalitous upon the rocks and mountains in the form of pictographs. Ibn Husham reports that certain pictograph sentences from 'Zabour' (one of the books of the Prophet Mani) in Yemen originated from the pre-Islamic period. Theses pictographs contain a prediction about the destiny of a land called Zamar/ Dhamar. Ibn Husham writes: 'Zamar/

---

[26] Wherry, Rev. E. M. A comprehensive commentary on the Quran: comprising Sale's translation & preliminary discourse, with additional notes & emendations... London, Trubner & Co., 1882-1886/ London, K. Paul, Trench, Trübner, & co., 1896.

[27] Ibn Husham, Ibid. Farsi version, vol. 1, pp. 42 to 46.

Dhamar signifies either Yemen or Sana'a.' (But in reality Zamar/ Dhamar is the name of a city in Yemen with more than 160,000 inhabitants).

قال ابن اسحق: و كان فى حجر باليمن فيما يزعمون كتاب بالزبور كتب فى الزمان الاول:

، لمن مُلكُ ذَمار؟ لحمير الاخيار

لمن مُلكُ ذمار؟ للحبشة الاشرار

لمن مُلكُ ذمار؟ لفارس الاحرار

لمن مُلكُ ذمار؟ لقريش التجار 28،

The art of inscribing in the Arabic alphabet used by the literate, educated, and the poet Odayy and his two brothers had been invented by the Manichean community as a branch of the Syriac alphabet to translate secretly the Manichean literature into Arabic for the usage of the local kings of Hira. Those local kings were the allies of the great kings of the Sassanid dynasty who did not have any respect or tolerance towards Manichaeism. In the same time, the Sassanid kings knew the existence of the Arabic alphabets from the bilingual poets of the family of Umra'ol Qays in Hira. The kings supposed that the unique usage of that Arabic alphabet was to inscribe the poetry. The last local king of the Lakhmid dynasty from the Monzar family was No'man ibn Monzar who was arrested by Khosrow Parviz – the great Sassanid King – and killed under the feet of an elephant in Ctesiphon. The real reason for that act of murder was never revealed; maybe Khosrow Parviz خسروپرویزساسانی discovered the attachment of No'man ibn Monzar to Manichaeism. After this event the alliance between the Sassanid empire and the kingdom of Hira broke down, and these two ancient allies ended up fighting against each other in the battle of Zo Ghâr ذوقار , in which the Persian army was defeated in front of its Arabic

---

adversary. It was an important historical event, and the Arabs considered it the vengeance of destiny against the egotist Sassanid kings.[29]

Ibn Nadim, a Manichean/Muslim historian, was a linguist and in his book Al-Fihrest الفهرست gives not only numerous detailed secrets about the teachings of the Prophet Mani (216-276 AD), but also a number of interesting information about the Nabataean and other pre-Islamic alphabets on the Arabian Peninsula.[30] For certain reasons that will be explained later, we can accept the important step of the Syriac alphabet, in the evolution of the Aramaic الآرامی and Nabataean النبطی alphabets, towards the invention of the first signs and letters of the Arabic Musnad المسند alphabet.

It is interesting to understand why the Manichean scribes became interested in Nabataean scripture. This fact is important, because the Nabataean alphabet was a forgotten style of inscription for many centuries, and around the time of the first appearance of Islam we see its renaissance. The reason, in our opinion, is that the majority of the texts written by prophets such as Habakkuk حبقوق , Jeremiah, and so on, were archived by the Gnostic population of the city of Qumran in Jordan, close to the shore of the Dead Sea بحرالميت , which was related to the civilisation of Petra.[31] These people, who were Essenians-Sedoughits, had been constantly persecuted by the Pharisees and Romans. They used multiple languages to write down their texts upon scrolls, parchment, bronze tablets, etc. They stored or hid their completed scriptures in the bottom of large jars and pots, which were placed in dark corners of mountain caves in Jordan. These people were expecting the arrival of an eschatological Saviour from

---

[29] Ahmad abi Ya'ghoub, Ibid. vol. 1, p.267.

[30] *Mohammad ibn Eshagh ibn Nadim.* Al-Fihrest/al-Fihrest ol Uloum. The book is written in 377 Hegira. al-Nadim, Ibn. *The Fihrest of al-Nadim.* Bayard Dodge, editor and translator, 1970, Columbia University Press.

[31] This subject will be explained in more detail in other chapters.

Arabia/Mecca (in the region of Pharan الفاران). The texts regarding these apocalyptical events were mainly named the 'Sohof é Ebrahim' صُحفِ ابراهيم.[32] This literature was used in Mecca by a group of monotheist people called Honàfâ.[33] Honàfâ, the followers of the religion of Abraham in Mecca, were a well-known people. They rejected the tribal traditions of the Bedouins of Arabia, and walked among the pilgrims of the Kabah to preach and teach them the lessons of the Sohof of Abraham (صحف ابراهيم).[34]

The Sohof of Abraham and Moses صحفِ ابراهيم و موسى were written teachings on pages called Zobor el Oulâ (زُبُرالاولى) , and (الصحف الاولى), Sohof el Oulâ. If we trust the writings of ibn Husham, then the head of the circle of the Hànif living in Mecca in the pre-Islamic period, contemporary to the birth time of Mohammad ibn Abdollah ibn Abdul-Motalleb, was

---

[32] It is probable that those texts were translated into Arabic and written in the Nabataean alphabet for the usage of the monotheist of Mecca, such Waraka ibn-Nowfel. Ibn Husham confirms – based on the report of Ibn Eshagh – that the Jewish priests, al-Ahbâr الاحبار, and the Christians monks, ar Rohban الرهبان , and the fortune-tellers called Kâhen الكاهن, predicted the arrival of a prophet. The Jewish priests and the Christians monks knew this fact because it was written in their respective books and manuscripts. Ibn Husham, Arabic version. Ibid, vol. I p.122.

[33] Hànif/ حنيف plural "Honàfâ حنفاء means monotheist related to the path of Abraham. This word is usually employed in the Quran twice in plural and ten times in singular form. It is used to describe the path of Abraham: Mellaté Ebrahim/ ملة ابراهيم: Abraham said: 'O my people, indeed I am free from what you associate with Allah. Indeed, I have turned my face towards He who created the heavens and the earth, as a Hànif and Muslim and I am not from the polytheist /moshrekin/ people; I am not of those who associate others with Allah.' S.6-v.79 Say, 'Indeed, my Lord has guided me to a straight path – a correct religion / دينًا قيمًا- the way of Abraham/ ملة ابراهيم, inclining towards truth. And he was not among those who associated others with Allah.' S.6 v.161 Mohammad received guidance to be on the path of Abraham: Then We revealed to you, [O Mohammad], to follow the monotheist path of Abraham, inclining towards truth; and he was not of those who associate with Allah. S.16 v.123.

[34] Waraka ibn Nowfel ورقة ابن نوفل , Obeydollah Jàhish عبيدالله جحيش , Othman ibn Howayrith عثمان ابن حويرث , Zeyd ibn Amr ibn Nàfil زيد ابن عمرو ابن نفيل . 'They made a circle and said to each other our people are in a wrong way. They took distance from the religion of their father Abraham, and prayed to the idols... They went to different places and preached about the religion of Abraham.' Ibn Husham, Ibid, Arabic version, vol. 1. p. 134.

Waraka ibn Nowfel.[35] He was an educated literate monotheist, and his presence in the life of Mohammad from the age of three years old onwards, is reported by ibn Husham.[36] According to ibn Husham, Waraka وَرَقة – as a multilingual scholar – studied a considerable number of books and scriptures. He was known as a monotheist Christian. He said once to Khadijeh, 'I read a lot of books. It is written in those books that a prophet will appear between these people, and now the time of his apparition is approaching.'[37]

The report of ibn Eshâgh ابن اسحاق given by ibn Husham ابن هُشام confirms this probability that Mohammad was an active member of the circle of Hàlf ol Fozoul حَلفُ الفضُول , and the group of Honàfâ الحُنَفاء in Mecca before his proclamation to be the messenger of Allah. Hence he may have somehow been in the company of the disciples of a private school, where they learned the 'science of the books', including reading, writing, preaching, narrating, reciting, studying, teaching, and discussing the religion of Abraham, in order to prepare for addressing the people of the region. This action was called Tahdith التحديث. The verse of the Quran attests that the prophetical mission of Mohammad started by the accomplishment of the duty of Tahdith, before the official annunciation of his prophecy (before he was forty years old).[38] It will be explained in the coming chapters that at least a part of the mission of Mohammad, a literate and educated

---

[35] Waraka ibn Nowfil was Christian, and was intensely studying the Books... Ibn Husham, Ibid. Arabic version, vol. 1. p. 115.

و كانت خديجه بنت خويلد قد ذكرت لورقة بن نوفل بن اسد بن عبد العزى ـ و كان ابن عمها، و كان نصرانيا، قد تتبع الكتب و علم من علم الناس...ـ

[36] Ibn Husham, Ibid. The report about the presence of Waraka in the life of the Prophet Mohammad is given in vol. 1 pp. 100 to 143.

[37] Ibn Husham Sirraton Nabbavieh, vol. 1, p.122-3/ Farsi translation, Tehran 1364. Eslamieh/Arabic edition V-I, p.115 Mo'asseà ton Nour/ Beyrout, 2004.

ـ[38]و اما بنعمة ربك فحدث. سوره "والضحى "آيه 11

But as for the favour of your Lord, report [it]. Surah 93, v: 11

individual related to the circle of the monotheists of Mecca, was to narrate texts of the teachings of the ancient prophets, particularly Abraham and Moses. According to ibn Husham there was a short gap of three years between the first verses revealed to Prophet Mohammad, and the second verses.[39] In fact this period was certainly much longer, because the first meeting with angels happened when he was five years old, and when he introduced himself as a messenger, he was forty years old. The first verse of 74th Surah commands Mohammad to start a new paradigm.

'O you who covers himself [with a garment], arise and warn. And your Lord glorify. And your clothing purify. And uncleanliness avoid. And do not confer favour to acquire more. But for your Lord be patient.' Surah 74, v: 1-7

و انذر عشيرتک الاقربين و اخفض جناحک لمن اتبعک من المومنين و ان عصوک فقل انی بری مما تعملون و توکل علی العزيز الرحيم الذی يراک حين تقوم و تقلبک فی الساجدين

He was, to use the analogy of a sleeping person, a messenger in a period of waiting. This was because the necessary conditions had not yet converged. '*O you who covers himself [with a garment], arise and warn.*' 'Qom'/arise/ قم is the moment of a new beginning in the life of Mohammad. '*Arise! And warn!*'

Verse 214 from the Surah 26 gives more precision about the strategy of his mission: '*Warn, your closest members of family.*'

'And warn, [O Mohammad], your closest kindred. And lower your wing to those who follow you of the believers. And if they disobey you, then say, "Indeed, I am disassociated from what you are doing."' Surah 26, v: 214 - 216.

---

[39] Ibn Husham, Ibid. Farsi version, Vol. 1, p. 158.

يا ايهاالمدثر قم فأنذر وربك فكبر و ثيابك فطهر والرجز فاهجر ولاتمنن تستكثر ولربك فاصبر. سوره المدثر. الايات 1-7

On the other hand, verse 94, Surah 15: *'Then declare what you are commanded'* confirms that even during that period of 'waiting' (being covered with a garment إدّثار), before he was forty years old, Mohammad was secretly giving personal guidance to people, but from a particular moment he was ordered to undertake his mission openly and loudly, and not in secret.

فاصدَع بما تومر و أعرض عن المشركين. إنا كفيناك المستهزئين. الذين يجعلون مع الله إلها آخر فسوف يعلمون. ولقد نعلم أنك يَضيقُ صدرُك بمايقولون. فسبح بحمد ربك و كن من الساجدين. واعبد ربك حتى يأتيك اليقين. سورة الحِجر. الايات 94-99

'Then declare what you are commanded and turn away from the polytheists. Indeed, We are sufficient for you against the mockers, Who make [equal] with Allah another deity. But they are going to. And We already know that your breast is constrained by what they say. So exalt [Allah] with praise of your Lord and be of those who prostrate [to Him]. And worship your Lord until there comes to you the certainty.' Surah15, v: 94-99

Syriac-Hijazi, important evidence

As we mentioned, the Hijazi alphabet, which evolved in Mecca (in the same way the Kufi style of inscribing was developed in Medina), was generated from Musnad Arabic style, and related to a particular branch of Syriac السريانى calligraphy. Here we present more details on this:

Figure 8 - Noun val Ghalam
The letter Noun is written in different styles in different languages.

The letter Noun in the Syriac alphabet, called Esterangela-style, is the painting of 'an ink-pot next to a pen'. Hence, for the Syriac-speaking people, the visual image of 'ink-pot + pen' reminds them of 'the art of inscribing and what a scribe is writing'. This meaning appears in the mind, only in the Esterangela-style of the Syriac alphabet, and not in any other alphabet such as Arabic العربى , Pahlavi الفهلوى , Aramaic الآرامى , Greek اليونانى and even other styles of Syriac script رسم الخط السريانى .

In fact this picture of the letter 'Noun' is described in a verse of the Quran.[40] This confirms that a certain and irrefutable relationship between certain parts of the Quranic literature and a Syriac culture existed. From other side, ibn Husham reports the event of the reconstitution of the cubic house of Kabah (five years before the public proclamation of Mohammad about his mission of prophethood) when during the excavation of the ancient foundation of Kabah, a document was discovered, written in the Syriac alphabet وَجَدوا بِالرُّكن كِتاباً بالسُّريانية which was read by a Jewish man.[41] This report regards the usage of the Syriac scriptures in Mecca in the pre-Islamic period.

According to this type of report the Syriac alphabet, a branch of Aramaic script, could be the origin of the invention of a particular new style

---

[40] Surah Noun val Ghalam. v: 1,2

41- قال ابن اسحاق: و حُدّثتُ أن قريشا وَجدوا فى الركن كتابا بالسريانيه فلم يدروا ما هو . حتى قراء لهم رجلٌ من يهود. فاذا هو: " أنا الله ذو بكة. خلقتها يومَ خلقتُ السموات و الارض. و صوّرتُ الشمس و القمر. و حفّتها بسبعة املاك حُنفاء. لاتزول حتى يزول اخشباها. مباركٌ لاهلها فى الماء و اللبن"

Ibn Husham, Ibid. Arabic version, vol. 1, p.117.

of calligraphy named 'Musnad' المسند. This new style was used by the scholars who were translating the texts of the old scriptures into Arabic. This was used mainly in Mecca, in parallel with the Arabic alphabet used by the group of Jewish scholars in Medina, who were developing another new style of writing (Rasmol khat رسم الخط) called Yahoudyyeh اليهودية. The style practised in Medina can be considered as a bridge between the Nabataean and Arabic calligraphy. These two independent styles of calligraphy for writing the Arabic alphabet in Mecca and Medina were employed before the appearance of Islam and the birth of Mohammad. The scribes of Medina were Jewish. The scholars of Mecca (Hànif) proclaimed themselves followers of the path of Abraham. This group was connected to the Christian/ Manichean community related to the Sedoughin community, which originated from Qumran, who joined Bosra (in Syria) and Hira after the decadence of Qumran.

The secret of the evolution of two different styles of Arabic calligraphy informs the nature of that particular messianic period, composed of a Christian (monotheist) and Mazdakite community on one side, and a Jewish community on the other, who were all expecting the apparition of a new prophet,[42] as per the prediction of the Pesher of Habakkuk. The attitudes of these two communities were opposite to each other towards this new prophet. According to the reports given by ibn Husham[43] the Jewish priests of Medina were mainly unhappy about that expected event, while the Hànif of Mecca were counting days and nights to witness the uprising of that

---

[42] ـ أحبار اليهود، و رهبان النصارى يتحدثون عن مبعثه. قال ابن اسحاق: و كانت الاحبار من يهود و الرهبان من النصارى و الكهان من العرب قد تحدثوا بامر رسول الله قبل مبعثه لما تقارب من زمانه. اما الاحبار من يهود و الرهبان من النصارى فعما وجدوا فى كتبهم من صفته و صفة زمانه و ماكان من عهد انبيائهم اليهم فيه...

Ibn Husham, Ibid. Arabic version, vol. 1, p.122.

[43] Ibn Husham, Ibid. Farsi version, vol. 1 p.117. Arabic version, vol. 1, p.110:

قال ابن اسحاق: بحيرا ينصح لابى طالب... قال: صدقتَ فارجع بابن اخيك الى بلده و احذر عليه يهود. فوالله لئن رأوه و عرفوا منه ما عرفتُآيَبَعْثَهُ شرا فانه كائن لابن اخيك هذا شان عظيم. فاسرع به الى بلاده. فخرج به عمه ابوطالب سريعا حتى اقدمه مكه حين فرغ من تجارته بالشام

42

Saviour, but feared the antipathy of certain priests among the Jewish community towards him. They kept their anticipation of a prophet as a secret between the members of their circle.

It was in that specific sphere of antagonism that the scriptures of the old predictions were translated into Arabic by the scholars of two different opposing communities.

One could imagine the possibility of the usage of the newborn Arabic alphabet in Hira and Syria (initially for the usage of the poets, and exported to Mecca by the poetry-narrators originating from Hira and Syria) by the circle of the wise people of Mecca to create a complete Arabic translation of the spiritual Manichean and Christian scriptures. This task of translating the teachings of the previous prophets and the spiritual masters into Arabic, and inscribing them in the Arabic alphabet, in secret, only for the members of the circle of Honàfâ, could be seen as the main reason for the invention and evolution of a very elaborate style of calligraphy in Mecca, called Hijazi. We should not forget the talent of Waraka to compose epic poems in the Arabic language. Ibn Husham mentions thirteen lines of a long poem, Qasideh القصيدة, written by Waraka about the imminent manifestation of the promised Saviour in the person of Mohammad.[44]

---

[44] This Qasideh – long poetry in an epic style – was composed by Waraka when Mohammad was twenty-five years old and returned back in company of a man called Meysareh from a trading trip to Sham-Syria, during which they met a monk (a fortune-teller) who declared to them that Mohammad was the awaited promised Saviour. Ibn Husham, Ibid., Arabic version, p.115 Three lines of the poetry of Waraka are composed as in the following lines:

بأنَّ محمداً سيَسود فينا ـ ويَخصم مَن يكون له حجيجا

ويظهر فى البلاد ضياء نور ـ يُقيم بهالبرية أن تموجا

و لو جَافَى الذى كرهت قريش ـ و لو عجَّت بمكة ها عجيجا

Waraka and the Honàfâ in Mecca

The relationship between the Hànif-circle and the evolution of the Arabic alphabet

This circle of Hànif lived in Mecca as a religious minority. Ibn Husham explains about them in the following lines:

'Once the Quraysh celebrated a feast for one of their idols. They worshipped it, turned around it, made the sacrifice for it; four people took distance from them and deliberated among them to make a new paradigm. They were Waraka ibn Nowfel ibn Asad ibn Abdul Ozza, Obaydollah ibn Johaysh, Othman ibn Howayrath, and Zeyd ibn Amr ibn Nafil. They talked between them and said to each other: By Allah your tribe is not on the right way, they went far in deviation from the religion of their father Abraham. They are worshipping a piece of stone which is unable to see, to hear, does not make any good or bad thing. O people think about yourselves. You are not on the right way. So these four people left (after this gathering) to different regions to talk about the religion of Abraham.'[45]

This confirms the fact that before Mohammad and in the pre-Islamic period, other people called Hànif (who were literate, educated, and monotheists) had access to the written teachings related to Abraham and propagated calmly and softly his religion in the Peninsula of Arabia. Their task was not easy and they were not very successful. But they were living amongst a mixture of monotheistic believers (who believed in only one true owner of the house of Kabah), Rabbol Beyt رب البيت and idol worshippers.[46] Ibn Husham gives more details about the activities of Waraka than his three

---

[45] Ibn Husham, Ibid. Arabic version, vol. 1, p.134.

[46] Abdul Motalleb went to visit Abrahah ibn Masroug to negotiate with him about his confiscated camels. He said to Abrahah, 'I am the owner of my camels, and the house (Kabah) has its owner as well, who will take care of it.' إنّى أنا ربُّ الإبل و إنّ للبيتِ ربٌّ سيمنعه . Ibn Husham, Ibid. Arabic version, vol. 1 p.32.

other friends. Waraka's life was dedicated to studying the teachings of the prophets of the Abrahamic lineage. He talked about Allah and the religious teachings with everybody in Mecca. Waraka was very protective of Mohammad and once, in the company of one of his friends, he brought Mohammad back to Abdul Motalleb when he had gone missing.[47] This confirms that people of the path of Abraham were watchful of Mohammad. We can suppose that on the way to Abdul Motalleb, Waraka talked to Mohammad about the universe, sky, earth, camels, mountains, deserts, trees, water, clouds, and so on, as the creatures created by only one Creator, who created mankind and taught him and guided him by the prophets to the right path, prophets such as Abraham and his successors.

Later on Mohammad received the order by an inner voice, Vahi الوحى, to call upon the polytheist people to change their ways and follow the religion of the monotheist path:

'And they were not commanded except to worship Allah, being sincere to Him in religion, inclining to truth حنفاء مخلصين له الدين *and to establish prayer and to give zakah. And that is the correct religion* ذلک الدین القمیة*.'Surah 98, v: 5.*

In order to call people to join the circle of the monotheist followers of the path of Abraham, the method employed by Mohammad was to recite sentences of the old Holy Books for the illiterate Bedouins of Mecca:

'A messenger from Allah, reciting purified scriptures صحفا مطهرة . *Within which are correct writings* فیها کُتُبٌ قیمة *.' Surah 98, v: 2-3.*

People of the Holy Books اهل الکتاب say: *'Be Jews or Christians so you will be guided.'* Say, *'Rather, we follow the monotheist path of Abraham,* مِلَّة ابراهیم حنیفاً *inclining towards truth, and he was not of the polytheists.' Surah 2, v: 135.*

---

[47] Ibn Husham, Ibid. v-1, p.101, Arabic version. Farsi version p.112.

The idol worshippers rejected the call of Mohammad, and from that moment onwards, the common life between the monotheists and polytheists of Mecca was broken.

Those who disbelieved among the people of the scriptures and the polytheists were not to be parted from disbelief until there came to them clear evidence, a messenger from Allah, reciting purified scriptures within which are correct writings. Nor did those who were given the scripture become divided until after there had come to them clear evidence. And they were not commanded except to worship Allah, being sincere to Him in religion, inclining to truth, and to establish prayer and to give zakat. And that is a serious and solid spiritual path. [48] Surah 98, v: 1 - 5.

Waraka ibn Nowfal ibn Asad ibn Abd-al Uzza ibn Qusay Al-Qurashi

As we have seen, according to the report of ibn Husham, Waraka was an educated man who was teaching the inhabitants of Mecca and preaching to them about the religion of Abraham. The teachings of Abraham must have been written in an old script, either on a scroll or on pages of a book, as it was used in the time of the monotheists of the Qumran community living on the shore of the Dead Sea. But Waraka needed to talk to the inhabitants of Mecca in the usual Arabic language; therefore he needed to translate those teachings and write them down, as the content of a Holy Scripture, with a new alphabet. They were written on non-attached papyrus pages, and placed on top of each other in a 'box of the Sacred Book', as

---

[48] 'Din' الدين often is translated to mean 'religion', but the Sanskrit root of the word means 'spiritual path' or 'method'. In addition 'shariat', which is an Arabic word, originally means 'path' or 'street' but in the Quranic jargon it is used to mean 'Legitimisation of a divine law that concerns social life'. This does not mean that it is an absolute law for eternity, rather a law for that time and place, which is more like a number of principles and may be modified by the law makers according to the developments of individuals and their society.

was in common use by the monotheists of Ethiopia. The content of this box were named 'Sohof é Ebrahim' (the Pesher of Abraham) صُحُفِ إبراهيم .

To inscribe the texts of the teachings of Abraham – the father of all prophets – on paper, could give dynamism to accelerate the evolution of the newborn Arabic Musnad alphabet to the Jazm alphabet and to the developed, elaborate Hijazi alphabet.

The presence of Waraka since the childhood of Mohammad has been reported by ibn Husham. Waraka took care of Mohammad because he had been certain about the apparition of Nâmous ol Akbar ناموس الاكبر [49], the promised eschatological Saviour in the person of Mohammad. Further, Waraka was the paternal first cousin of Khadijeh. Waraka and Khadijeh were also second cousins of Mohammad. Their paternal grandfather Asad ibn Abd-al-Uzza was Mohammad's matrilineal great-great-grandfather. Waraka ibn Nowfel lived in Mecca before the time of the coming of Islam. He was related to the school of Bosra and its Christian-Manichean community. He was also expecting the apparition of the promised Saviour. This Saviour, by the name of Pharghalitous (Paracletus), was predicted by Mani and Jesus. As we mentioned previously, Waraka's first presence in the life of Mohammad, as reported by ibn Husham, was from the moment that Halimeh Sa'dieh حليمة السعدية brought Mohammad back from the desert to Mecca when he was only three years old. This is the complete version of ibn Husham:[50]

---

[49] When Waraka heard the report of Mohammad's vision in the cave of Hira he said to Khadijeh: 'Ghoddous, Ghoddous, قدّوس قدّوس . I swear to Whom who detains the life of Waraka in his hands, if what you are reporting to me is true, the same Namous ol Akbar, ناموس الاكبر who has visited Moses, also came to visit Mohammad, and he is in fact the Prophet for this community. Tell him to have strength in his mission,' Ibn Husham, Ibid. Farsi version, vol. 1, p-155. Arabic version, vol. 1, p.143.

[50] Ibn Husham, Ibid. Arabic version, vol. 1, p.100. Ibid. Farsi version, vol. 1, p.112.

'She gave him back to his grandfather Abdul Motalleb. But one day Abdul Motalleb lost any trace of little Mohammad who was playing with the children in the street. He looked at every corner and did not find Mohammad. He became very sad and upset. He went to the Kabah and put his hand upon the Hajar ol Aswad, wept and requested Allah to bring back Mohammad. At the end of the day he saw Waraka ibn Nowfel walking in the street from the desert to the Kabah holding the hand of Mohammad. Waraka was one of the educated masters of the circle of the "spiritual chivalry" named "fozoul";[51] to which Mohammad was also related from the age of fifteen years.'

He was alone, poor and an orphan, when at the age of twenty, Mohammad met Khadijeh, a cousin of Waraka, and began to work for her in her trading company. Five years later, Mohammad married Khadijeh and was thus related to Waraka through marriage into his family. When Mohammad was about twenty-eight years old Abu Talib brought Ali (one of his four children, called Taleb, Aghil, Ja'far, and Ali), to the house of Mohammad and Khadijeh.

Waraka was an educated, knowledgeable, and gentle chevalier who owned many books written in various languages, which he was able to read and study. He could write different alphabets including Arabic. His presence in the life of Mohammad, Khadijeh, and Ali was very important. After the event of the apparition of the angel in the cave of Hera in Jabal al Nour, Waraka was the first person who attested that Mohammad was the waited promised eschatological Saviour, and the Prophet of Allah.[52]

---

[51] Ibn Husham, Ibid. Arabic version, vol. 1, p. 82.

Mohammad ibn Sa'd, *Tabaqat ol Kobra* vol. 1. Translated by Haq, S. M. *Ibn Sa'd's Ketab al-Tabaqat al-Kabir*, p.54. Delhi: Ketab Bhavan. *Encyclopaedia of Islam*, Online ed., *Waraka ibn Nowfel* Mohammad ibn Eshaq, *Sirat Rasul Allah*. Translated by Guillaume, A. (1955). *The Life of Mohammad*, p. 107. Oxford: Oxford University Press. Bukhari 1:1:3. See also Bukhari 4:55:605; Bukhari 9:87:111; Muslim 1:301.

[52] Ibn Husham, Ibid. p.117.

Travel to Bosra in Syria

As we have already mentioned in this book, contrary to the majority of the inhabitants of Mecca whose religion was based on idol worshipping, the family of Mohammad was monotheist and was connected to the spiritual centre of Bosra in Syria. Abu Talib, the father of Ali and the uncle of Mohammad, organized a trip to Bosra in the company of twelve-year-old Mohammad to meet Bahira Georgious.[53] They travelled with a caravan to a monastery. When they reached their destination, the highest master of that monastery, Bahira Georgious, welcomed Abu Talib and Mohammad into his retreat. Bahira asked Abu Talib about the relationship between him and his young companion of the road. Abu Talib replied: 'He is my son.' Bahira responded: 'It is not possible, because his father should already be dead.' In fact Mohammad was like a son to Abu Talib. But Bahira had read in his book about the particular physical signs on the body of the anticipated Prophet, and he was looking for this specific sign on Mohammad's body, between his shoulders. The fact that Mohammad at the age of twelve years, in the presence of his uncle Abu Talib, was in solitude inside the monastery confirms the spiritual dependency of Mohammad and Abu Talib to Bosra and its spiritual masters.[54] Mohammad travelled in the company of Abu Talib to be initiated into the spiritual order of the circle of Bahiras.[55] Abu Talib himself was certainly an initiated individual connected to the monastery of Bosra, and trusting of Bahira, to have brought Mohammad with him. If this was not the case, surely he would never have allowed

---

[53] Ibn Husham, Ibid. Arabic version, vol. 1, pp 109 to110.

[54] Those masters were named Bahira – the carriers of the burden of prophetic heritage in the line of St John the Baptist, Jesus, Mani, up to the time of Mohammad.

[55] This old spiritual tradition still exists in certain Sufi orders, according to which during the ceremony of initiation the men undress their chests and shoulders, and bow in front of the spiritual master, and give him their hands to receive the Baraka of the guidance.

Mohammad to show his bare shoulders to Bahira. Bahira assigned Abu Talib to take care of Mohammad, because he was the promised Prophet.[56]

The esoteric experience of Mohammad

During this messianic period, the monotheists of Mecca, who were related to the monastery of Bosra in Syria, expected the apparition of a Saviour at the end of their long period of waiting. Events such as the meetings of Mohammad (once in the presence of his uncle Abu Talib when he was twelve years old, and once in the presence of Meysareh ميسرة when he was twenty-five years old) with the monks in Syria, and their confirmation about the fact that Mohammad matched all of the descriptions of the awaited prophet,[57] plus the certainty of Waraka about Mohammad being the bearer of the divine burden of an eschatological Saviour, confirms that a close circle around Mohammad – the Honàfâ of Mecca – recognised him as the Prophet of the 'End of time' (Akher oz Zaman رسول الآخرالزمان), but he was still young at that time. After Khadijeh bint Khovaylad خديجه بنت خويلد explained to Waraka the opinion of an old monk from Bosra about Mohammad to Meysareh مَيسَرة when he had seen Mohammad, Waraka answered to Khadijeh: 'Listen, it is true that this Mohammad is the prophet of this community (Ummah الامة), and I know that he is "the awaited prophet" for these people. This is his time and the

---

[56] The monastery of Bosra in the south of Syria has a very important place in the hidden history of Islam. People who were waiting for the apparition of the awaited Prophet proclaimed by Jesus and Mani were depending upon this spiritual sanctuary, such as Salman é Farsi, who after the apparition of Mohammad became one of the important companions of Mohammad. The life events of Salman é Farsi سلمان فارسى, who originated from a Zoroastrian family, converted to Christianity and later on to the monastery of Bosra, are explained in detail by ibn Husham. Ibid. Arabic version, vol. 1 p.128-134. Farsi version, vol. 1, pp 139-146. The masters of this monastery were not believers in the Trinity, and they were the inheritors of the teachings and the books of the successors of Mani. Their Gospel was different to the official version of the books of the Byzantine Church.

[57] Ibn Husham, Ibid. Arabic version, vol. 1, p.113 and p.115.

period for him to appear.'[58] But they still had to wait some years, because
for the Quraysh tribe the age of maturity was forty years. Before reaching
this age, men were still considered young and not mature. Men under forty
years old did not have the right to attend the gatherings and the assemblies
of the old men in a place called Dar on Nadouh دارالندوة . This rule was
founded first by Qusay ibn Kolab, one of the ancestors of Mohammad.
Mohammad spent his time in seclusion and waiting between the ages of
thirty-five and forty. One time in the cave of Hera, when he was already
forty years old, he had an important spiritual contemplation in which an
angel ordered him to: éghrà' اقراء – 'read loudly' or 'recite the written
texts.'[59] Mohammad was shocked by the unexpected apparition of the

---

[58] Ibn Husham, Ibid. Arabic version, vol. 1, p.115.

[59] The Muslim reporters say that while Mohammad – at the age of forty – was meditating
during the month of Ramadan in the cave of Hera غار الحراء on the mountain called 'an
Nour/light' جبل النور the shape of a phantom (a kind of a non-material being/an angel)
appeared to him and ordered him to read/recite إقراء . Ibn Husham, Ibid. Farsi version,
vol. 1, pp.152 -153. Arabic version, vol. 1, p.142.

The shape, who had a green written parchment ديباج in his hands, repeated three times the
same order to Mohammad. Mohammad recited loudly the four inscribed verses:

اقرا باسم ربک الذى خلق .خلق الانسان من علق .اقرا وربک الاکرم .الذى علم بالقلم .علم الانسان ما لم يعلم
سورة العلق .الايات5-1

*'Recited in the name of your Lord who created – created man from a clinging substance. Recite, and your
Lord is the most Generous – Who taught by the pen – taught man that which he knew not.'* Surah 96
v: 1-5

Mohammad was trembling and could not stay longer in the cave. He ran away towards the
house of Khadijeh.

In the end of the month of Ramadan, Mohammad left the cave and went to visit the
Kabah. He met Waraka who was turning around the House of Allah. Waraka asked him
about his particular experience. Mohammad talked with him and explained in detail every
single moment of that event. He kissed the forehead of Mohammad and told him what he
had said to Khadijeh about Namous ol Akbar. Ibn Husham, Ibid. Farsi version, vol. 1,
p.155.

According to the reporters, after this event, up to the time that he received a new wave of
the inner voice (Nedâ-Vahi) there was a period of three years of silence during which he
did not receive any other order. In concordance with our analysis, which we will see in this

mighty angel and replied: 'What do I read?'[60] After this event, Mohammad left the cave quickly, running away from the mountain called Jabal an Nour جبل النور to the house of Khadijeh.[61]

'Upon hearing this Khadijeh went to visit her cousin Waraka ibn Nowfel who was converted to the Nasranyyaf[62] النصرانية, had read a lot of books, and also learnt from the people of the books اهل الكتاب such as the Torah and the Evangelium. Khadijeh gave him the information about the experience of Mohammad concerning what he had heard and what he had witnessed. Waraka ibn Nowfel said: "Goddous, Goddous. I swear to the one who has the control upon the life of Waraka if what you said to me O Khadijeh

---

book, this period lasted much longer than only three years. In fact, Mohammad had this experience at a young age when he was not yet able to read or write. But following the guidance that he received during that mystical experience to 'Read, Recite,' he started a long period of education in Syria. At the end of that period of preparation to carry the hard responsibility of a divine mission on his shoulders he had to wait for the passage of time until he reached the age of forty years, to receive – according to the local tradition – permission to speak. When he had a new experience during which he received the order to go and proclaim his prophetic mission to his tribe, he was able to read/recite قرائت and to narrate تلاوت . The four sentences following the first revelation to Mohammad 'éghrà' are seen by all of the Muslim reporters and Quran interpreters as the beginning of the Quran. These four sentences talk about the creation and education of mankind; his education by pen in relation to the knowledge that he does not know and must learn.

60ـ قال رسول الله: فجائنى جبرئيل- و أنانائم- بنمط من ديباج فيه كتابٌ. فقال اقراء! قلتُ ما أقرأ. فغطنى به حتى ظننت أنه الموت. ثم ارسلنى فقال: اقراء. قلت ماذا اقراءُ... فقال: اقراء باسم ربك الذى خلق... فقراتها. ثم انتهى فانصرف عنى و هببت من نومى فكانما كُتِبَت فى قلبى كتابا. فخرجت ..." Ibn Husham, Ibid.

. Arabic version. Vol-1. P. 142 قَالَ جَابِرٌ : أَلَا أُخْبِرُكَ بِمَا حَدَّثَنَا رَسُولُ اللهِ صَلَّى اللهُعَلَيْهِ وَسَلَّم ، وَقَالَ فِي آخِره " : فَرَفَعْتُ رَأْسِيفَرَأَيْتُ شَيْئًافَجُدْثْتُ مِنْهُ ،فَأَتَيْتُ خَدِيجَة ، فَقُلْتُ : دَثْرُونِيفَدَثَّرُونِي وَصَبُّوا عَلَيَّ مَاءً بَارِدًا إِلَى آخِره " . و فى صحيح الامام ابوحسين مسلم كتب : جابربن عبدالله انصارى و كان من اصحاب رسول الله قال رسول الله و هو يحدث عن فترة الوحى ... فرجعت فقلت "زملونى زملونى. فدثرونى. فانزل الله تبارك و تعالى ياايها المدثر قم فانذر وربك فكبر و ثيابك فطهر و الرجز فاهجر. (المدثر. الايات 5-1). صحيح بخارى. دار صادر. بيروت. جلد الاول. ص.77.

61 Ibn Husham, Ibid. Arabic version, p.142.

62 Nasranyyat النصرانية means Christianity. But as we will see in the coming chapters there is a difference between monotheist Christianity and the official Christian church based on the principle of the Trinity.

has happened, the Nâmous Akbar came to him (Mohammad), the same who came to Moses. And he is the Prophet for this Ummah. Go and tell him to be strong.'" And Khadijeh returned to Mohammad and informed him about the opinion of Waraka.[63]

Later on Mohammad went to the Kabah and there he met Waraka. Waraka repeated the same sentences that he had said to Khadijeh once again to Mohammad; that he is finally the Prophet who was announced and promised by previous other prophets.[64] After this meeting and conversation, Mohammad returned back to his house.[65]

By looking at all of these events reported by ibn Husham we understand that the mission of Mohammad as a prophet started from the age of forty. But before reaching this crucial age, he was already a prophet, hiding his mission. According to the report of ibn Husham, his first meeting with the angels was when he was only about three to five years old,[66] when he was just an 'Ummi, illiterate little boy'الأُمَّى not yet able to read any text nor to inscribe any sentence, and unable to know the definition of faith.[67] Mohammad explained a miraculous meeting with the angels to his

---

[63] Ibn Husham, Arabic version, vol. 1, Ibid. p.143.

[64] In the Gospel of Yohànnàs (Saint John apostle) was written: 'When Monhàmànnâ – who will be sent to you from Ràbb, and Saint Spirit, comes to you He is coming from his Rabb and He will be my witness.' Ibn Husham adds this complementary explanation: in the Syriac language Monhàmànnà is Mohammad, and in Roman (Greek) language its equivalent is 'Bargàlis'. Ibn Husham, Ibid. Arabic version, vol. 1, p.140.

[65] Ibn Husham, Arabic version, Ibid. vol. 1, p.143.

[66] Ibn Husham, Ibid. Arabic version, vol. 1, p.100-101.

[67] وكذلك أوحينا إليك روحا من أمرنا ما كنت تدري ما الكتاب ولا الإيمان ولكن جعلناه نورا نهدي به من نشاء من عبادنا وإنك لتهدي إلى صراط مستقيم /سوره الشّورى –آيه 52

'And thus We have revealed to you an inspiration of Our command. You did not know what is the Book or [what is] faith, but We have made it a light by which We guide whom We will of Our servants. And indeed, [O Mohammad], you guide to a straight path' Surah 42, v:52

grandfather Abdul Motalleb[68] when Halimeh (his wet nurse) brought him back unexpectedly from the desert to Mecca. From the age of about three years, a long period of spiritual and cultural education started in the life of Mohammad in the company of the circle of the wise Hànif, both in Mecca and in Syria.

Historians have confused the time marking the beginning of the prophecy of Mohammad which began with his first meeting with the angels, with the proclamation of his mission at the age of forty. At the age of forty, Mohammad was an educated, literate, mature gentleman able to read the texts (tàlâwàt التلاوة), to recite the scriptures (garâ'àt القرائة) from the books, and to remind/teach (zekr الذكر) the contemporary inhabitants of Mecca the written tales of the lost people and civilisations. As we will see more in detail in further chapters, when he proclaimed loudly and openly to be the Prophet of Allah, the owner of the house of Ka'bah (Rabbol Beyt), his adversaries and the disbelievers told him: 'O Mohammad, you are just a literate man able to read the old written texts of the former people, which are dictated by other people to you and you take note of them;[69] and you

---

[68] Mohammad explained: *'I am the invitation of my father Abraham and the annunciation of my brother Jesus. When my mother was pregnant of me, a light emanated from her, shedding the palaces of Shâm – Bosra/Syria. I got milk in the tribe of Bani Sa'd ibn Bakir. Once I and a brother of milking of mine were looking after the sheep when two men dressed with the white clothes came to me bringing a golden plate full of snow. They captured me and opened my chest and brought out my heart and took away from my heart a little black point and washed my heart and inside of my chest with the snow.'* Ibn Husham, Ibid. Arabic version, p.100-101.

[69]و قال الذين كفروا ان هذا الا افک افتراه و اعانه عليه قوم آخرون فقد جانوا ظلما و زورا و قالوا اساطير الاولين اكتتبها فهی تملی عليه بکره و اصيلا. سورة الفرقان آيه 4-5

And those who disbelieve say, 'This [Quran] is not except a falsehood he invented, and another people assisted him in it. But they have committed an injustice and a lie. And they say, "Written legends of the former peoples which he has written down, and they are dictated to him morning and afternoon."' S.25 v.4-5

In the commentary of the Quran by ibn Kathir, these verses are explained by this manner: *'He (Mohammad is taking the copy/Estansakhà/* استنسخها *early in the morning and late in the evening the texts of the former people ...'* p.95. The commentary of ibn Kathir, Ismail ibn Omar ibn Kathir al-Qorashi al-Dameshqi. Edition: Dar Tayyebeh. 2002.

are a talented poet.[70] But until you levitate in front of our eyes to the sky to bring a book by your hands, we don't give any credence to your proclamation to be a prophet sent by Allah.'[71]

It is true that the majority of the inhabitants of Mecca were illiterate nomadic Bedouins, but there is no doubt that the Holy Books, written in different languages, such as diverse Gospels, the Torah, or the Enjil of Mani, existed in Mecca as well Medina, Syria, Jordan, Yemen, and Ethiopia (الحبشه), and were in the possession of Honàfâ (monotheists, followers of Abraham) as well as 'Ahl ol Ketab' (Jewish, Christian, Manichean, Sabian, and Zoroastrian).

After the dawn of Islam, for the first time, Mohammad taught, in Arabic, the people of Mecca and the surrounding regions (to whom a Holy Book in the Arabic language had never before been revealed) the content of the preceding Holy Books such as the صحف موسی Sohof of Moses, Sohof of Abrah صحف ابراهيم , Zobor owla زبر الاولی , Om ol Ketab ام الكتاب .

Inscribing the verses from the public proclamation of the Prophethood by Mohammad

According to the reports, from the recitation of the first revealed verse to Mohammad, Ali ibn abi Talib, the cousin of Mohammad who lived in his house as his disciple and was usually in his cousin's company,[72] was

---

[70]و ما هو بقول شاعر .قليلا ما تومنون .سوره الحاقه .آيه 41

It is not the words of a poet, there are only a few people who believe to this. Surah 69, v:41

[71]ترقی فی السما ولن نومن لرقيک حتی تنزل علينا كتابا نقروه قل سبحان ربی هل كنت الا بشرا رسولا .سوره الاسراء آيه 93

...Or you ascend into the sky. And [even then], we will not believe in your ascension until you bring down to us a book we may read. Surah 17, v:93

[72] Ibn Husham reports that Ali in company of Mohammad went to the valley of Mecca to pray, and it was just a secret between him and Mohammad. He was hiding his actions out of faith to the Prophecy of Mohammad- because it was not yet announced openly and

charged with the responsibility of writing down all the sentences of the Surahs in the Arabic alphabet following a chronological order. As explained previously, it is clear that the Arabic alphabet existed already as a settled art in Mecca. Ali accomplished this important mission perfectly in Mecca and in Medina, before and after migration, by writing down one by one all the sentences revealed to Mohammad and then passing them back to Mohammad. We should be aware that the problem of the collation of the Quranic verses was one of the main concerns occupying the mind of Mohammad. As it is noted in the Quran:

O Mohammad move not your tongue with it, to hasten with recitation of the Quran. Indeed, upon Us is its collection and junction of its sentences. So when We have realised its assemblage, then follow the order of its collection. Then upon Us is its explanation.' Surah 75, v:16 - 19.[73]

Jalal od Din Soyouti in his book (الاتقان فى علوم القرآن) *Al-Itghan fi Oloum él Quran* says: 'According to the opinion of Ghazi Aboubakr in his book called *al-Intesâr* الا نتصار the person to whom Allah revealed the Quran collected it. He (the collector) ordered somebody else to write down the Quran, but he did not write it by himself. And once it was completely collected and written as a book under two covers, nothing of its content was missing. And the order of its composition was established according to the original divine order, as the prophet made it in that manner in the building of each Surah.'[74]

---

publicly- from his father and his uncles and family and the Quraysh. ibn Husham. Ibid. vol-1. p.148-149. Arabic version.

[73] Qoran, قْران in this sentence is the equivalent of the word of Jàm'. It means to join together the pieces of a puzzle. To bring together and to collect in order to assemble. We must differentiate between the word of "qorân" قْران , used in these cited verses, and Kor'an قرآن used as the name of the book of Mohammad in other places.

[174] الاتقان فى علوم القرآن ـ جلال الدين سيوطى ـ جلد اول ـ صفحه 63 ـ

'Ali made a copy from the original manuscript of Prophet Mohammads' Quran. He wrote down the verses in chronological order of the revelation of each verse, and added their meanings. It is said in a Revayàt (cited by ibn Shahr Ashoub ابن شهرآشوب) that Ali collected what was in the house of the Prophet. Because the Prophet had said: "Ali, this is the ensemble of the book of Allah. Take it with you." So Ali collected it as it was written on different pieces of paper and wrapped them up in a large robe (such as an àbâ) and brought it to his house. When Mohammad passed away Ali dedicated his time to stay in the house and put the verses of Quran in an order as it was said by Allah.[75]

"Kalbi" الكلبى who was a reporter said: "When Mohammad died, Ali stayed in his house and collated the Quran according to the chronology of the revelation.'[76]

Where did Ali learn to read and write?

It seems that while Mohammad recited and narrated the verses to the people of the Arabian Peninsula as a prophet during a period of more than

---

الذى نذهب اليه أن جَمَع القرآن الذى انزلهُ الله، و آمر بإثبات رسمه .ولم ينسخه .و لا رفعَ تلاوته بعد نزوله هذا بين الدفتين .وأن ترتيبه و نظمه ثابت على ما نظمَهُ الله تعالى ورتّبَهُ عليه رسوله من آىَالّسُوَر

al-Itghan- vol.I, p.63. In those quotations neither Ghazi Aboubakr, nor Jalal od din Soyouti talk about Ali, as the writer of the Quran. But they precise that Mohammad collected and asked "somebody else" to write them down, however in p.291 of the same book al-Itghan Vol-1, Jalal od din Soyouti mentions the name of Ali as the writer of the Quran.

75ـ أَخَذَهُ عَمّا كان عند النبى .و أضافَ إليه التنزيل و التأويل .كما فى الرواية :ماكان فى بيت النبىفَأَخَذَهُ على بِأمر الرسول حيث قال "ياعلى !هذا كتابُ الله .خُذْهُ إليك فِجَمعَهُ علىَ فى ثوبٍ و مَضَى إلى منزله فَلَمّاقَبَضَ النبى، جَلَسَ علىّ فَلأَقَّهُ كَما أنزَلَ الله و كان به عالماً " و هذه الرواية رواها ابن شهرآشوب "التمهيد فى علوم القرآن .ج اول .ص. 291.

At-Tamhidfi Oloum el Korân: vol. 1 p.291. The révayat is cited from 'Ibn Shar Ashoub'.

76ـ لَمّاتَوَقّى رسول الله،قَعَدَ على بن ابى طالب فى بيته فِجَمعَهُ علىترتيب نزولِهِ .التمهيد فى علوم القرآن .جلد اول -صفحه 290

Ibid, vol. 1 p.290.

twenty years (610 AD - 632 AD), at the same time Ali ibn abi Talib (his cousin) inscribed those sentences.

The question is: where and when did Ali learn to inscribe the very specific and elaborate language of the Quran, using only the non-adequate Arabic alphabet (without points and using fifteen letters for writing twenty-eight letters of the alphabet) in a correct manner and in accordance with the complicated grammatical rules of a mixture of the Syriac-Aramaic-Arabic languages? There is no doubt that the Muslim community, regardless of the diverse Islamic denominations, unanimously confirm Ali's faculty of writing and reading.[77] So who was teacher and educator of Ali ibn abi Talib ibn Abdul Motalleb على ابن ابى طالب ابن عبدالمطلب [78]?

77- بابُ صلح الحديبية فى الحديبية. حدثنى عبدالله بن معاذ العنبرى حدثنا أبى حدثنا شُعبة عن ابى اسحاق قال: سمعتُ البَراء بن عازب يقول كتب على بن ابى طالب الصلح بين النبى و بين المشركين يوم الحديبيه. فكتبَ: "هذا ما كاتب عليه محمدرسول الله". فقالوا "لاتكتب رسول الله. فلونعلم أنك رسول الله لما نقاتلك. فقال النبى لعلى:"امحه"! فقال :"ماانا بالذى امحاه". فمحاه النبى بيده هذه الرواية 268 رواها امام ابو عبدالله البخارى فى كتابه :الصحيح. و رواها ايضاً الامام ابوحسين المسلم فى كتابه الصحيح. باب الجهاد و السير.

Abu Hossein al- Muslim, Sahih Muslim, vol. 3, p.688 Dar os Sâder.Beyrout .

'Mohammad dictated and Ali wrote down the peace treaty of Hodaybieh الحديبية ' Ibn Husham, Ibid., Farsi version, vol. 2, p.216.

قال رسول الله : أنَا مَدينة العِلم و علىّ بابُها . حديث روى الطبرانى فى "المعجم الكبير (11061) "والحاكم فى "مستدركه (4637) "وابن المقرئ فى "معجمه (175) "والسهمى فى "تاريخه" (65) والخطيب فى "تاريخه" (655/3)وابن المغازلي فى "مناقب على (120) "وابن حبان فى "المجروحين (130/1) "وابن عدى فى "الكامل (311/1)"والعقيلى فى "الضعفاء (149/3) "وأبو نعيم فى "المعرفة (88/1) "من طرق عنه صَلَّى اللهُ عَلَيْه وَسَلَّم أنه قال " إِنَا مَدينةُالْعِلْم وَعَلِيٍّ بَابُها ، فَمَنْ اَرَادَالْعِلْمْ فَلْيَأْ تِهِ مِنْ بَابِهِ"

This sentence is attributed to the prophet Mohammad as a Hadith os Sahih الصحيح . It is reported by all of the Shiite reports, and a considerable quantity of the Sunni reporters as well.

78 Ahmad ibn abi Ya'ghoub mentions the names of the Mohammad's scribes from the beginning to the end and he introduces a letter of Prophet Mohammad to the Yemenit people. The scribes of Mohammad according to Ahmad ibn abi Ya'ghoub are: Ali ibn abi Talib على ابن ابيطالب, Othman ibn Affan عثمان بن عقان , Amr ibn Âs ibn Omayyeh عمرو بن العاص بن الامية, Mo'âviieh ibn abi Sofian معاوية ابن ابى سفيان , Sharhabil ibn Hasaneh شرحبيل بن حَسَنة, Abdollah ibn Sa'd ibn abi Sarh عبدالله ابن سعد ابن ابى سرح , Moghayra tibn Sho'ba مغيرة ابن شعبة , Ma'z ibn Jabal معاذ ابن جبل , Zeyd ibn Thabit زيد ابن ثابت , Hanzala tibn Rabi' حنظلة ابن ربيع , Obayy ibn Ka'b أبىّ ابن كعب, Jahim ibn Silt جهيم ابن الصلت , Hasin Nomayri حصين النميرى . Tarikh Ya'ghoubi, Farsi version, vol. 1, p. 446. Ahmad ibn abi

We have seen already how the Quran rejects the false idea that Mohammad was an illiterate man.[79] The Quran introduces Mohammad as the best example for the Muslim community, and encourages every Muslim to behave according to the model of Mohammad.[80] Notably, the Quran advises explicitly that Muslims write down their contracts. Therefore the guide of the Muslim community needed to be an educated and literate person to inspire his followers fully. In accordance with the Quran, even the non-believers considered that Mohammad was able to write and to read the scriptures.

The Quran qualifies Mohammad with different qualities such as light, guide, warner, announcer, and so on.[81] One of the most important descriptions of Mohammad in the Quran is 'a person who is teaching',[82] who did indeed teach the Book and Wisdom الكتاب و الحكمة يعلمهم to those who were living in ignorance. He was teaching the science of writing-reading-reciting-narrating-understanding-studying the Books containing the Wisdom, yo'àlémohom ol Ketab val hikmat, الكِتاب و الحِكمَة يُعَلِّمُهُم and training to clean (yozakihem يُزَكِّيهِم) his disciples from the darkness of

---

Ya'ghoub talks also about the letters of Mohammad to the Kings of the neighbouring countries such as Persia and Byzance. Ibid. pp. 442-444.

[79] See section entitled 'Invention and evolution of the Arabic alphabet.'

[80] Ignas Goldziher, *Le dogme et la loi de l'Islam*, Paris 1920, Farsi translation by Ali Naghi Monzavi. Edition Kamanghir. Second publication. 1357: 1978: P. 32 footnote pp. 56-57 'Mohammad was seen by the Muslims as a hero, with the highest qualities of the best individual. Following the life style of Mohammad is the most important objective of each Muslim. The foundation of the Islamic ethic is the life style of Mohammad.'

81ـ يَا أَيُّهَا النَّبِيُّ إِنَّا أَرْسَلْنَاكَ شَاهِدًا وَمُبَشِّرًا وَنَذِيرًا . وَدَاعِيًا إِلَى اللَّهِ بِإِذْنِهِ وَسِرَاجًا مُنِيرًا /سوره احزاب آيات 45 و 46

O Prophet, indeed We have sent you as a witness and a bringer of good tidings and a warner. And one who invites to Allah, by His permission, and an illuminating lamp. S.33 v.45-46

82ـ لَقَدْ مَنَّ اللَّهُ عَلَى الْمُؤْمِنِينَ إِذْ بَعَثَ فِيهِمْ رَسُولًا مِنْ أَنْفُسِهِمْ يَتْلُوا عَلَيْهِمْ آيَاتِهِ وَ يُزَكِّيهِمْ وَيُعَلِّمُهُمُ الْكِتَابَ وَ الْحِكْمَةَ وَإِنْ كَانُوا مِنْ قَبْلُ لَفِي ضَلَالٍ مُبِينٍ .سوره آل عمران آيه 164

Certainly did Allah confer [great] favour upon the believers when He raised among them a Messenger from themselves, reciting to them His verses and purifying them and teaching them the Book and wisdom, although they had been before in manifest error. S.3 v-164

Ignorance الجاهلية . His cousin Ali, who lived like his own son in his house, was amongst his first devoted pupils even before the proclamation of his prophecy.[83]

What did Ali learn from his teacher Mohammad?

Ali learned the 'science of the Book', Elm ol Ketab علم الكتاب.[84] This science includes writing and inscribing (kitâbàt كتابت) as a kâtib, كاتب scribe, reading (tàlàwàt ol Ketab تلاوت الكتاب) and reciting (ghara'àt ol Ketab قرائت الكتاب) as a ghâri القارى , and studying from the book (yadresoun al Ketab يدرسون الكتاب). Mohammad knew all these techniques before the birth of Ali and familiarised Ali with them.

Twenty three years before Hegira (the start of the Islamic calendar) and ten years before proclamation of Mohammad's prophecy Ali was born. His father was called Abu Talib (one of the uncles of Mohammad) and his mother was named Fatimah. Three years after Mohammad's marriage with Khadijeh, when Mohammad was twenty-eight years old, and sometime after Ali's birth, Abu Talib brought Ali to his cousin's house, where he grew up under the observation and care of Mohammad and his wife Khadijeh.[85] Later on Ali and Fatima, (the daughter of Mohammad and Khadijeh), married and gave birth to Hassan, Hussein, Zeynab, and Ommé Kolthoum. Ali was a disciple and follower of Mohammad.

---

[83] Ibn Husham, Ibid. Arabic version, vol. 1, p.140. Farsi version, vol. 1, p.160: Ali was the first man of the Muslim community who attested the prophetic mission of Mohammad. Khadijeh was the first Muslim woman. Mohammad and Ali were praying together in the valley of Mecca.

[84] وَيَقُولُ الَّذِينَ كَفَرُوا لَسْتَ مُرْسَلًا قُلْ كَفَى بِاللَّهِ شَهِيدًا بَيْنِي وَبَيْنَكُمْ وَمَنْ عِنْدَهُ عِلْمُ الْكِتَابِ . سوره رعد .آيه 43

And those who have disbelieved say, 'You are not a messenger.' Say, [O Mohammad], 'Sufficient is Allah as Witness between me and you, and [the witness of] whoever has science of the book.' Surah 13, v: 43

[85] Ibn Husham. Ibid.Arabic version, vol-1. p. 148

From the age of three until he was twelve years old, Ali lived in the house of Mohammad and Khadijeh. The early life of Ali corresponds with the age of Mohammad from twenty-eight to forty. For the first seven of those twelve years, Mohammad was continuously travelling between Syria north of Mecca and Yemen south of Mecca, as a trade manager. He worked in the trading company of Khadijeh until he was thirty-five. During the period of Mohammad's travels as a businessman, which started when he was twenty years old (five years before he was married to Khadijeh and eight years before the birth of Ali), he was in close contact with the wise monotheists of the regions surrounding Mecca. Afterwards he stopped travelling for five years in order to stay in Mecca and spend his time mainly between the house of Khadijeh and the cave of Hera حراء in Jabal on Nour الجبل النور , outside Mecca, to meditate. In this time Ali was in his service, bringing him food and drink, but in an absolute secrecy as is stated by ibn Husham.[86] Mohammad was his master, teacher, inspirer, guide, educator, and trainer. Mohammad taught Ali, in particular the specific language of the Holy Book and its grammar, plus the art of calligraphy. The talent of a sincere disciple such as Ali and the qualities of a talented master such as Mohammad created from Ali a trustworthy scribe who gained the responsibility to redact the sentences of the Quran, from the first moment of revelation, when he was very young (about ten or twelve).

It is important to understand that the language of the first part of the verses of the Quran did not correspond with the usual spoken Arabic language of the Quraysh tribe. It was more related to Syriac-Aramaic literature, totally foreign for the Bedouins of Mecca. In consequence, in order to write it correctly, it was not enough for the scribe just to know the

---

[86] Ibn Husham explains that Mohammad was learning the manner in which to do the ablution, prayers, (including all of the sentences of incantation to say during the prayers and the bodily movements and actions in prayers, and time of prayers, and the direction to orient his attention, etc...) from the Angel Gabriel, and did teach them exactly to his wife Khadijeh –Arabic version ibid- vol.I p.147 and to Ali – ibid-p. 148, 149, out of the eyes of the father of Ali and his uncles and his tribe. Ibid. Farsi version. Vol-1 p.161

Arabic alphabet, but to have a complete knowledge of the grammatical aspects of the language. This is very important, particularly when we see that the oldest examples of the Quran, in Hijazi and Kufi scriptures, are written without the usage of points on any letters of their alphabet and just on the base of fifteen letters for writing down the usual twenty-eight Arabic letters. This shows that Ali must have had a teacher to instruct him all of the subtle secrets of this art. In a sentence attributed to Ali he says: 'Whoever taught me "one letter" – (the secret of the science of the letters) – made me forever his servant.'[87] And in a Hadith attributed to Mohammad he says, 'I am the city of the knowledge, and Ali is the gate of this city.'[88]

From the first moment of its revelation, the verses of the Quran were inscribed by Ali up until the end of the period of revelation (a few months before the death of Mohammad). This was the first version of the Quran, which was recorded according to the rhythm (flow) of the chronology of revelation. During the last months of the life of Mohammad and under his observation and order, Ali managed to write down a new version of the Quran in which the verses were arranged in a different sequence and classification in the frame of 114 chapters, Surahs, with specific names and titles. This book was the Quran, the final version written in the lifetime of

---

87ـ "مَن عَلّمَنى حرفاً، قد صَيّرنى عبداً" ـ من تعلمت منه حرفاً صرت له عبداً. ملا محمدباقر المجلسى. بحارالانوار، ج77، ص165

'Man Alamani harfa, ghad sayarani abdâ' – Mohammad Baghar Majlesi, Bihâr ol Anwar, vol. 77, p.165.

88ـ قال رسول الله:" انا مدينة العلم و علىّ بابها فَمَنْ أَرَادَ الْعِلْمَ أَتِّيهِ مِنْ بَابِهِ " كما نقول من قبل، هذا الحديث حديثٌ صحيحٌ متواترٌ رَواهُ الرُّوات عَلَى التّواتر. الطبراني في "المعجم الكبير" (11061) "والحاكم في "مستدركه " (4637)وابن المقرئ في "معجمه" (175) "والسهمي في "تاريخه"و الخطيب في "تاريخه" (655/3) "وابن المغازلي في "مناقب علي" (120) "وابن حبان في "المجروحين" (130/1) "وابن عدي في "الكامل" (311/1) " والعقيلي في "الضعفاء" (149/3) "وأبو نعيم في "المعرفة".

See footnote 72

Mohammad, by the hand of Ali, according to the whole archive of the revealed verses and sentences.[89]

It is clear that the complete version of the Book of Mohammad called the Quran was written twice by the hand of Ali under Mohammad's observation. The first version was according to the chronology of revelation, and the second version was in the form and shape of a book assembled during the last months of the life of Prophet Mohammad in Medina.[90] This last version was the official version of the Holy Book of the Muslim community (See the page 5). Before his death Mohammad announced it to his companions: 'I am going to die and will leave amongst you two important heritages: the Book of Allah, and my étràt العترة – Ahl él bayt اهل البيت – family. Be attached tightly to both of them, in order to be protected by Allah (from any division and deviation).'[91]

We understand (according to the révâyâts and reports) that from this final version of the Quran written by Ali, Mohammad assigned Zeyd ibn

---

[89] The reporters confirm that Mohammad himself was getting guidance from the angel of revelation to assemble the Quran in this manner.

[90] Mohammad returned back from his last pilgrimage to Mecca which was called 'Haj jatol Védâ' – farewell pilgrimage. On the way back from Mecca to Medina he stopped in a place called al Ghadir and gave a very long speech. This speech is called 'Khotbato Haj jatol Veda', in which he announced that it was the last 'Hajj' that he would do, that in the coming years the Muslims would no longer be in his company, and he had accomplished his mission to transmit the divine messages to his Ummah. Ibn Husham, Ibid, second volume pp. 373-380.

[91] Hadith Nabavi cited by Zeyd ibn Argham, reported by al Mulem in his book *Sahih*. Hadith as-Sagàlayn is cited by many reporters: Al-Termazhi ; as-Sonan, vol. 5 in the chapter titled 'al-Managhib fil Ahlol bayt en Nabbi'. Ahmad Hanbal. Al-Musnàd, vol. III, p.14, 17, 26, 59. Hâkim says in Al-Mustadrak, vol. 3 p.109 that this Hadith is Sahih according to Muslim and Bokhari in their books called *Sahih*. Mohammad Baghir el Majlesi, Bihâr ol Anwar, vol. 3 p.106.

حديث الثقلين وهو قول النبي صلى الله عليه وآله : إني تارك فيكم الثقلين : كتاب الله ، وعترتي أهل بيتي ، ما إن تمسكتم بهما لن تضلوا بعدي أبدا "ما هو حديث الثقلين حديث الثقلين أخرجه الإمام مسلم في صحيحه عن زيد بن أرقم أن النبي قال :وأنا تارك فيكم الثقلين أولهما كتاب الله فيه الهدى والنور فخذوا بكتاب الله وأستمسكوا به قال زيد :فحث على كتاب الله ورغب فيه ثم قال :وأهل بيتي أذكركم الله في أهل بيتي أذكركم الله في أهل بيتي أذكركم الله في أهل بيتي" أخرجه الإمام مسلم في صحيحه

Thabit[92] to make a copy and to give to Abu Bakr, the oldest Sheikh of all the companions of the Muslim community. As we mentioned, it is certain that Ali gathered all of the sentences that he had collected from the beginning of Islam until the death of Mohammad in the form of a book. It was the most complete example of the Quran, known as 'al-Moshaf ol Ali'.[93] By this fact, one can conclude that people such as Zeyd ibn Thabit and Hafsah bint Omar, who learned the art of writing in Medina, must have copied a complete version of the Quran by order of Mohammad during his life. That original example could not be any other one than the book collected by Ali and certified by Mohammad himself.[94]

Prophet Mohammad spent the last moments of his life in his house in Medina where he was lying in his bed while Ali was taking care of him. Abu Bakr, Omar, Othman, the chiefs of the tribes, the companions of Mohammad from Mohajeroun and Ansâr were all present at the moment Mohammad closed his eyes and passed away. The army of the Muslim community under the leadership of Zeyd ibn Haritheh was ready to confront the Byzantine warriors.

After the death of Prophet Mohammad, Ali, who then was around the age of thirty-five, took the body of Mohammad to wash and cover it with white linen and bury him. Meanwhile the companions of Mohammad, including Mohajeroun and Ansâr, after much deliberation decided to vote in favour of Abu Bakr becoming the first Caliph of the Muslim community in Saghifeh[95] Bani Sâedeh سقيفة بنى ساعدة in Medina.

---

[92] A young scribe from Medina.

[93] Ibn en Nadim in his book Al Fihrest confirms that he has seen by his own eyes the Moshaf of Ali. Ibn Nadim adds that due to the passage of the years, some pages of this example of the Quran have been lost and disappeared. History of the Quran- Mahmoud Ramiar, pp. 368-369.

[94] http://www.birmingham.ac.uk/news/latest/2015/07/quran-manuscript-22-07-15.aspx

[95] Saghifeh: place with a roof top, i.e. gathering place.

Abu Bakr (the first Caliph) and his example of the Quran

In conclusion, we can say that the copy of the Quran of Abu Bakr was in his house until the end his life, and passed after his death ابوبکر to Omar ibn Khattab عمربن الخطاب , the second Caliph, and remained in the possession of his daughter, Hafseh bint Omar حفصة بنت عمر , after Omar's sudden assassination. She brought this heritage to the third Caliph, Othman عثمان بن عفان, who then gave it back to Zeyd ibn Thabit (زید بن ثابت) as the most exact example of the Quran. Othman ordered all those who had a personal copies of the Quran to bring their books to an assembly of literate companions of Prophet Mohammad, in order to compare with the Quran of Hafseh bint Omar. Ali also brought his version. After making the comparison, Othman ordered all the other versions to be burned, and asked Zeyd and the assembly of the scribes to make multiple copies of the one official version of 'the Book of Allah' in order to give it to those who recited (Ghari), to read according to that one and only version. Only two copies were not burned in this assembly: the Quran of Ali and the Quran of Hafseh. They both took back their own books and returned to their houses. This confirms the similarity of their Moshafs (the other name for the Quran) with the official version of the Holy Quran.

We can suppose that the reason Ali brought his own version to that assembly was to certify the accuracy of the version of Hafseh during the comparison with his original book. This would be because Hafseh had made a personal copy for herself during the period of her possession of the Quran of Abu Bakr, and Ali and Othman wanted to avoid any mistake.[96]

As we have mentioned, according to our exploration and analysis, either the Quran which passed from Zeyd to Hafsah to Othman is a copy of the Quran written in the time of Prophet Mohammad under his care by Ali, copied in Medina by Zeyd ibn Thabet, and given as a gift to Abu Bakr; or

---

[96] As we will see, the personal example of Hafsah, copied by a scribe from the example of Abu Bakr, was also burned in 45 AH, after the death of Hafsah.

both examples (the Quran of Ali and the Quran of Zeyd) were copied from another source, which should have been only written by Prophet Mohammad himself.

Kufi style

In the period of the third Caliph the scribes in Medina wrote the verses of the Quran in the frame of a book by using the 'Kufi style'. The Kufi style is in fact the elaboration of the technique of the scribes in Medina but it is somehow related to the city of Kufah, which is a city in Mesopotamia[97] located on the banks of the Euphrates River.

The city was founded in 637 AD by the order of the second Rashidun Caliph Omar ibn al-Khattab, a few years after the conquest of Ctesiphon, the capital of the Sassanid kingdom, by one of the companions of the prophet Sa'd ibn abi Waqqa سعد ابن ابی وقّاص.

In the beginning, Sa'd founded Kufah as a simple encampment adjacent to the Lakhmid Arab city of al-Hīra, and later incorporated it as a city of seven divisions.[98] Omar, who assigned the Jewish land in Arabia to his warriors, ordered the relocation of the Jews of Khaybar الخيبر in Medina to a strip of land in Kufah in 640 AD. Omar was assassinated in Medina on 7th November 644 AD and his successor Othman replaced him. The first official version of the Quran was written in this period under the order of the third Caliph Othman in the Kufi style of the Arabic alphabet. One of the oldest examples of the Quran, kept in Tashkent in Uzbekistan, supposed to be the original Quran of Othman, or a close copy of it, confirms that it was written in Kufi style. This style was used by Zeyd ibn Thabet to inscribe the Book of Allah. Although this style is named Kufi style, Zeyd ibn Thabet learned it

---

[97] Kufah (الكوفة *al-Kūfah*) Iraq, is about 170 kilometres south of Baghdad, and ten kilometres north-east of Najaf.

[98] Non-Arabs knew the city under alternate names: *Hīra* and *Aqulah*, before the consolidations of 'Abdu l-Mālik in 691. Kufah was the final capital of 'Alī ibn Abī Ṭālib.

when he went to the Jewish school of Medina, on the advice of Mohammad, to learn to read and write the Arabic alphabet. Perhaps the teachers and instructors of the same school of Medina were among the Jewish community who went from Medina to Kufah, by order of Omar ibn Khattab.

Some quotations about the writing of the Quran

Hadith as-Sagàlayn, is one of the well-known "sayings" of the Prophet Mohammad. He says: "I leave –after my death- for you two heavy things: the Book of Allah, and my "Etràt" (family)/ or "Sunnat" (tradition). This hadith إنّى تاركٌ فيكم الثّقلين: كتاب الله و عترتى (أو سنّتى). –which is cited by many reporters[99] – is an important proof confirming the existence of the Quran as a finalized book, in the lifetime of the Prophet Mohammad. Jalal od Din Soyouti in his book *al-Itghan* says: 'There exists the "ijma'" (opinion of the high religious authorities – doctors in the Islamic law – unanimously) and the "revayat" (reports about the Islamic events regarding the time of the Prophet) confirming the fact that the verses of the Quran are "towghifi" (fixed according to the will of the Prophet, and not decided by the people themselves) and it is actually a certain fact, without any doubt in it. Regarding the 'Ijma" the experts such as Zarkeshi in his book *al-Borhan* and 'Abu Ja'far Zobay in his book *al-Monâsebât* say: 'The order of verses and the Surahs are done according to the guidance of the Prophet without any doubt; and regarding the "revayat" we mention the "revayat of Zeyd" saying: "we were somewhere near to the prophet and were collecting the verses upon pieces of paper.'[100]

---

[99] Al-Termazhi ; as-Sonan, vol. 5 in the chapter titled 'al-Managhib fil Ahlol bayt en Nabbi.' Ahmad Hanbal. Al-Musnàd, vol.III, p.14, 17, 26, 59. Hâkim says in Al-Mustadrak, vol.3 p.109 that this Hadith is Sahih according to Muslim and Bokhari in their books of 'Sahih. Mohammad Baghir el Majlesi, Bihâr ol Anwar, vol. 3 p.106.

[100] Soyouti, Al-Itghan, vol. 1, p.62.

عبدالرحمن بن الكمال ابى‌بكر بن محمد سابق‌الدين الخضيرى الأسيوطى . الاتقان فى علوم القرآن. مركز الدراسات القرآنية. 1426 هجرى. المجلدات 7.

Morteza Alam ol Hoda as reported by Tabarsi says: 'The Quran that was gathered and collected in the time of the Prophet is similar to the Book which exists in our time. Certain companions of the prophet such as Abdollah ibn Mas'oud and Obayy ibn Kà'b and others, made two examples of the Quran in the time of the prophet, and they read it from the beginning to the end multiple times. So it confirms the fact that the Quran was already gathered as a book (in the time of the Prophet Mohammad), not spread on different pieces.'[101] "There existed some companions of the Prophet who were inscribing the Quran while it was revealed to the Prophet (sentence by sentence), either under his order or by their own decision, completely or partially. In concordance with a general opinion between Muslims, those who wrote the Quran in its totality, they were five people".[102] Anas ibn Malik mentions the names of four of the Quran-collectors in the time of the Prophet, namely Obayy أُبَىّ ابن كَعب, Mà'zh ibn Jabal معاذ ابن جبل, Abou Zeyd ابو زيد, Zeyd ibn Thabit" زيد بن ثابت . "We understood that the Quran was already written in the life period of the Prophet, piece by piece upon papers, bones, the skin of the palm trees... later on Abu Bakr ordered to bring together all of those written pieces to make out of them one book".[103]

Imam Abu Abdollah al Mohasebi in his book *Fahm os Sonan Ma Nassoh* says: 'The writing of the Quran is not a new case. It was done under the order of the prophet himself. They were written on the papers one by one, and they were kept in the house of the Prophet Mohammad. But Abu Bakr collected all of those papers and attached them to each other by ropes'[104].

---

[101]Tabarsi, At-Tafsir ol-Majma'ol Bayan, vol. 1, p.15 fànn ol khâmès.

ابو على فضل بن الحسن الطبرسى. تفسير مجمع البيان فى تفسير القرآن. 20 المجلد. ترجمة الفارسية 30 المجلد.

[102] Allameh Rafe'I; E'jaz ol Quran, p.36.

اعجاز القرآن. مصطفى صادق الرافعى. دانشنامه جهان اسلام. مبحث "اعجاز القرآن".

[103]-Manna' Ghattan. Mabaheth fi Oloum él Quran.(مباحث فى علوم القرآن. مكتبة وهبة. القاهرة) P.74 .

[104]Zarghani, Mànâhel ol-Erfan fi Quran, Beyrout; 2008, vol. 1 p.242.

Ghazi Aboubakr in his book *al-Intisâr* wrote: 'We follow this way that the Quran was collected and written and recited by the order of the person to whom it was revealed, between two covers, totally without any missing part.'[105]

Baghavi in his book *Sharh os Sunnah* says: 'The companions of the Prophet collected between two covers (as a book) the Quran which was sent by Allah to His Messenger without any addition or deletion.'[106]

In summary, these quotations state that, the Quran as a book existed in the lifetime of Mohammad. Actually the word 'Ketab' does not mean separate texts, written upon bones, skins of palm trees and stones, but 'one collected ensemble of the text between two covers' i.e. one thing which exists on its own.[107]

Some reporters stress on the name of Zeyd between all of the Quran collectors among the companions of the Prophet. Certainly, Zeyd was a literate individual, educated in the Jewish school of the Arabic language and inscribing in Medina. The problem with Zeyd is that he was from the group of Ansâr among the companions of Prophet Mohammad who converted to Islam after the migration of the Prophet to Medina, and as a consequence he missed the thirteen years of revelations of the Quran, which took place in Mecca. Therefore, in order to accomplish the task of inscribing the Quran, he needed to make copies of the verses of the Quran that were

---

مناهل العرفان فى علوم القرآن. محمدعبدالعظيم الزرقانى. دارالكتاب العربى. بيروت. 2 مجلد. بيروت. 1995/ الطبعة الثانى 2008 .

[105] Soyouti, Ibid, vol. 1, p.63.

[106] Soyouti, Ibid, vol. 1, p.63.

[107] Abul Gasem Khoii, Tafsir ol- Bàyân, Arabic version, p. 271.

البيان فى تفسير القرآن. ابوالقاسم خويى. النجف الاشرف. 413 هـق. ترجمه فارسى هاشم زاده هريسى.

Bukhari, Sahih. (كتاب صحيح. البخارى)Ketab ol Fazael. Chapter of Fazâél ol Ansar, vol. 6, p.106. and his book Ketab ot Tafsir. Chapter about the companions of the Prophet.

revealed in Mecca, and written by another scribe. Actually, a complete example of the Quran should have existed from the first revelation to the last verse revealed in Medina, written by a person who was present, educated eyewitness from the beginning, and in the company of Mohammad, such as Ali. Also, according to the reports, Ali inscribed the Quran, even though he had not learned the art of inscribing in any school in Medina. As we have shown before, he had learned it in another school in Mecca, whose calligraphic-style was different from the style of the scribes in Medina. Thus his Quran was written in another type of calligraphy/it means Hijazi style.

Figure 9 - The Quran in Tashkent[108]

Figure 10 - The Quran of Topkapi Museum, Istanbul

---

[108] This was one of the oldest known copies of the Quran, written in Kufi style, رسم الخط (الكوفی),before the discovery of the Quran of Tübingen.

The recent determination of the age of the oldest Quran examples, in the Tübingen and Birmingham Universities, which are both inscribed in Hejazi style, confirms that this model of writing was older then the Kufi style used by the team of Zeyd to write down the example known as the Quran of Othman.

The examples in the Topkapi Museum in Turkey, and in Tashkent in Uzbekistan, are both written in Kufi style, following the scribe model of the Quran of Othman.

Therefore, the oldest examples of the Quran currently held in Tübingen and Birmingham should be considered somehow related to Ali ibn abi Talib.[109]

Summary

So in summary we can conclude the following:

a) The Quran existed already as 'one book' in the lifetime of Mohammad;

b) It was written in Hijazi style;

c) It was inscribed by Ali;

d) The teacher of Ali was Mohammad himself;

e) Mohammad was a literate man and learned to inscribe Arabic calligraphy in Mecca in a Christian-Manichean school of the circle of the Hanifs, connected to the monastery of Bosra in the south of Syria;

f) Waraka ibn Nowfel was an educated monotheist in Mecca and taught the lessons according to Abraham from the old written scripture called Sohof é Ebrahim.

---

[109] In this 'Hijazi scribe style' رسم الخط الحجازى other examples of the Quran exist as well in Paris, Berlin, and St Petersburg. The examples of the Quran written in Hijazi style are not complete, but only contain some Surahs and verses.

The similarity of the content of the two examples of Quran (in Kufi and in Hijazi)

Despite the fact that the calligraphy of the examples of the Quran of Birmingham and Tübingen are related to a different school of inscribing from the copies of the Quran related to the Quran of the third Caliph, the formulation of the sentences in the frame of the verses and Surahs are absolutely similar to each other. It seems as if one of them is a copy of the other, or both of them are copies of yet another example. As mentioned previously, in the period of the third Caliph, two examples of the Quran existed and were used for scribing an officially recognise d unique example of the Quran: the Moshaf of Hafsah bint Omar, one of the wives of Prophet Mohammad and the Moshaf of Ali ibn abi Talib, cousin of Prophet Mohammad.

In this case the two versions of the Quran (Hijazi and Kufi), have been inscribed in accordance with another older, original book. This is the reason that they look similar to each other with regard to the name and number of the Surahs and verses.[110]

---

[110] The different examples of the Quran written in Hijazi style are not complete.

How was the Quran collected in the time of the prophet?

Ibn Hajar said: 'Nàsâii reported by true evidence, sanad é sahih, from one of the companions of the Prophet called Abdollah ibn Amr ibn al-As who said, "I collected the Quran, and read it each night. People told the Prophet of this and he said: 'read it once a month.'"[111]

Hâkim on Nayshabouri reported from Zeyd ibn Thabet who said: 'We were with the Prophet of God, and we collected the Quran from the robe.' And Nayshabouri adds: 'This is an exact report according to Moslem and Bukhari, even if they did not mention it in their books named Sahih.'[112] It confirms again that the Quran was collected in the lifetime of the Prophet.[113]

The author has discovered a tradition in some Muslim countries, particularly in Africa, which sheds some light on this issue. It concerns the box containing the Quran. Keeping the Quran in a box relates to a very old tradition, preceding Islam, which was used by the Christian-Manichean scribes to inscribe the Gospels on different papers, and place them one by one upon each other in the correct order, and then put them in the box.[114] This ancient tradition was certainly known by the traders of Mecca who travelled between Mecca and Ethiopia, and Mecca and Syria, and could have been transmitted to the scribes in the time of the emergence of Islam in Mecca as well. Therefore, the box contained the unbound pages of Quran. The Quran was therefore in the box in its entirety but not in the form of a bound or tied book.

---

[111] Fat hol-Bâri, vol. IX, p.47; As Sonan ol Kobrâ, An-Nésâii, vol. V, p.24; Ahmad Hanbal. Mosnàd, vol. II, p.163; Sahih, Ibn Habban, vol. III, p.33.

[112] Al-Mostadrak alas Sahihayn, vol. II, p.611; Ahmad Hanbal. Mosnad, vol. V, p.185; at Termazhi. Sàhih, vol. 0, p.390.

[113] Jalal od Din Soyouti in his book al-Etghan, vol. I, pp.62-63 gives more reports in this sense.

[114] Recently in Middle Egypt the researchers found very old examples of the Gospels of the Apostles of Jesus in Coptic language. 'The Gospel of Judas', from Codex Tchakos, Rudolphe Kasser, Marvin M. Meyer, Gregor Wurst.

Figure 11 - The box of the Quran

Figure 12 - The pages containing the Quranic verses[115]

Therefore, it could be concluded that the use of this method of writing the texts on non-attached pages, and keeping them together in one place, inside a box, corresponds with an intermediary state in the transitional period of the writing of the Quran. This manner of preserving the verses could have been the most suitable method, because of the gradual nature of revelation of the sentences of the Quran during a period of twenty-three years.

To summarise:

a) The verses were revealed gradually over a long period,

---

[115] This corpus of the non-attached pages contains the verses of the Quran. The box of the Quran is on display in the British Museum in London.

b) They were written one after another on paper,

c) They were placed upon each other in a box.

Thus as a consequence they remained collected and gathered next to each other in one place, but at the same time they did not yet make a 'real book', because they were not yet fixed and settled in their final arrangement. 'The Book' could not be completed before bringing each verse into its exact final position. This could not be done until the end of the period of revelation. Once everything was ordered in its exact place, and it was enframed, the scribes could attach the single sheets to each other by threads.

To better understand the process of final positioning of the verses, we can say that the Quran (as it is today in the hands of the Muslims) was certainly rearranged by Mohammad himself. For instance, the first verses supposed by the majority of the Muslim community to be introduced by Mohammad as the initial moment of the revelation are the following five:

'Recite in the name of your Ràbb[116] who created. Created man from a viscid substance. Recite, and your Ràbb is the most Generous. Who taught by the pen. Taught man that which he knew not.' Surah 96, v:1-5

From a chronological point of view these verses should be placed in the opening part and first chapter of the Quran. But they constitute a part of the 96th Surah of the Quran, with an additional part composed of some fourteen other verses which were revealed at another time to the Prophet:

'No! [But] indeed, man transgresses. Because he sees himself self-sufficient. Indeed, to your Lord is the return. Have you seen the one who forbids, a servant when he prays? Have you seen if he is upon guidance, or enjoins righteousness? Have you seen if he denies and turns

---

[116] Rább can be translated as 'Master', 'Lord', 'Guide'. We have chosen to keep 'Ràbb' because the term has a unique and authentic notion in its original expression.

away? Does he not know that Allah sees? No! If he does not desist, We will surely drag him by the forelock, A lying, sinning forelock. Then let him call his associates; We will call the angels of Hell. No! Do not obey him. But prostrate and draw near [to Allah].' Surah 96, v: 6-19

The majority of Muslims believe that in the second moment of the revelation Mohammad recited these seven verses:

'O you who covers himself [with a garment], arise and warn. And glorify for your Ràbb. And your clothing purify. And uncleanliness avoid. And do not confer favour to acquire more. But for your Lord be patient.' Surah 74, v:1-7

But in the Quran the place given to these verses is not in the second paragraph. They are just a part of Surah 74, composed of an ensemble of fifty-six verses, introduced and recited by Mohammad during different years.

Gradual steps in completion of the Quran

Therefore we can differentiate certain steps in the process of the completion of the Quran as a book:

a) The revelation to Mohammad, and recitation by Mohammad;

b) Inscribing the recited sentences by a scribe close to Mohammad, from the beginning to the end;

c) Taking a new copy of those verses upon paper in order to place them on top of each other and collect them in a box;

d) Fixing the sentences in their final position in the frame of Surah;

e) Making from all of the Surahs an ensemble in the form of a book, including the attachment of the pages to each other by thread and needle, and covering them with a hard cover made from animal skin.

It could be concluded that:

a.) The Quran was revealed to Mohammad by Vahi;

b.) The Quran was recited by Mohammad;

c.) The Quran was written by Ali on paper;

d.) The single pages of the Quran were placed upon each other in 'the box of the Quran'.

In the last year of Mohammad's life, the whole Peninsula of Arabia, from Yemen in the south to Bosra/Syria in the north, was already under the flag of Islam, and the newborn religion was established. During this period, some literate companions of the Prophet Mohammad -under his observation- were working to make a finalised Book as the unique authoritative valid version of the Quran. Hence, even before the final "Farewell pilgrimage" حجة الوداع of the Prophet Mohammad to Mecca (in company of the majority of the Muslim community, in March 632 AD) the final example of the Quran was in a box. After leading the ceremony of pilgrimage, the Prophet Mohammad returned back to Medina. He assigned and instructed those people able to inscribe, to come and write down a copy for themselves from the original example contained in a box. Zeyd ibn Thabet and some other people made copies for themselves and for some of the companions such as Abu Bakr, and so on. In the time of the third Caliph and under his order, the majority of the examples of the Quran were destroyed, once they had been compared to each other, apart from the "Moshaf of Abu Bakr", the "Moshaf of Ali", and the official version which became the original example of the Quran (written in the Kufi alphabet) to be copied by the governmental scribes and sent all over the empire to be recited by the narrators.

Hafsah bint é Omar

Hafsah bint é Omar[117] was one of Mohammads' wives, whose father was Omar ibn Khattab (second Caliph) and whose mother, Zeynab, was a sister of Othman ibn Matoun (one of the companions of Mohammad). She was born five years before the birth of Islam and eighteen years before Hegira. Her marriage to Mohammad was her second marriage, after the death of her first husband (Khonays ibn Hozafeh Sahmi), two months before the battle of Ohod in Medina, in the third year after Hegira, and she died forty one years after Hegira. She was not in the camp of the companions of Ali.[118]

According to ibn Sà'd in his book *At Tàbàghât ol Kobra*, Hafsah following the advice of Mohammad, learned to read and write under the teaching of a woman called Shàfâ bint é Abdullah Adàvieh, who was one of the literate people during the Period of Ignorance in the Peninsula of Arabia.[119] This means that Hafsah was a literate person living in the house of Mohammad in Medina.

The Moshaf of Hafsah

As we have mentioned, a written example of the Quran, from the period of the first Caliph Abu Bakr, and inherited by Omar after the death of Abu Bakr, remained in the possession of Hafsah after the sudden and unexpected assassination of Omar by Abou Lo ابولوء لوء فيروزان .

117- حفصة بنت عمر بن الخطاب- ولدت خمسة اعوام قبل البعثة و ماتت شعبان 41 ق.هـ/ 602 م. - إحدى زوجات النبي محمد، وابنة الخليفة الثاني عمر بن الخطاب وشقيقة الصحابي عبد الله بن عمر. أسلمت حفصة في مكة، ثم هاجرت مع زوجها الأول خنيس بن حذافة السهمي إلى المدينة المنورة، ثم تزوجها النبي محمد بعد وفاة زوجها الأول إثر جروح أصابته في غزوة بدر. توفيت حفصة في شعبان 41 هـ بالمدينة في أول خلافة معاوية بن أبي سفيان، وصلى عليها مروان بن الحكم أمير المدينة في ذلك الحين، ودفنت في البقيع، ونزل في قبرها أخواها عبد الله وعاصم.

118- فقد روى أبو عبد الله البخاري أن نساء النبي محمد كان حزبين، حزب فيه عائشة وحفصة وصفية و سودة، والآخر فيه أم سلمة وباقي نساء النبي محمد. فتح الباري، كتاب الهبة، باب 8. 51 من أهدى إلى صاحبه وتحرى بعض نسائه دون بعض، 243\5

119- ابن سعد، الطبقات الكبرى، ج 8، ص 84، بيروت 1405/1985.

In the period of the third Caliph, Othman ibn Affan, while the authorities decided to make one official unique version of the Quran and gave the mission of the redaction and collection of the verses and Surahs of the Quran into the form of a book to a group of literate individuals under the leadership of Zeyd ibn Thabit, Hafsah was invited to bring that example of the Quran to the Caliphate's house.

According to Mohammad Ismaeil Bukhari[120] and ibn abi Davoud,[121] at the end of that procedure, Othman ordered all of the diverse examples of the Quran to be put into the fire, apart from the Moshaf of Hafsah (and the Moshaf of Ali). Ali received his book back, as Hafsah also received hers, and her book remained in her possession until the end of her life. We know that Abu Bakr and Omar were illiterate all their lives, which signifies that the example of the Quran known as the Moshaf of Hafsah could not have been written by either of them. This book was called Moshaf é Hafsah only because it was in the possession of Hafsah, and not because it was written or collected by Hafsah.

According to Mohammad Ismail é Bukhari, and ibn abi Davoud[122], Hafsah assigned a scribe to make a copy of her inherited example of the Quran for herself, because she thought it would be necessary to release her heritage from Omar to the third Caliph Othman.

Ibn abi Davoud stated that Hafsah asked her scribe to consult her before writing verse number 238 of the second Surah, and to inscribe that sentence according to a frame that she would explain.[123] Zobayr ibn Bakkar,[124] Ahmad

---

[120] Sahih, volume V, pp 210-211.

[121] *Ketab ol masáhif* pp 15-16.

[122] *Ketab ot Tarikh ol kabir* volume six, 6th chapter, second section page 330; ibn abi Davoud *Ketab ol Masahif* pp 95-97

[123] *Ketab ol Masahif*, pp 96-97.

[124] Al Muntakhab min ketab é Azwaj on Nabi, p. 40.

ibn Yàhiâ Balazari,[125] and ibn abi Davoud[126] state that after the death of Hafsah the Mayor of Medina, a man named Màrvân, recuperated the book of Hafsah from the possession of her brother and destroyed it. This was in order to avoid any risk of the existence of two different versions of the Quran. It is not clear which example of the Quran was destroyed – the original one which was the heritage of Abu Bakr and Omar, or the personal example of Hafsah copied from that original one, or both of them.[127]

Although the first Caliph, was illiterate companion of Mohammad, he retained an example of the Quran which was copied by Zeyd, from the basic, authentic, and original Quran in the time of the Prophet Mohammad. After the death of Abu Bakr, Omar (the second Caliph) who also was illiterate, inherited this example and brought it to his house, which was used by his literate daughter Hafseh. According to ibn abi Davoud,[128] one of the first actions of Othman – third Caliph- was to call Zeyd ibn Thabet and order him to make an official version of the Quran in concordance with the Abu Bakr's example. Ibn abi Davoud[129] mentions that for the first time Zeyd was invited by the second Caliph (Omar) to make one official example of the Quran, and his work in the time of Othman (third Caliph) was in continuity with his work in the time of Omar. Nevertheless, Zeyd needed to have an original example of the Quran with a direct connection to the time of Mohammad, in order to avoid any lack of agreement about its authenticity.

---

[125] Jomal min Ansabil Ashraf, second volume, P. 60.

[126] *Ketab ol Masahif*, p.28.

[127] Encyclopaedia of Islam; The foundation of the Muslim world. The article about Hafsah bint Omar ibn Khattab, p. 6314

[128] *Ketab ol Masahif* pp.28-32.

[129] ibid. pp.12-16.

Who was Zeyd?

Zeyd ibn Thabit (610-660 AD) was one of the Ansâr[130] who joined the camp of the companions of Mohammad in Medina. He was a scribe skilled in diverse languages such as Hebrew, Kaldani, and Syriac. After the death of Prophet Mohammad and during the period of Abu Bakr, the Muslim community fell into great trouble and long internal wars in the course of which a considerable number of Muslims, including the companions of Mohammad, were killed. After the battle of Yamameh,[131] in which certain important knowers of the Quran died, Abu Bakr gave Zeyd the task of making one unique official example of the Quran. Zeyd accomplished this task and made a book named 'Moshaf', which he brought to Abu Bakr. In the face of his death Abu Bakr gave that book to Omar, and after Omar's assassination his daughter Hafsah brought it to Othman, the third Caliph, and (as stated above) Othman ordered Zeyd again to make an assembly of the scribes to write down the only official version of the Quran; this version was redacted according to the dialect of the Quraysh tribe.

Where did Zeyd learn to write?

During the time of Prophet Mohammad in Medina, after migration from Mecca (the Hijra/ in 622 AD which ended with the conquest of Mecca in 630 AD), Zeyd joined the circle of the Muslim scribes and was one of the scribes

---

[130] Ansâr: inhabitant of Medina who gave hospitality to the companions of Mohammad when they fled from Mecca.

[131] The Battle of Yamama was fought in December 632 AD as part as the Ràddà Wars (Apostate Wars الحرب الردّة) on the plain of Aqraba in the region of Al-Yamama (in present-day Saudi Arabia), between the forces of Abu Bakr and Musaylimah مسيلمة or Musaylimah bin Ḥabīb مسيلمة بن حبيب, a self-proclaimed prophet. More than 450 Muslims – including 58 companions of Mohammad who knew totally or partially the Quran by heart – were killed. Ibn Kathīr, Dameshghi Esmael ibn 'Omar (2000), ed. *al-Miṣbā ḥal-munīr fī tahdhīb tafsīr Ibn Kathīr* 1, Riyadh, Sa'udi Arabia: Darussalam, p. 68.

of Prophet Mohammad alongside Ali. During the time of Abu Bakr and Omar, Zeyd taught the Quran to the Muslim people.

Zeyd was born in Mecca, even though his family originated from Medina, and belonged to a branch of the Khazraj tribe. His birth date was two years after Mohammad's proclamation about his prophetic mission, and eleven years before migration to Medina. According to Zahabi[132] and ibn Abdol,[133] when in Medina Mohammad asked Zeyd (who was then eleven years old) to go to the Jewish school to learn how to write. Mohammad intended Zeyd to develop as a scribe and knowledgeable person in the matter of the Quran, and a notable companion for the coming generations after his death. This was why he ordered Zeyd not to take part in several battles such as Badr and Ohod. Ibn Sà'd[134] writes that Zeyd was one of the four people who collected and wrote down the Quran in the time of Prophet Mohammad. He was known as an Âlim (wise) during his life, and, according to ibn Sa'd,[135] after his death Abu Horayreh ابوهريرة said: 'Today the Âlim of the Muslim community passed away, and we hope he will be replaced by ibn Abbas.' This confirms that Zeyd always had the recognition of Abu Horayreh.[136] Abu Horayreh was one the knowledgeable Jewish scribes who converted to Islam in Medina and joined the circle of the companions of Mohammad. Zeyd was not related to the

---

[132] In his book *Sayr é A'lâm on Nobàlâ*, second volume, p428.

[133] Birr in his book *Al Esti'âb fil Mà'rifàt el Ashâb*, second volume, p. 539.

[134] In his book *Tabaghat ol Kobrâ*, second volume, p.340.

[135] ibid, p344.

[136] 'Abd ar-Ramān ibn akhr ad-Dawsī al-Azdī (Arabic: عبد الرحمن بن صخر الدوسي الأزدي; 603AD–681), born 'Abd ash-Shams (Arabic: عبد الشمس), but better known by the surname (*kunyah*) Abu Hurairah (Arabic: أبو هريرة, *Abū Hurayrah*, 'Father of the Kitten'), (603AD-681 AD) was a knowledgeable Jew born in Yemen who converted to Islam three years before the death of Mohammad. His conversion happened after the battle of Kheybar. Abu Hurairah spent three years in company of Mohammad and went on expeditions and journeys with him. It is estimated that he narrated around 5,375 Hadith. Abu Hurairah has been described by some Muslims as having a photographic memory. He is known as the most prolific narrator of Hadith in Sunni Hadith compilations. Sahih Bukhari Volume 001, Book 003, Hadith 118.

Jewish tribes of Medina, but he did study in the Jewish school there, and he learned the Hebrew and Syriac languages and alphabets.[137] Ibn Masoud and Obayy ibn Kà'b, two of Mohammad's companions, attested that they had personally heard and learned about seventy Surahs of the Quran directly from the mouth of Mohammad, while Zeyd was still a child and playing with Jewish children in the school of the Jewish community in Medina.[138]

This is important because it shows that the example of the Quran which was introduced in the time of the third Caliph Othman was written in a style called Kufi calligraphy, related to the style of the Arabic alphabet used originally by the Jewish scribes in Medina.

After the end of the period of the third Caliph, Zeyd stayed in Medina and one year later, after the Caliphate of Ali, he passed away.

Why it was important to make one version of the Quran

The Quran is the cornerstone of the foundation of the Muslim community. The personal copies of the Quran were written in a heterogenic order, which could have risked the breaking down of the unity of the Muslim community from the beginning. Over the passage of time, each version could have been given a sacred aspect with each version having its supporters all asserting its authenticity. By destroying all of the diverse versions except the examples of Ali and Hafsah, the third Caliph guaranteed the unity of the community after him regarding the holiness of one sacred book.

But we should know that the texts of the verses were not only written on paper, which is easy to burn and destroy. The scribes were writing the verses of the Quran (before the appearance of the official version) on rocks and stones in the mountainous regions of the Peninsula of Arabia. Many verses of the Quran remained intact even after the strict governmental order of the third

---

[137] Zahabi, ibid, second volume p.428. Ibn Abdol Birr, ibid p.539.

[138] Ahmad ibn Hanbal. Mosnad. First volume. Pp 389-405-442; Azody neyshabouri. Al-Izah. P.519; Seyed Ali Khan. Darajat or Rafi'àh. P.22.

Caliph. Nowadays, we are discovering more and more of these types of petroglyphs in the far corners of Arabia. These ancient verses of the Quran – dating from the first century of Hegira – are extremely valuable and need to be treated with great care.

In figure 13 we introduce one of these petroglyphs to stress the importance of the unity of the text. It is perhaps one of the oldest verses of the Quran recently discovered in the region of Mecca, carved on a stone in the mountains, in a decorative elaborated Hijazi style. The author of this petroglyph text is a man called Abdullah ibn Emareh. The scripture is dated by the author at 48 H, which corresponds to 703 AD.

48 AH. Abdollah ibn

Emâreh

سنه اربع و ثمين هجری

Figure 13 - Petroglyphs (Arabic stone scripture – Saudi Arabia)
Dated by its scribe signed Abdollah ibn Emareh. 48 after Hegira.
Elaborated Hijazi style, decorated with the painting of a cow.[139]

The following points should be noted about the petroglyph:[140]

a) The text is written in a Hijazi style.
b) It is similar to the text of the Qurans of Birmingham and Tübingen.
c) The calligraphy is elaborate and decorative.

---

[139] Text written in Hijazi script upon a rock in Arabia, 16 years after the Prophet's death.
[140] The original is already published in *Les routes d'Arabie*, Louvre edition, Paris 2008.

d) It is written on a rock and is similar in style to the paintings of the prehistoric people living in those regions and in Africa.

e) The painting shows the shape of a cow, upon which Abdollah ibn Emareh has inscribed a sentence he dates as the year 48 after Hegira. The sentence seems to be a verse from the second Surah of the Quran called Surah tol Baghareh, the Surah of the Cow.

The reality about this sentence is that it does not fit correctly and exactly either with any verse in the Surah of the Cow, or with any other in the whole Quran. In other words, the scribe wrote one sentence in which he gathered two parts of two sentences of the Surah of Baghareh, verses 21 and 189, in one place, because he had mistakenly mixed them up in his mind. This confusion caused by poor memory was a danger to the correct reporting of the very long verses of the Quran.

Section Two

The relevance of tales, legends, and historical events stated in the Quran

The meaning of Sahifeh صحیفه and Ostoureh اسطوره

In the eyes of the majority of his contemporary inhabitants of Mecca and the Bedouin of the Arabian Peninsula, Mohammad, son of Abdullah, was just a 'legend- reader' who read and narrated the tales and legends from some old books (Kotob) and scrolls (Sohof). The Arabic word for legend and tale is Ghesseh-قصه.

Mohammad himself did not deny the fact that one aspect of his mission was to narrate, tàlâwàt تلاوت and to recite, ghàrâ'àt قرائت the tales /Ghesseh- for his audience. However, a point of discordance between Mohammad and those who had no conviction about his mission evolved around the source of those tales and legends. That is, the faithless thought that he was reading tales from the 'ancient written manuscripts' of the ancient people. On the contrary, Mohammad stressed the importance of the sacred aspect of the texts he was reading from. More specifically, Mohammad introduced the valuable purified written manuscripts of the sohof é motahareh صُحُفٍ مُطَّهره and sohof él oulâ الصحف الاولى', while his adversaries accused him of using the common written legends of the ancient people, which are also referred to as 'àsâtir ol àwàlin' أساطيرُ الاوَّلين. But beyond this challenge concerning the value of the sources those tales were derived from, Mohammad was seen as a 'text reader' and not a simple 'story teller'. This distinction between a story teller and a text reader is of importance as it implies that Mohammad could read, contrary to the claims of some Muslim authorities that hold on to their belief that he was illiterate.

87

Reference to the purified manuscripts and meaningful books in the Quran: Sohof é Motahareh, Kotob ghayemeh

A number of the verses of the Quran contain a chain of historical events that took place on the Arabian Peninsula and the territories around it, from the very ancient times to the period of Mohammad's appeal. The way these events are introduced resembles the spread of pieces of a large puzzle within the frame of the Quranic sentences. Therefore, in order to put them together correctly, one should take into consideration the chronological aspect of their occurrence.

In the Quran, Mohammad, son of Abdullah, is introduced as a messenger from the Lord of the universe whose main mission is to read, in Arabic, the texts of the authentic manuscripts (Sohof), and the meaningful books and texts (Kotob).

A Messenger from Allah, reciting purified scriptures, Sohof. Within which are correct writings, Kotob.[141]

In the Quran, the manuscript of Abraham and the manuscript of Moses are referred to as the old scriptures, Sohof.

Indeed, this is in the former (ancient) scriptures, the scriptures of Abraham and Moses.[142]

According to the Quran, when Mohammad, son of Abdullah, recited the sentences of his book which contained the old manuscripts, the non-

---

[141] Surah 98, v: 2-3 Sohof is the plural of Sahifeh. Sahifeh means the pages of papers/papyrus containing the line by line written texts. Kotob is the plural of Ketâb meaning the written texts, such as the books.

رسولٌ مِن الله يتلوا صحفا مطهره. فيها كتب قيمه. سورة البينة. الايات 2 و 3

[142] Surah 87, v:18-19

إنَّ هذا لفىالصحف الاولى صحف ابراهيم و موسى سورة الاعلى الايات 18و19

believers of the Quraysh tribe criticised him by stating that reading the old manuscripts could not be a convincing reason to consider a person, such as Mohammad, a prophet. Furthermore, they added that they would be able to do the same thing as Mohammad did, if they wished to do so, as it was just a matter of reading the texts of the existing asâtir.[143]

> *Even when they come to you arguing with you, those who disbelieve say: 'This is not but written legends of the former peoples, àsâtir ol àwàlin':*[144] *And when our verses are recited to them, they say: 'We have heard. If we willed, we could say [something] like this. This is not but written legends of the former peoples.'*[145]

Nevertheless, the fact that the people who were critical of Mohammad, and stressed the common value of his source of inspiration (referring to the old written texts), gives us an important clue about the regular speeches of Mohammad: that they were extracted from written texts, not verbal accounts. At the same time, the faithless pretended to be capable of reading the same texts and give lectures similar to the speeches of Mohammad. This illustrates that during this period access to those texts was not a complicated affair and was just a matter of understanding the language of those manuscripts, which were written in a different language to Arabic.

---

[143] Asâtir, plural of Ostoureh, is derived from the route of sàtr, means the written line of the texts. Sàtàrà means writing down. Asatir, the written legends, is described by 'awalin'. Awalin means old scriptures of the primitive people and tribes, or 'the old fashioned written tales remaining from very ancient times.'

[144] Surah 6, v:25:

حتى اذا جائوك يجادلونک يقول الذين کفروا إن هذا الا اساطير الاولين سورة الانعام الايه 25

[145] Surah 8, v: 31

و إذا تثلى عليهم آياتنا قالوا :قد سمعنا .لو نشاء لقلنا مثل هذا إن هذا الا اساطير الاولين سورة الانفال الايه 31

It is certain that during this period, there were number of knowledgeable people[146] who were able to read, study, and understand the sacred books written in the Aramaic, Syriac, and Hebrew languages living on the Arabian Peninsula. The Jewish patriarch, for instance, could easily read the texts of the Bible (the Old and New Testaments) to the Jewish community. However, if among those people there had been someone who was not able to understand a language other than Arabic, he or she would not have been able to comprehend the meaning of the speech. The faithless among the people of the Quraysh tribe did not believe in the text of the Torah and considered it to be an accumulation of legendary tales, simply written in an old-fashioned style. Given that they thought Mohammad was reading to them the same content as in these legendary tales, but simply in an Arabic version, they did not accept the holiness of the Quran.

The stories in the Quran and their relationship to historical events

The language in which the Quran was recited among the people of the Quraysh tribe was Arabic. These people were living in the city (Balad) of Mecca situated in the desert of Pharan on the western side of the Arabian Peninsula. The Quran is composed of historical reports of lost civilisations and people. Besides these historical reports, which are introduced in the frame of tales and legends (ghésàs), the Quran furthermore contains reports regarding the entire life of Mohammad, which includes his birth, his childhood, his familial state, his economic situation in different phases of life, his studies and his process of learning different subjects, his development to the age of maturity, the beginning of his mission, the evolution of his situation in Mecca from the moment of the declaration of his mission to the people, all the way up to the migration from Mecca to

---

[146] Their names will be quoted from the book of Ibn Husham Sirat-on Nabavyieh in other chapters.

Medina, his battles with the invaders of Medina, his victorious conquest of Mecca, his conversations with people of diverse religions and paths, and the last moments of his life. The last part of the Quran finishes with the successful accomplishment of his mission, before his death,[147] which occurred twenty-three years after the beginning of the public announcement of his prophethood.

Another part of the Quran contains tales and legends that can be found in the Bible, while yet another part talks about events that were never reported in the Bible, particularly those related to the history of the Arabian Peninsula. One part of the Quran even opposes the sayings of the Bible.

Setting up the foundation of the Quran

Tales that are common to both the Bible and the Quran

There are many tales that are common to both the Bible and the Quran. They are as follows:

- the creation of the universe by the unique Creator in six days
- the discussion in the world of the angels about the creation of a new creature on earth
- the creation of Adam and Eve, staying in the garden of Eden and being prohibited to approach the tree of the Garden

---

[147] Surah 110, v:1-3

الاتقان فى علوم القرآن.جلال ال الدين سيوطى. ج اول. ص 27

It is said the last Surah in the Quran is 'Nasr'. Jalalodin Soyouti, 'al-Itghan', vol.1 p.27.

When the victory of Allah has come and the conquest, and you see the people entering into the religion of Allah in multitudes, then exalt [Him] with praise of your Lord and ask forgiveness of Him. Indeed, He is ever accepting of repentance.

اذا جاء نصرالله والفتح و رايت الناس يدخلون فى دين الله افواجا فسبح بحمدربك و استغفره انه كان توابا سورة
النصر الايات 1-3

- the temptation of Adam and Eve by Eblis (Satan), falling into the trap of disobedience and being expelled from the garden of Eden
- the fight between the children of Adam and the assassination of one by the other
- the time of Noah and the inundation of the earth by a flood and the resulting elimination of all living creatures except for those on the boat with Noah
- the tale of Abraham
- the tale of Lut, the tale of the companions of Shabbat – the fishers of Saturday on the border of the sea
- the tale of Jacob and Joseph
- the tale of the Pharaoh and the children of Israel
- the tale of Moses and Aaron and Samaritan
- the tale of Talout (Saul), Jalout (Goliath), Davoud (David)
- the tale of Solomon and the Queen of Sabah
- the tale of Jonas and the whale
- the tale of Job
- the tale of Zachary and the extraordinary birth of John the Baptist
- the tale of Saint Mary and the extraordinary birth of Jesus
- the tale of all of Jesus's miracles
- the tale of the last supper
- the tale of the apostles.

Tales that are written only in the Quran

As mentioned before, there are indeed tales that are contained only in the Quran, and which are not mentioned in the Bible. Some of the tales are as follows:

- the tale of the companions of Okhdoud
- the tale of the companions of the cave
- the tale of the companions of the village
- the tale of Zol Gharnayn and Yaghog and Maghog

- the tale of Moses meeting with an unknown master
- the tale of the lost people of the Arabian Peninsula – Aâd, Samoud, tribe of Tobbà'
- the tale of the companions of the elephant
- and the tale of the Quraysh.

Tales in the Quran that contradict the stories in the Bible

In addition to the tales that were mentioned above, there are also tales that are contained in both the Quran and the Bible, yet their content varies. One example is the case of Jesus. The majority of what is written in the Quran about Jesus is contrary to what is written in the New Testament. For instance, the Quran explains that the tale of Jesus's crucifixion, as outlined in the four Gospels, was just a divine plan to distract the attention of wrongdoers away from Jesus. According to the Quran, those who believed that Jesus was crucified were following their own idea based on an illusion. According to the Quran Jesus was never arrested, never crucified, and never killed. While the Quran does not condemn the opinion of those who believe in the crucifixion, it is strongly opposed to the opinion of those who violate the principle of monotheism and divide the unity of the unique Creator of the universe into the principle of Trinity. The Quran criticises the opinion of the official church according to which Jesus should be considered as the personification of God, who is to be worshipped by men.

The relationship between the tales of the Quran and the Bible

Because of the manner in which certain tales are introduced in the Quran, it may sometimes be advisable to consult the Bible in order to better understand the entire event. This is because, the Quran explains an event in Arabic terminology in a rather mysterious and hidden way. It is therefore necessary to study the Bible in Hebrew in order to get a wider, deeper, and more open version of the matter, as the Quran simply extracts a compact, summary version of a very detailed Biblical story.

To illustrate this point, we will make a comparison of the tale of Noah as it is stated in the Quran and the Bible.

The Bible tells the tale of Noah as follows:

In the six hundredth year of Noah's life, in the second month, on the seventeenth day of the month, on this day, all the springs of the great deep were split, and the windows of the heavens opened up. And the rain was upon the earth for forty days and forty nights. On this very day, Noah came, and Shem and Ham and Japheth, Noah's sons, and Noah's wife and his sons' three wives with them, into the ark. They, and every beast after its kind, and every domestic animal after its kind, and every creeping thing that creeps on the earth after its kind, and every fowl after its kind, every bird of every wing. And they came to Noah to the ark, two by two of all flesh in which there is the spirit of life. And those who came male and female of all flesh came, as God had commanded him, and the Lord shut him in. Now the Flood was forty days upon the earth, and the waters increased, and they lifted the ark, and it rose off the earth. And the waters became powerful, and they increased very much upon the earth, and the ark moved upon the waters. And the waters became exceedingly powerful upon the earth, and all the lofty mountains that were under the heavens were covered up.

Fifteen cubits above did the waters prevail, and the mountains were covered up. And all flesh perished that moved upon the earth, among the fowl, and among the cattle, and among the beasts, and among all creeping creatures that creep upon the earth and all mankind. Everything that had the breath of the spirit of life in its nostrils, of all that were on the dry land, died. And it [the Flood] blotted out all beings that were upon the face of the earth, from man to animal to creeping thing and to the fowl of the heavens, and they were blotted out from the earth, and only Noah and those with him in the ark survived. And the water prevailed upon the earth a hundred and fifty days, And God remembered Noah and all the beasts and all the cattle that were with him in the ark, and God caused a spirit to pass over the earth, and the waters subsided. And the springs of the deep were closed, and the windows of the heavens, and the rain from the heavens was withheld. And the waters receded off the earth more and more, and the water diminished at the end of a hundred and fifty days. And the ark came to rest in the seventh month, on the seventeenth day of the month, on the mountains of Ararat.

In the Quran, the tale of Noah is explained in verses 25 to 49 from the Surah 11, Hud, in the following lines:

And We had certainly sent Noah to his people, [saying], 'Indeed, I am to you a clear warner. That you not worship except Allah. Indeed, I fear for you the punishment of a painful day.' So the eminent among those who disbelieved from his people said, 'We do not see you but as a man like ourselves, and we do not see you followed except by those who are the lowest of us [and] at first suggestion. And we do not see in you over us any merit; rather, we think you are liars.' He said, 'O my people have you considered: if I should be upon clear evidence from my Lord while He has given me mercy from Himself but it has been made unapparent to you, should we force it upon you while you are averse to it? And O my people, I ask not of you for it any wealth. My reward is not but from Allah. And I am not one to drive away those who have believed. Indeed, they will meet their Lord, but I see that you are a people behaving ignorantly. And O my people, who would protect me from Allah if I drove them away? Then will you not be reminded? And I do not tell you that I have the depositories [containing the provision] of Allah or that I know the unseen, nor do I tell you that I am an angel, nor do I say of those upon whom your eyes look down that

Allah will never grant them any good. Allah is most knowing of what is within their souls. Indeed, I would then be among the wrongdoers.'

They said, 'O Noah, you have disputed us and been frequent in dispute of us. So bring us what you threaten us, if you should be of the truthful.' He said, 'Allah will only bring it to you if He wills, and you will not cause [Him] failure. And my advice will not benefit you - although I wished to advise you - If Allah should intend to put you in error. He is your Lord, and to Him you will be returned.' Or do they say [about Prophet Mohammad], 'He invented it'? Say, 'If I have invented it, then upon me is [the consequence of] my crime; but I am innocent of what [crimes] you commit.' And it was revealed to Noah that, 'No one will believe from your people except those who have already believed, so do not be distressed by what they have been doing. And construct the ship under our observation and our inspiration and do not address me concerning those who have wronged; indeed, they are [to be] drowned.' And he constructed the ship, and whenever an assembly of the eminent of his people passed by him, they ridiculed him. He said, 'If you ridicule us, then we will ridicule you just as you ridicule. And you are going to know who will get a punishment that will disgrace him [on earth] and upon whom will descend an enduring punishment [in the Hereafter].' [So it was], until when Our command came and the oven overflowed, We said, 'Load upon the ship of each [creature] two mates and your family, except those about whom the word has preceded, and [include] whoever has believed.' But none had believed with him, except a few. And [Noah] said, 'Embark therein; in the name of Allah is its course and its anchorage. Indeed, my Lord is Forgiving and Merciful.' And it sailed with them through waves like mountains, and Noah called to his son who was apart [from them], 'O my son, come aboard with us and be not with the disbelievers.' [But] he said, 'I will take refuge on a mountain to protect me from the water.'

[Noah] said, 'There is no protector today from the decree of Allah, except for whom He gives mercy.' And the waves came between them, and he was among the drowned. And it was said, 'O earth, swallow your water, and O sky, withhold [your rain].' And the water subsided, and the matter was accomplished, and the ship came to rest on the [mountain of] Judiyy. And it was said, 'Away with the wrongdoing people.' And Noah called to his Lord and said, 'My Lord, indeed my son is of my family; and indeed, your promise is true; and You are the most just of judges!'

He said, 'O Noah, indeed he is not of your family; indeed, he is [one whose] work was other than righteous, so ask Me not for that about which you have no knowledge. Indeed, I advise you, lest you be among the ignorant.' [Noah] said, 'My Lord, I seek refuge in You from asking that of which I have no knowledge. And unless You forgive me and have mercy upon me, I will be among the losers.' It was said, 'O Noah, disembark in security from Us and blessings upon you and upon nations [descending] from those with you. But other nations [of them] We will grant enjoyment; then there will touch them from Us a painful punishment.' That is from the news of the unseen which We reveal to you, [O Mohammad]. You knew it not, neither you nor your people, before this. So be patient; indeed, the [best] outcome is for the righteous.[148]

Each of the two versions of the same tale have their own particularities, but we find certain sentences that are quite similar to each other, when taking

---

[148] و لقد ارسلنا نوحا الى قومه اني لكم نذير مبين. ان لا تعبدوا الا الله اني اخاف عليكم عذاب يوم اليم. فقال الملا الذين كفروا من قومه ما نراك الا بشرا مثلنا و ما نراك اتبعك الا الذين هم اراذلنا بادي الراي و ما نرى لكم علينا من فضل بل نظنكم كاذبين. قال يا قوم ا رايتم ان كنت على بينة من ربي و آتاني رحمة من عنده فعميت عليكم ا نلزمكموها و انتم لها كارهون. و يا قوم لا اسئلكم عليه مالا ان اجري الا على الله و ما انا بطارد الذين آمنوا انهم ملاقوا ربهم و لكني اراكم قوما تجهلون. و يا قوم من ينصرني من الله ان طردتهم ا فلا تذكرون. و لا اقول لكم عندي خزائن الله و لا اعلم الغيب و لا اقول اني ملك و لا اقول للذين تزدري اعينكم لن يؤتيهم الله خيرا الله اعلم بما في انفسهم اني اذا لمن الظالمين. قالوا يا نوح قد جادلتنا فاكثرت جدالنا فاتنا بما تعدنا ان كنت من الصادقين. قال انما ياتيكم به الله ان شاء و ما انتم بمعجزين. و لا ينفعكم نصحي ان اردت ان انصح لكم ان كان الله يريد ان يغويكم هو ربكم و اليه ترجعون. ام يقولون افتراه قل ان افتريته فعلي اجرامي و انا بريء مما تجرمون. و اوحي الى نوح انه لن يؤمن من قومك الا من قد آمن فلا تبتئس بما كانوا يفعلون. و اصنع الفلك باعيننا و وحينا و لا تخاطبني في الذين ظلموا انهم مغرقون. و يصنع الفلك و كلما مر عليه ملاء من قومه سخروا منه قال ان تسخروا منا فانا نسخر منكم كما تسخرون. فسوف تعلمون من ياتيه عذاب يخزيه و يحل عليه عذاب مقيم. حتى اذا جاء امرنا و فار التنور قلنا احمل فيها من كل زوجين اثنين و اهلك الا من سبق عليه القول و من آمن و ما آمن معه الا قليل و قال اركبوا فيها بسم الله مجراها و مرساها ان ربي لغفور رحيم و هي تجري بهم في موج كالجبال و نادى نوح ابنه و كان في معزل يا بني اركب معنا و لا تكن مع الكافرين. قال سأوي الى جبل يعصمني من الماء قال لا عاصم اليوم من امر الله الا من رحم و حال بينهما الموج فكان من المغرقين. و قيل يا ارض ابلعي ماءك و يا سماء اقلعي و غيض الماء و قضي الامر و استوت على الجودي و قيل بعدا للقوم الظالمين. و نادى نوح ربه فقال رب ان ابني من اهلي و ان وعدك الحق و انت احكم الحاكمين. قال يا نوح انه ليس من اهلك انه عمل غير صالح فلا تسئلن ما ليس لك به علم اني اعظك ان تكون من الجاهلين. قال رب اني اعوذ بك ان اسئلك ما ليس لي به علم و الا تغفر لي و ترحمني اكن من الخاسرين. قيل يا نوح اهبط بسلام منا و بركات عليك و على امم ممن معك و امم سنمتعهم ثم يمسهم منا عذاب اليم. تلك من انباء الغيب نوحيها اليك ما كنت تعلمها انت و لا قومك من قبل هذا فاصبر ان العاقبة للمتقين/ سوره هود. الايات 25-49

97

into consideration the frame and specific characteristics of the two different languages, namely Hebrew and Arabic.

The Torah:

God caused a spirit to pass over the earth, and the waters subsided. And the springs of the deep, as well as the windows of the skies were closed, and the rain from the skies was withheld. And the waters receded off the earth more and more, and the water diminished at the end of a hundred and fifty days. And the ark came to rest in the seventh month, on the seventeenth day of the month, on the mountains of Ararat.

The Quran:

And it was said, 'O earth, swallow your water, and O sky, withhold [your rain].' And the water subsided, and the Order was accomplished, and the ship came to rest on the [mountain of] Judiyy. And it was said, 'Away with the wrongdoing people.' Surah 11, v:44

The Quran points out that before the revelation of this tale in the frame of the Quran, Mohammad and his people were not familiar with it, and they learned from an invisible source:

That is from the news of the unseen الغيب *which We reveal to you, [O Mohammad]. You knew it not, neither you nor your people, before this.*[149]

Mohammad did not invent any tales, he merely introduced in the Arabic language, tales already reported in the Old Testament[150], originated

---

[149] Surah 11, v: 49

[150] T.C. Mitchell. *The Bible in the British Museum*, The British Museum Press, 1988

from the written literature of the Sumerian civilisation [151](6000 years ago). This tale was well known by the Hebrew speaking people, Ahl ol Ketab اهل الكتاب (the People of the Books) of both Jewish and Christian communities, whereas the majority of the inhabitants of Mecca (such as the Quraysh tribe) and the nomadic Bedouins of the desert in the peninsula of Arabia did not understand any language other than Arabic.[152]

Another example is the tale of Abraham

The stories in both the Quran and the Torah can be summarized briefly as follows: Three unknown people appeared in the desert. Abraham saw them, invited them to his tent, and prepared some food for them by killing a cow. During the feast, the three travellers announced to Abraham that his wife, who had already experienced menopause, would have a son, within one year. When Abraham's wife heard the news, she laughed. After receiving the good news, fear left the heart of Abraham and quietness took its place. He asked his guests what was their purpose for being in that region. They replied that they were sent to the wrongdoing people. From this Abraham understood that the people of the city of Sodom and Gomorrah would be punished and started to negotiate with the unknown visitors in order to attempt to change their mind. However, the Quran does not specify the manner of Abraham's negotiation with his guests. For this, the reader has to study the text of the Torah.

---

[151] George, Andrew R., trans. & edit. *The Epic of Gilgamesh*, Penguin Books

[152] It is important to differentiate between unawareness: gheflat غفلت and ignorance: jaheliat- جاهليت. Gheflat is a type of ignorance which can be solved by learning when somebody wants to study that matter. On the contrary, there exists another type of ignorance which cannot be solved because an ignorant person thinks that the borders of the world correspond with the limits of his knowledge, so he does not need to learn more. The Quran describes this matter in this sentence: *You and your people were unaware of the existence of this tale (or the reality of this affair) before you learnt it thanks to the revelation.*

Quran:

And when the fright had left Abraham and the good tidings had reached him, he began to argue with Us concerning the people of Lot.[153]

Torah:

And Abraham approached and said, 'Will You even destroy the righteous with the wicked? Perhaps there are fifty righteous men in the midst of the city; will You even destroy and not forgive the place for the sake of the fifty righteous men who are in its midst? Far be it from You to do a thing such as this, to put to death the righteous with the wicked so that the righteous should be like the wicked. Far be it from You! Will the Judge of the entire earth not perform justice?' And the Lord said, 'If I find in Sodom fifty righteous men within the city, I will forgive the entire place for their sake.' And Abraham answered and said, 'Behold now I have commenced to speak to the Lord, although I am dust and ashes. Perhaps the fifty righteous men will be missing five. Will You destroy the entire city because of five?' And He said, 'I will not destroy if I find there forty-five.' And he continued further to speak to Him, and he said, 'Perhaps forty will be found there.' And He said, 'I will not do it for the sake of the forty.' And he said, 'Please, let the Lord's wrath not be kindled, and I will speak. Perhaps thirty will be found there.' And He said, 'I will not do it if I find thirty there.' And he said, 'Behold now I have desired to speak to the Lord, perhaps twenty will be found there.' And He said, 'I will not destroy for the sake of the twenty.' And he said, 'Please, let the Lord's wrath not be kindled, and I will speak yet this time, perhaps ten will be found there.' And He said, 'I will not destroy for the sake of the ten.' And the Lord departed when He finished speaking to Abraham, and Abraham returned to his place.[154]

Quran:

---

[153] Surah 11, v: 74

[154] Genesis - 18

[The visitors said], 'O Abraham, give up this [plea]. Indeed, the command of your Lord has come, and indeed, there will reach them a punishment that cannot be repelled.'[155]

Actually We brought out of the city whoever living from the righteous people, but We did not find there more than just one house of the righteous people (Muslim).[156]

However, the report of the destruction of the cities (Sodom and Gomorrah) exists in both the Quran and the Torah.

Another example is the tale of Joseph in the Quran and the Torah. The Torah tells the tale of Joseph as follows:

It came to pass at the end of two full years, which Pharaoh was dreaming, and behold, he was standing by the Nile. And behold, from the Nile were coming up seven cows, of handsome appearance and robust flesh, and they pastured in the marshland. And behold, seven other cows were coming up after them from the Nile, of ugly appearance and lean of flesh, and they stood beside the cows [which were] on the Nile bank. And the cows of ugly appearance and lean of flesh devoured the seven cows that were of handsome appearance and healthy; then Pharaoh awoke. And he fell asleep and dreamed again, and behold, seven ears of grain were growing on one stalk, healthy and good. And behold, seven ears of grain, thin and beaten by the east wind, were growing up after them. And the thin ears of grain swallowed up the seven healthy and full ears of grain; then Pharaoh awoke, and behold, a dream. Now it came to pass in the morning that his spirit was troubled; so he sent and called all the necromancers of Egypt and all its sages, and Pharaoh related to them his dream, but no one interpreted them for Pharaoh.[157]

---

[155] Surah 11, v: 76

يا ابراهيم. اعرض عن هذا انه قدجاء امرربک و إنهم آتيهم عذاب غير مردود   سورة هود الايه 76

[156] Surah 51, v: 35- 36

فأخرجنا من كان فيها من المؤمنين فما وجدنا فيها غير بيت من المسلمين / سورة   والذاريات الاية 36-

[157] Genesis -41

In contrast, the Quran tells the story as follows:

And [subsequently] the king said, 'Indeed, I have seen [in a dream] seven fat cows being eaten by seven [that were] lean, and seven green spikes [of grain] and others [that were] dry. O eminent ones, explain to me my vision, if you should interpret visions.'[158]

The Torah continues the story:

And Pharaoh said to Joseph, 'I have dreamed a dream, and there is no interpreter for it, but I have heard it said of you [that] you understand a dream, to interpret it.' And Joseph replied to Pharaoh, saying, 'Not I; God will give an answer [that will bring] peace to Pharaoh.' And Pharaoh said to Joseph, 'In my dream, behold, I was standing on the bank of the Nile. And behold, seven cows of robust flesh and handsome form were ascending from the Nile, and they pastured in the marshland. And behold, seven other cows were ascending after them, emaciated and of very ugly form and with meagre flesh; I have not seen such ugly ones throughout the entire land of Egypt. And the meagre and ugly cows devoured the first seven healthy cows. And they went inside them, but it was not known that they had gone inside of them, for their appearance was as ugly as in the beginning; then I awoke. Then I saw in my dream, and behold, seven ears of grain were growing on one stalk, full and good. And behold, seven ears of grain, hardened, thin, and beaten by the east wind, were growing up after them. And the thin ears of grain swallowed up the seven good ears of grain; I told the necromancers, but no one tells me [its meaning].' And Joseph said to Pharaoh, 'Pharaoh's dream is one; what God is doing He has told Pharaoh. The seven good cows are seven years, and the seven good ears of grain are seven years; it is one dream. And the seven meagre and ugly cows coming up after them are seven years, and the seven empty ears of grain, beaten by the east wind, will be seven years

---

[158] Surah 12, v: 43

و قال الملك إنى أرى سبع بقرات سمان ياكلهن سبع عجاف و سبع سنبلات خضر و أخر يابسات ياايهاالملاء افتونى فى روياى ان كنتم للرويا تعبرون سورة يوسف. الاية 43

of famine. It is this matter that I have spoken to Pharaoh; what God is about to do He has shown Pharaoh.

Behold, seven years are coming, great plenty throughout all the land of Egypt. And seven years of famine will arise after them, and all the plenty will be forgotten in the land of Egypt, and the famine will destroy the land. And the plenty will not be known because of that famine to follow, for it [will be] very severe. And concerning the repetition of the dream to Pharaoh twice that is because the matter is ready [to emanate] from God, and God is hastening to execute it. So now, let Pharaoh seek out an understanding and wise man and appoint him over the land of Egypt. Let Pharaoh do [this] and appoint officials over the land and prepare the land of Egypt during the seven years of plenty. And let them collect all the food of these coming seven good years, and let them gather the grain under Pharaoh's hand, food in the cities, and keep it. Thus the food will remain as a reserve for the land for the seven years of famine which will be in the land of Egypt, so that the land will not be destroyed by the famine.' The matter pleased Pharaoh and all his servants.[159]

While the Quran continues the tale in the following manner:

[He said], 'Joseph, O man of truth, explain to us about seven fat cows eaten by seven [that were] lean, and seven green spikes [of grain] and others [that were] dry - that I may return to the people; perhaps they will know [about you].' [Joseph] said, 'You will plant for seven years consecutively; and what you harvest leave in its spikes, except a little from which you will eat. Then will come after that seven difficult [years] which will consume what you saved for them, except a little from which you will store. Then will come after that a year in which the people will be given rain and in which they will press [olives and grapes].[160]

---

[159] Genesis 42

[160] Surah 12, v: 46 - 49.

The beginning and the end of the Surah 12 (Joseph) in the Quran, contains certain information which could help us to better understand the model of the explanation of the Quran.

Alif, Lam, Ra. These are the verses of the clear Book. Indeed, We have sent it down as an Arabic Quran that you might understand. We relate to you, [O Mohammad], the best of stories in what We have revealed to you of this Quran although you were, before it, among the unawares.[161]

There was certainly in their stories a lesson for those of understanding. Never was the Quran a narration invented, but a confirmation of what was before it; and a detailed explanation of all things; and guidance and mercy for a people who believe.[162]

These verses remind us of what has also been explained in the tale of Noah, namely that the Quran is not simply an invented narration by Mohammad, but the Arabic recitation of the content of a Holy Book preceding the Quran, just in a non-Arabic version, thereby confirming it. From these details that are mentioned inside the Quran, we can conclude that Mohammad was unaware of these tales or events before learning about them through an invisible source, and before he introduced them to the people of his tribe.[163]

قَالَ تَزْرَعُونَ سَبْعَ سِنِينَ دَأَبًا فَمَا حَصَدتُّمْ فَذَرُوهُ فِي سُنبُلِهِ إِلَّا قَلِيلًا مِّمَّا كُلُونَ ثُمَّ أْتِي مِن بَعْدِ ذَٰلِكَ سَبْعٌ شِدَادٌ كُلْنَ مَا قَدَّمْتُمْ لَهُنَّ إِلَّا قَلِيلًا مِّمَّا تُحْصِنُونَ ثُمَّ أْتِي مِن بَعْدِ ذَٰلِكَ عَامٌ فِيهِ يُغَاثُ النَّاسُ وَفِيهِ يَعْصِرُونَ   سورة يوسف الايات
49-46

[161] Surah 12, v: 1 - 3.

الر تِلْكَ آيَاتُ الْكِتَابِ الْمُبِينِ إِنَّا أَنزَلْنَاهُ قُرْآنًا عَرَبِيًّا لَّعَلَّكُمْ تَعْقِلُونَ نَحْنُ نَقُصُّ عَلَيْكَ أَحْسَنَ الْقَصَصِ بِمَا أَوْحَيْنَا إِلَيْكَ هَٰذَا الْقُرْآنَ وَإِن كُنتَ مِن قَبْلِهِ لَمِنَ الْغَافِلِينَ   سورة يوسف الايات 3-1

[162] Surah 12, v: 111.

لَقَدْ كَانَ فِي قَصَصِهِمْ عِبْرَةٌ لِّأُولِي الْأَلْبَابِ مَا كَانَ حَدِيثًا يُفْتَرَىٰ وَلَٰكِن تَصْدِيقَ الَّذِي بَيْنَ يَدَيْهِ وَتَفْصِيلَ كُلِّ شَيْءٍ وَهُدًى وَرَحْمَةً لِّقَوْمٍ يُؤْمِنُونَ   سورة يوسف الآية 111

[163] This shows a cultural process that includes three steps: reading the writings in Hebrew or another language such as Syriac, translating the texts into an Arabic version, and reciting

In the Surah 'Tâ Hâ' we discover more details regarding this:

TÂ HÂ We have not sent down to you the Quran that you be distressed. But only as a reminder for those who fear (disobedience towards Allah). Surah 20, v.1-3.[164]

The method of education according to the Quran

Anzàlnâ, meaning 'we have sent down', is derived from Enzâl - إنزال أنزَلَ - يُنزِلُ -which means sending. This word is employed in the jargon of the Quran in order to explain the way by which the Quran was transmitted to Mohammad, for it to be recited by him, little by little, to the Arabic-speaking people. In fact, the Quran divides this process of preaching the Quran into three distinct steps:

- the first step consists of Mohammad learning the content of an existing book[165] أُمُّ الكتاب

- the second step consists of repeating the sentences in order to memorise them.

- the third step consists of Mohammad preaching the Book that he had taught to the people, according to the way an invisible source had inspired him over a period of twenty-three years.

---

them in Arabic. This clarifies one important point, namely that certain tales in the Quran existed before being taught and sent (ànzàlà) to Mohammad.

[164] Surah 20, v: 1 -3.

طه ما انزلنا عليک القرآن لتشقى الا تذكره لمن يخشى. سوره طاها. الايات 1-3

[165] سورة "آل عمران"- الايه 7؛ سورة "الرعد"- الاية 39؛ سورة الزخرف – الاية 4.

وانه فى "ام الكتاب" لدينا لعلى حكيم. سورة الزخرف. الايه 4

مجمع البيان فى تفسير القرآن. فضل بن حسن طبرسى. ج 9. ص 60. تهران ناصرخسرو 1372. چاپ سوم

The first and second steps, correspond with the period of learning in which the teacher teaches, and the disciple learns: Ar Ràhmân, Allàm al Quran الرحمن عَلَّم القُرآن, meaning 'God taught the Quran'.[166] This teaching is qualified as Enzâl, 'sending at once from up to down', because the teacher is situated, due to his knowledge, in a higher place than his disciple. In this process, the teacher gives a very important scripture or book to his disciple and advises him at once to read and study it, also referred to as éghrà' إقرء 'read'.[167] The student then has the scripture in his possession and learns it chapter by chapter, slowly and calmly, in order to memorise it by heart. This step of learning is called Tanzil تَنزيل - نَزَّلَ-يُنَزّلُ, the gradual sending from up to down but not all at once. At the end of this process the disciple gains the ability to recite the book by heart, without reading from the text: Allàmà ho-l bàyân عَلَّمَهُ البَيان , that is, 'He did teach him bàyân'.[168] Bàyân, or 'eloquence', is the art of speech or speaking about a matter in detail. The origin of the word is 'bayn' which means among or between, or the distance between two or multiple pieces. Bàyân is equivalent to the capacity of someone to express his mind by using words in the frame of sentences.

The last step is the period of preaching, which occurs when the disciple is absolutely ready to accomplish his mission and awaits the order of his invisible source to begin his actions and announce his message. The Quran also mentions the case of Yàhiâ (John the Baptist) and Jesus, who received the Book in their childhood and announced their mission of prophethood some years later.

'O John, take the Scripture with energy.' And We gave him mandate in his childhood. Surah 19, v: 12.[169]

---

[166] Surah 55, v: 1, 2.

[167] Surah 96, v: 1.

[168] Surah 55, v: 4.

[169] يا يحيى خذ الكتاب بقوه و آتيناه الحكم صبيا سورة مريم الاية 12

Allah said: 'O Jesus, Son of Mary, remember My favour upon you and upon your mother when I supported you with the Pure Spirit and you spoke to the people in the cradle and in maturity; and [remember] when I taught you writing and wisdom and the Torah and the Gospel.' Surah 5, v: 110.[170]

Often, reporters on this matter do not make any distinction between the moment a person is visited by an angel who announces to him that he is a chosen individual by divine destiny to become a messenger of God, and the moment that he receives the order to go to the people and proclaim loudly that he is God's messenger.[171] Jesus and Yàhiâ are two examples of this, as they gained awareness of their future task (in their childhood) a long time before actually starting their mission (at the age of about thirty). From the moment they understood their mission, they started to prepare themselves to accomplish it. But at first, just like every other little child, they were not able to read or write; they did not even know the meaning of certain concepts such as faith, wisdom, and guidance. All the knowledge of these matters they acquired during different stages of learning.

Recite! And your Lord is the most Generous, Who taught by the pen. He taught man that which he knew not. Surah 96, v: 3 - 5.[172]

Two Surahs of the Quran explain in detail this period of learning and evolution: (1) Surah 93, Vad duhâ and (2) Surah 94, Inshirâh.

ـ 170اذ قال الله " يا عيسى ابن مريم اذكر نعمتى عليک و على والدتک اذ ايدتک بروح القدس تكلم الناس فى المهد و كهلا و اذ علمتک الكتاب و الحكمه و التورات و الانجيل سورة المائده الآية 110

171 Sahih al-Bukhari. Dar Sader: Beryrout; vol. 1 pp.76- 77.

ـ 172اقرا و ربک الاكرم الذى علم بالقلم علم الانسان ما لم يعلم سورة العلق الآيات 3- 5

(1) By the morning brightness. And [by] the night when it covers with darkness. Your Lord has not taken leave of you, [O Mohammad], nor has He detested [you]. And the Hereafter is better for you than the first [life]. And your Lord is going to give you, and you will be satisfied. Did He not find you an orphan and give [you] refuge? And He found you lost and guided [you], And He found you poor and made [you] self-sufficient. So as for the orphan, do not oppress [him]. And as for the petitioner, do not repel [him]. But as for the favour of your Lord, report [it]. Surah 93, v:1 - 11[173]

(2) Did We not expand for you, [O Mohammad], your breast? And We removed from you your burden; which had weighed upon your back. And raised high for you your repute. For indeed, with hardship [will be] ease. Indeed, with hardship [will be] ease. So when you have finished [your duties], then stand up [for worship]. And to your Lord direct [your] longing.[174] Surah 94, v:1-8

Hence, the method of education to which these sentences of the Quran refer is clear and transparent. That is, going to school from childhood in order to learn reading and writing through the alphabet, words, sentences, wise tales, history, and so forth, as well as the contents of various books and scriptures, by making copies line by line, using a pen, on pages of parchment.

Nun. By the pen and what they inscribe, Surah 68, v: 1.[175]

[by] a Book inscribed. In parchment spread open. Surah 52, v: 2, 3.[176]

---

[173]والضحى و الليل اذا سجى ماودعك ربك و ماقلى وللاخره خير لك من الاولى و لسوف يعطيك ربك فترضى الم يجدك يتيما فاوى ووجدك ضالا فهدى ووجدك عائلا فاغنى فامااليتيم فلاتقهر و اما السائل فلا تنهر واما بنعمه ربك فحدث سوره والضحى الآيات 1- 11

[174]الم نشرح لك صدرك ووضعنا عنك وزرك الذى انقض ظهرك و رفعنا لك ذكرك فان مع العسر يسرا ان مع العسر يسرا فاذا فرغت فانصب و الى ربك فارغب سورة الانشراح الايات 8-1

[175]نون و القلم و ما يسطرون سورة القلم 1-

[176] و كتاب مسطور فى رق منشور سورة الطور الايات 2 و 3

Do you have a book, ketâb, in which you learn? Surah 68, v: 37.[177]

And We had not given them any scriptures which they could study, and We had not sent to them before you, [O Mohammad], any warner. Surah 34, v: 44.

Be pious scholars of the Lord because of what you have taught of the Scripture/Books - al Ketab and because of what you have studied - taught.[178] Surah 3, v: 79.[179]

From what is written in the Quran about Mohammad, it seems his childhood was similar to those of the other prophets. In his early life, Mohammad did not know anything about faith, about books, or about how to read or write. It was during this period that the Angel of God visited him.

And thus We have revealed to you an inspiration of Our command. You did not know what is the Book or [what is] faith, but We have made it a light by which We guide whom We will of Our servants. And indeed, [O Mohammad], you guide to a straight path. Surah 42, v: 52.[180]

And thus We have sent down to you the Book. And those to whom We [previously] gave the Book believe in it (yours). And among these [people of Mecca] are those who believe also in it. And none reject Our verses except the disbelievers. And you were not able to read or recite[181] *before this moment any book, nor did you inscribe one with your*

ـ [177]ام لکم کتاب فیه تَدرُسون؟ سوره القلم آیه 37

[178] Tadrosoun یدرسُ دَرَسَ to teach. School is madreseh مَدرسه Teacher is modàrres مُدَرّس.

[179]کونوا ربانیین بما کنتمْتُعَلِمُون الکتاب و بما کنتم تدرسون سورة آل عمران الآیه 79

[180] و کذلک اوحینا الیک روحا من امرنا ماکنت تدری ماالکتاب و لاالایمان و لکن جعلناه نورا نهدی به من نشاء من عبادنا و انک لتهدی الی صراط مستقیم سوره الشوری آیه 52

[181] تلاوت ـ یتلوا تلی Tàlà - yàtlou - tàlâwàt reading loudly, reciting. خَط ـ یَخُطّ ـ خَطّ khàttà – yàkhotto - khat inscribing the text with the pen on the paper.

right hand. Otherwise the falsifiers would have had [cause for] doubt. Rather, it (the Quran) is distinct verses [preserved] within the breasts of those who have been given knowledge. And none reject Our verses except the wrongdoers. Surah 29, v: 47 - 49.[182]

According to the Quran, Mohammad achieved all these steps of education and reached the stage of maturity. At the age of forty, he was ready to accomplish his divine mission for which he had prepared himself for many years: reciting the Book in Arabic to a group of people who did not have the benefit of lessons of the other prophets' scriptures because they did not know any language other than Arabic.

They (people of Mecca) complain: 'The Book was only sent down to two groups (Jew and Christian) before us, but we were of their study unaware,' Or lest you say, 'If only the Book had been revealed to us, we would have been better guided than they (Jew and Christian)', So there has [now] come to you a clear evidence from your Lord and a guidance and mercy. Surah 6, v: 156-157.[183]

And this [Quran] is a Book We have revealed [which is] blessed, so follow it and fear Allah that you may receive mercy. Surah 6, v: 155.[184]

The explanations in the Quran clarify perfectly that Mohammad offered the people of Arabia the necessary potential to learn and to study, in pure Arabic, the content of the preceding Books (scriptures) which were the source of education for Jewish, Christians and other communities, who

---

[182]وكذلك انزلنا اليك الكتاب فالذين آتيناهم الكتاب يومنون به ؛ و من هولاء مَن يومن به .و ما يجحد بآياتنا الاالكافرون .و ماكنت تتلوا من قبله و لا تخطه بيمينك .اذا لارتاب المبطلون .بل هو آيات بينات فى صدور الذين اوتواالعلم و ما يجحد بآياتنا الا الظالمون سوره العنكبوت. الايات 47-49

[183]أن تقولوا انما انزل الكتاب على طائفتين من قبلنا و إن كنا عن دراستهم لغافلين او تقولوا لو انا انزل علينا الكتاب لكنا هدى منهم فقد جائكم بينه من ربكم و هدى و رحمه سوره الانعام آيه هاى 156، 157

[184]او هذا كتاب انزلناه مبارك فاتبعوه و اتقوا لعلكم ترحمون سوره الانعام آيه 155

were reading and writing texts in other languages. As such, the similarities between some parts of the Quran and the Bible are no accident.

In the Quran, a part of the Surah Tâ Hâ is about Moses and goes as follows:

And has the story of Moses reached you? When he saw a fire and said to his family, 'Stay here; indeed, I have perceived a fire; perhaps I can bring you a torch or find at the fire some guidance.' And when he came to it, he was called,[185] 'O Moses! Indeed, I am your Lord, so remove your sandals.[186] Indeed, you are in the sacred valley of Tuwa.[187] And I have chosen you, so listen to what is revealed [to you]. Indeed, I am Allah. There is no deity except Me, so worship Me and establish prayer for My remembrance. Indeed, the Hour is coming - I almost conceal it - so that every soul may be recompensed according to that for which it strives. So do not let one avert you from it who does not believe in it and follows his desire, for you [then] would perish. And what is that in your right hand, O Moses?' He said, 'It is my staff; I lean upon it, and I bring down leaves for my sheep and I have therein other uses.' [Allah] said, 'Throw it down, O Moses.' So he threw it down, and thereupon it was a snake, moving swiftly. [Allah] said, 'Seize it and fear not; We will return it to its former condition. And draw in your hand to your side; it will come out white without disease - another sign, That We may show you [some] of Our greater signs. Go to Pharaoh. Indeed, he has transgressed.' [Moses] said, 'My Lord,

---

[185] نودی Noudi yà is derived from Nédâ/ inner voice. The outer voice is Sédâ. The inner voice – Nédâ – is heard inside of the brain, and it does not involve the ear itself. Nédâ can be heard only by the person to whom the vibration is propagated. وحی / Vahi is a particular type of Nédâ. The Quran talks about Zakhary and Mary when they were alone in the corner of their place of prayer, being visited by Gabriel. They heard an inner voice i.e. Nédâ. Even if other persons are present in the same room at the same time they do not perceive any voice.

[186] نعليک =نعلین +ک -

Na'l means 'fer à cheval'/horseshoe. Na'layn means a couple of Na'l for both feet; the rustic shoes of the shepherds. Na'layk means your shoes. This word does not have an Arabic origin.

[187] وادی المقدس طوی -

expand for me my breast [with assurance] And ease for me my task. And untie the knot from my tongue. That they may understand my speech. And appoint for me a minister[188] from my family – Aaron, my brother. Increase through him my strength. And let him share my task. That we may exalt You much. And remember You much. Indeed, You are of us ever Seeing.[189]

The Torah states:

1 Now Moses was keeping the flock of Jethro his father-in-law, the priest of Midian; and he led the flock to the farthest end of the wilderness, and came to the mountain of God, unto Horeb. 2 And the angel of the LORD appeared unto him in a flame of fire out of the midst of a bush; and he looked, and, behold, the bush burned with fire, and the bush was not consumed. 3 And Moses said: 'I will turn aside now, and see this great sight, why the bush is not burnt.' 4 And when the LORD saw that he turned aside to see, God called unto him out of the midst of the bush, and said: 'Moses, Moses.' And he said: 'Here am I.' 5 And He said: 'Draw not nigh hither; put off thy shoes from off thy

---

- [188] و اجعل لی وزیرا من اهلی

وزیر / Vàzir means administrator and advisor of the King. Equal to a prime minister in our time. Vazir is not an Arabic word, it is borrowed from the Persian–Aramaic languages. In the Sassanid period, contemporary to the time of Mohammad, the Vazirs were sometimes more famous than the king. Bouzarjomehr/Bozorg Mehr é Vazir was one the very well-known advisors of the Sassanid emperors and a manager of the Persian territory. According to Shahnameh this Vazir was an intellectual Wiseman in conflict with the wise Indian philosophers who invented the game of chess / Shatouranga.

[189] Surah 20, v: 9 - 35.

وَهَلْ أَتَاكَ حَدِيثُ مُوسَىٰ ؟ إِذْ رَأَىٰ نَارًا فَقَالَ لِأَهْلِهِ امْكُثُوا إِنِّي آنَسْتُ نَارًا لَعَلِّي آتِيكُم مِّنْهَا بِقَبَسٍ أَوْ أَجِدُ عَلَى النَّارِ هُدًى. فَلَمَّا أَتَاهَا نُودِيَ "يَا مُوسَىٰ إِنِّي أَنَا رَبُّكَ فَاخْلَعْ نَعْلَيْكَ إِنَّكَ بِالْوَادِ الْمُقَدَّسِ طُوًى وَأَنَا اخْتَرْتُكَ فَاسْتَمِعْ لِمَا يُوحَىٰ إِنَّنِي أَنَا اللَّهُ لَا إِلَٰهَ إِلَّا أَنَا فَاعْبُدْنِي وَأَقِمِ الصَّلَاةَ لِذِكْرِي إِنَّ السَّاعَةَ آتِيَةٌ أَكَادُ أُخْفِيهَا لِتُجْزَىٰ كُلُّ نَفْسٍ بِمَا تَسْعَىٰ. فَلَا يَصُدَّنَّكَ عَنْهَا مَن لَّا يُؤْمِنُ بِهَا وَاتَّبَعَ هَوَاهُ فَتَرْدَىٰ. وَمَا تِلْكَ بِيَمِينِكَ يَا مُوسَىٰ ؟ قَالَ: "هِيَ عَصَايَ أَتَوَكَّأُ عَلَيْهَا وَأَهُشُّ بِهَا عَلَىٰ غَنَمِي وَلِيَ فِيهَا مَآرِبُ أُخْرَىٰ. قَالَ: "أَلْقِهَا يَا مُوسَىٰ. فَأَلْقَاهَا فَإِذَا هِيَ حَيَّةٌ تَسْعَىٰ. قَالَ: "خُذْهَا وَلَا تَخَفْ سَنُعِيدُهَا سِيرَتَهَا الْأُولَىٰ. وَاضْمُمْ يَدَكَ إِلَىٰ جَنَاحِكَ تَخْرُجْ بَيْضَاءَ مِنْ غَيْرِ سُوءٍ آيَةً أُخْرَىٰ. لِنُرِيَكَ مِنْ آيَاتِنَا الْكُبْرَى اذْهَبْ إِلَىٰ فِرْعَوْنَ إِنَّهُ طَغَىٰ. قَالَ رَبِّ اشْرَحْ لِي صَدْرِي وَيَسِّرْ لِي أَمْرِي وَاحْلُلْ عُقْدَةً مِّن لِّسَانِي يَفْقَهُوا قَوْلِي. وَاجْعَل لِّي وَزِيرًا مِّنْ أَهْلِي هَارُونَ أَخِي اشْدُدْ بِهِ أَزْرِي وَأَشْرِكْهُ فِي أَمْرِي. كَيْ نُسَبِّحَكَ كَثِيرًا وَنَذْكُرَكَ كَثِيرًا إِنَّكَ كُنتَ بِنَا بَصِيرًا سورة/ طه 9 - 35

feet, for the place whereon thou standest is holy ground.' 6 Moreover He said: 'I am the God of thy father, the God of Abraham, the God of Isaac, and the God of Jacob.' And Moses hid his face; for he was afraid to look upon God.

7 And the Lord said: 'I have surely seen the affliction of My people that are in Egypt, and have heard their cry by reason of their taskmasters; for I know their pains; 8 and I am come down to deliver them out of the hand of the Egyptians, and to bring them up out of that land unto a good land and a large, unto a land flowing with milk and honey; unto the place of the Canaanite, and the Hittite, and the Amorite, and the Perizzite, and the Hivite, and the Jebusite. 9 And now, behold, the cry of the children of Israel is come unto Me; moreover I have seen the oppression wherewith the Egyptians oppress them. 10 Come now therefore, and I will send thee unto Pharaoh, that thou mayest bring forth My people the children of Israel out of Egypt.' 11 And Moses said unto God: 'Who am I, that I should go unto Pharaoh, and that I should bring forth the children of Israel out of Egypt?' 12 And He said: 'Certainly I will be with thee; and this shall be the token unto thee, that I have sent thee: when thou hast brought forth the people out of Egypt, ye shall serve God upon this mountain.' 13 And Moses said unto God: 'Behold, when I come unto the children of Israel, and shall say unto them: The God of your fathers hath sent me unto you; and they shall say to me: What is His name? What shall I say unto them?' 14 And God said unto Moses: 'I AM THAT I AM'; and He said: 'Thus shalt thou say unto the children of Israel: I AM hath sent me unto you.' 15 And God said moreover unto Moses: 'Thus shalt thou say unto the children of Israel: The Lord, the God of your fathers, the God of Abraham, the God of Isaac, and the God of Jacob, hath sent me unto you; this is My name for ever, and this is My memorial unto all generations.' And the Lord said unto him: 'What is that in thy hand?' And he said: 'A rod.' 3 And He said: 'Cast it on the ground.' And he cast it on the ground, and it became a serpent; and Moses fled from before it.

4 And the Lord said unto Moses: 'Put forth thy hand, and take it by the tail – and he put forth his hand, and laid hold of it, and it became a rod in his hand – 5 that they may believe that the Lord, the God of their fathers, the God of Abraham, the God of Isaac, and the God of Jacob, hath appeared unto thee.' 6 And the Lord said furthermore unto him: 'Put now thy hand into thy bosom.' And he put his hand into his bosom; and when he took it out, behold, his hand was leprous, as white as snow. 7 And He said: 'Put thy hand back into thy bosom.' And he put his hand back into his bosom; and when he took it out of his bosom, behold, it was turned again as his other flesh. 8 'And it shall come to pass, if they will not believe thee, neither hearken to the voice of the first sign, that they will believe the voice of the latter sign. 9 And it shall come to pass, if they will not believe even these two signs, neither hearken unto thy voice, that thou shalt take of the water of the river, and pour it upon the dry land; and the water which thou takest out of the river shall become blood upon the dry land.' 10 And Moses said unto the Lord: 'Oh Lord, I am not a man of words, neither heretofore, nor since Thou hast spoken unto Thy servant; for I am slow of speech, and of a slow tongue.'

11 And the Lord said unto him: 'Who hath made man's mouth? Or who maketh a man dumb, or deaf, or seeing, or blind? Is it not I the Lord? 12 Now therefore go, and I will be with thy mouth, and teach thee what thou shalt speak.' 13 And he said: 'Oh Lord, send, I pray Thee, by the hand of him whom Thou wilt send.' 14 And the anger of the Lord was kindled against Moses, and He said: 'Is there not Aaron thy brother the Levite? I know that he can speak well. And also, behold, he cometh forth to meet thee; and when he seeth thee, he will be glad in his heart. 15 And thou shalt speak unto him, and put the words in his mouth; and I will be with thy mouth, and with his mouth, and will teach you what ye shall do. 16 And he shall be thy spokesman unto the people; and it shall come to pass, that he shall be to thee a mouth, and thou shalt be to him in God's stead. 17 And thou shalt take in thy hand this rod, wherewith thou shalt do the signs. [190]

In the above section the Torah states:

'Moses, Moses.' And he said: 'Here am I.' 5 And He (God) said: 'Don't approach further, put off your shoes, for the place whereon you stand is holy ground.'

Similarly, the Quran says:

---

[190] Torah, Exodus, chapter 3,4

O Moses Indeed Me I am your Lord, put off your shoes indeed you are standing on the holy valley of Tova. Surah 20, v: 12

The Torah states:

'What is that in your hand?' And he said: 'A rod.' 3 And He said: 'Cast it on the ground.' And he cast it on the ground, and it became a serpent; and Moses fled from before it. 4 And the LORD said unto Moses: 'Put forth your hand, and take it by the tail' – and he put forth his hand, and laid hold of it, and it became a rod in his hand.

And the Quran states:

(God said to Moses) and what is that in your right hand, O Moses?' He said, 'It is my staff; I lean upon it, and I bring down leaves for my sheep and I have therein other uses.' [Allah] said, 'Throw it down, O Moses.' So he threw it down, and thereupon it was a snake, moving swiftly. [Allah] said, 'Seize it and fear not; We will return it to its former condition.' Surah 20, v: 17-18

When the contents of two books are so similar to each other, as here, one can imagine there to be two possibilities: either the similarity is due to coincidence; or the second book is inspired by the older, or preceding one. What is, however, not acceptable is to imagine that the older book is inspired by the more recent, or the second book.

In the ensemble of the verses of the Quran, we find a very close relationship with the Bible. This hypothesis is proven to be correct because it is backed up by the writings in the Quran. For instance, this sentence: *'the earth we will let it as heritage to the righteous people'* exists both in Zabour (Psalm of David) and the Quran. It is clear that the Psalm cannot be copying this sentence from the Quran one thousand five hundred years before the revelation of the Quran. Therefore, the origin of this sentence definitely resides in the Psalm. The Quran itself testifies this fact by confirming: *We wrote in Zabour, Psalm – after Zekr, Torah, 'the earth we will let it as heritage to the righteous people'.*[191]

This type of similarity also exists between the Quran and the New Testament, as we read in the first chapter of the Gospel of Saint Luke. Besides the story of Moses in the Bible, there are other stories that are common to both the Quran and the Gospel.

The tale of Zacharias in the Gospel and the Quran

The Gospel according to Luke says:[192]

There was in the days of Herod, king of Judaea, a certain priest named Zacharias, of the course of Abijah: and he had a wife of the daughters of Aaron, and her name was Elisabeth. 1:6 And they were both righteous before God, walking in all the commandments and ordinances of the Lord blameless. 1:7 And they had no child, because that Elisabeth was barren, and they both were now well stricken in years. 1:8 Now it came to pass, while he executed the priest's office before God in the order of his course, 1:9 according to the custom of the priest's office, his lot was to enter into the temple of the Lord and burn incense. 1:10 And the whole multitude of the people were praying without at the hour of incense. 1:11 And there appeared unto him an angel of the Lord standing on the right side of altar of incense.

1:12 And Zacharias was troubled when he saw him, and fear fell upon him. 1:13 But the angel said unto him, Fear not, Zacharias: because thy supplication is heard, and thy wife Elisabeth shall bear thee a son, and thou shalt call his name John. 1:14 And thou shalt have joy and gladness; and many shall rejoice at his birth. 1:15 For he shall be great in the sight of the Lord, and he shall drink no wine nor strong drink; and he shall be filled

---

[191] Surah 21, v:105

و لقد كتبنا فى الزبور ـمن بعد الذكر ـأن الارضَ يرثُها عبادىَ الصالحون.   سورة الانبياء. الايه 105

[192] Gospel according to Luke. Chapter 1

with the Holy Spirit, even from his mother's womb. 1:16 And many of the children of Israel shall he turn unto the Lord their God. 1:17 And he shall go before his face in the spirit and power of Elijah, to turn the hearts of the fathers to the children, and the disobedient to walk in the wisdom of the just; to make ready for the Lord a people prepared for him. 1:18 And Zacharias said unto the angel, Whereby shall I know this? For I am an old man, and my wife well stricken in years.

1:19 And the angel answering said unto him, I am Gabriel, that stand in the presence of God; and I was sent to speak unto thee, and to bring thee these good tidings. 1:20 And behold, thou shalt be silent and not able to speak, until the day that these things shall come to pass, because thou believedst not my words, which shall be fulfilled in their season. 1:21 And the people were waiting for Zacharias, and they marvelled while he tarried in the temple. 1:22 And when he came out, he could not speak unto them: and they perceived that he had seen a vision in the temple: and he continued making signs unto them, and remained dumb. 1:23 And it came to pass, when the days of his ministration were fulfilled, he departed unto his house. 1:24 And after these days Elisabeth his wife conceived; and she hid herself five months, saying, 1:25 Thus hath the Lord done unto me in the days wherein he looked upon me, to take away my reproach among men.

The Quran, Surah 19, verses 1 to 25, states: [193]

Kâf, Hâ, Yâ, 'Ayn, Sâd. [This is] a mention of the mercy of your Lord to His servant Zechariah. When he called to his Lord a private supplication. He said, 'My Lord, indeed my bones have weakened, and my head has filled with white, and never have I been in my supplication to You, my Lord, unhappy. And indeed, I fear the successors after me, and my wife has been barren, so give me from Yourself an heir. Who will inherit me and inherit from the family of Jacob. And make him, my Lord, pleasing [to You]. [194]

---

[193] The tale of Zachariah is mentioned in different Surahs. Here we refer to Surah 19 (Miryam) and 3 (Aâl é Imran).

[194] Surah 19, v: 1- 6.

At that, Zachariah called upon his Lord, saying, 'My Lord, grant me from Yourself a good offspring. Indeed, You are the Hearer of supplication.' So the angels called him while he was standing in prayer in the Mehrab:[195] 'Indeed, Allah gives you good tidings of John,[196] confirming a word from Allah and [who will be] 'Sayyed'[197] honourable, 'has our[198] preserved [from each temptation], and a prophet from among the righteous.' He said, 'My Lord, how will I have a boy when I have reached old age and my wife is barren?' The angel said, 'Such is Allah; He does what He wills.' He said, 'My Lord, make for me a sign.' He Said, 'Your sign is that you will not [be able to] speak to the people for three days except by gesture. And remember your Lord much and exalt [Him with praise] in the evening and the morning.[199]

'O Zachariah, indeed We give you good tidings of a boy whose name will be John. We have not assigned to any before [this] name.' He said, 'My Lord, how will I have a

---

[195] محراب، مهراب Mehrab/praying place inside the Temple/ Mosque. In Jerusalem the Temple Mehrab was the altar of incense. Mehrab is a word used in the Quran in the tale of Zechariah. It is written by this style mehrab- محراب being derived from Hàràbà/fighting. In this case the word of Mehrab -محراب-signifies the place for fighting (the ego, the devil). But an older vocabulary related to the architecture of the temples exists as well which is mehrab -مهراب but written differently. It is a composed word based on Mehr - مهر - meaning sun, and Ab or âveh - آب - meaning temple, altar. It is rooted in the culture of the Mages and Mithraicism in Ancient Persia.

[196] John, St. John the Baptist. In the Quran his name is Yahia -یحیی -, which is the same name used in Aramaic employed by the Mandean Sabian, the followers of the religion in which St John the Baptist, Yahia-یحیی - is considered as the last prophet sent by God. The Arabic version of the other John – the Apostle John – is Youhanna -یوحنا . Yahia -یحیی - can be derived from the word Hayy -حَیَ -, meaning life, alive being. The Quran states that nobody before Yahia -یحیی - had been called by this name.

[197] Sayyed- سید-is equal to honourable. This word is employed rarely in the jargon of the vocabularies of the Quran. In Islamic culture sayyed-سید" is the qualification of those whose paternal ancestors descend from the children of Ali – Fatima (daughter of Mohammad son of Abdollah).

[198] Hasour -حصور –means being protected inside a castle. It is derived from Hàsàrà – حصَر-encircling, encircled. Hasour is a qualification for the very advanced seekers on the path of the substantial evolution whose heart is strongly preserved from each type of devilish temptation. This quality is attributed only to Yahia.

[199] Surah 3, v: 38 - 41.

boy when my wife has been barren and I have reached extreme old age?' [An angel] said, 'Thus [it will be]; your Lord says, 'It is easy for Me, for I created you before, while you were nothing.' '[Zachariah] said, 'My Lord, make for me a sign.' He said, 'Your sign is that you will not speak to the people for three nights, [being] sound.' So he came out to his people from Mehrab (the prayer chamber) and made them known without talking (by giving signs)²⁰⁰ to exalt [Allah] in the morning and afternoon. [Allah] said, 'O John, take the *Scripture with determination.' And We gave him judgement [while yet] a boy. And affection from Us and purity, and he was fearing of Allah. And dutiful to his parents, and he was not a disobedient tyrant. And peace be upon him the day he was born and the day he dies and the day he is raised alive.*²⁰¹

We can see the similarity between this story in the Quran and the Gospel as follows:

The Gospel:

And Zacharias said unto the angel, 'Whereby shall I know this? For I am an old man, and my wife well stricken in years.' 1:19

The Quran:

He said, 'My Lord, how will I have a boy when my wife has been barren and I have reached extreme old age?' Surah 19, v: 8

The Gospel:

---

²⁰⁰ فاوحى اليهم fà owhâ élày hem. He let them know his orders without using his tongue for talking. Communicating in a 'dumb' manner.

²⁰¹ Surah 19, v: 7 - 15.

And behold, you will be silent and not able to speak, until the day that these things shall come to pass. And when he came out, he could not speak unto them... and he continued making signs unto them, and remained dumb. 1:23

The Quran:

He said, 'Your sign is that you will not speak to the people for three nights, [being] sound.' So he came out to his people from Mehrab (the prayer chamber) and made them known without talking (by giving signs) to exalt [Allah] in the morning and afternoon. Surah 19, v: 10, 11

The tale of Mary according to the Gospel and the Quran

We can observe the same similarities in the tale about Mary in the Gospel and the Quran.

The Gospel according to Luke states:

Now in the sixth month (after the pregnancy of Elisabeth) the angel Gabriel was sent from God unto a city of Galilee, named Nazareth, 1:27 to a virgin betrothed to a man whose name was Joseph, of the house of David; and the virgin's name was Mary. 1:28 And he came in unto her, and said, Hail, thou that art highly favoured, the Lord is with thee. 1:29 But she was greatly troubled at the saying, and cast in her mind what manner of salutation this might be. 1:30 And the angel said unto her, Fear not, Mary: for thou hast found favour with God. 1:31 And behold, thou shalt conceive in thy womb, and bring forth a son, and shalt call his name JESUS. 1:32 He shall be great, and shall be called the Son of the Most High: and the Lord God shall give unto him the throne of his father David: 1:33 and he shall reign over the house of Jacob for ever; and of his kingdom there shall be no end. 1:34 And Mary said unto the angel, How shall this be, seeing I know not a man? 1:35 And the angel answered and said unto her, The Holy Spirit shall come upon thee, and the power of the Most High shall overshadow thee: wherefore also the holy thing which is begotten shall be called the Son of God.

1:36 And behold, Elisabeth thy kinswoman, she also hath conceived a son in her old age; and this is the sixth month with her that was called barren. 1:37 for no word from God shall be void of power. 1:38 And Mary said, Behold, the handmaid of the Lord; be it unto me according to thy word. And the angel departed from her. 1:39 And Mary arose in these days and went into the hill country with haste, into a city of Judah; 1:40 and entered into the house of Zacharias and saluted Elisabeth. 1:41 And it came to pass, when Elisabeth heard the salutation of Mary, the babe leaped in her womb; and Elisabeth was filled with the Holy Spirit; 1:42 and she lifted up her voice with a loud cry, and said, Blessed art thou among women, and blessed is the fruit of thy womb. 1:43 And whence is this to me, that the mother of my Lord should come unto me? 1:44 For behold, when the voice of thy salutation came into mine ears, the babe leaped in my womb for joy. 1:45 And blessed is she that believed; for there shall be a fulfilment of the things which have been spoken to her from the Lord.

The Quran says:

'And mention, [O Mohammad], in the Book [the story of] Mary, when she withdrew in seclusion from her family to place facing east. She placed a screen (to screen herself) from them. Then We sent to her Our Spirit,[202] and he represented himself to her in form of a man in all respects. She said, 'Indeed, I seek refuge in the Most Merciful from you, [so leave me], if you should be fearing of Allah.' He said, 'I am only the messenger of your Lord to give you [news of] a pure boy.' She said, 'How can I have a boy while no man has touched me and I have not been unchaste?' He said, 'Thus [it will be]; your Lord says, "It is easy for Me, and We will make him a sign to the people and a mercy from Us. And it is a matter [already] decreed."' So she conceived him, and she withdrew with him to a remote place. And the pains

---

[202] Rouh -روح –means Spirit, Holy Spirit, Gabriel, the Angel of Revelation.

of childbirth drove her to the trunk of a palm tree. She said, 'Oh, I wish I had died before this and was in oblivion, forgotten.' But he called her from below her, 'Do not grieve; your Lord has provided beneath you a stream.' [203]

The Gospel:

And Mary said unto the angel, 'How shall this be, seeing I know not a man?' 1:35

The Quran:

She said, 'How can I have a boy while no man has touched me and I have not been unchaste?' Surah 19, v: 20

Torah, Gospel, Forghân

Although the resemblance between the Quran and the Bible is astounding, it should not lead us to the conclusion that the content of the Quran is merely inspired by the tales of the Bible and confirms the Old and New Testaments. As we mentioned before, certain parts of the Quran do not correspond to the Biblical texts and are sometimes even in opposition to them. As a consequence, we should not only take into consideration the importance of the Bible in the research of the source of the Quranic tales, but also consider other written texts such as 'Sohof', 'Zobor' and 'Kotob', totally out of the frame of the Bible, as sources of the verses of the Quran. The Quran specifically mentions the name of another book (Ketâb) besides the Bible (New and Old Testaments), which is called 'al-Forghân':

---

[203] Surah 19, v: 16 - 24.

(O Mohammad,) He - (Allah) - has sent down upon you 'the Book' - نَزَّلَ عَلَيْكَ الْكِتَابَ -, *on the side of truth* بِالْحَقِّ - *(not on the side of wrongness* - بالباطل -)*; confirming* مصدقا - *what was before it; and He had sent down before (your Book) the Torah and the Enjil (Gospel)* وَأَنْزَلَ التَّوْرَاةَ وَالْإِنْجِيلَ مِنْ قَبْلُ *as guidance for the people* هُدًى لِلنَّاسِ *. And he had sent down Al- Forghân* وَأَنْزَلَ الْفُرْقَانَ. Surah 3, v: 3, 4[204]

Forghân: Name and description

Forghân means an instrument to differentiate between two categories of values: "khayr" الخير (positive); "shàrr" الشرّ (negative). Each Holy Book has the character of Forghân and can be qualified as al-Forghân, because by reading it, the reader is able to distinguish between actions and intentions that are increasing or decreasing the inner energy of the individual on his/her path of the substantial evolution. Forghân is used as a general name for all Holy Books, referring to their common qualities.

Besides this general meaning, al-Forghân is used as a pure name to indicate one of the Holy Books revealed by God/Allah to one of his prophets, to give guidance to the community of mankind regardless of time and place.

The Great is God who had sent down to his Abd, al-Forghân, in order to become a guide for people of both worlds. Surah 25, v: 1[205]

This verse is in fact at the beginning of the Surah 25, which is titled al-Forghân.

But to whom had God sent down al-Forghân? To his Abd, which refers to a person who has reached the ultimate point of his seeking towards his Creator and as a result is named Abdollah. He is a worshipper of Allah

---

204-نَزَّلَ عَلَيْكَ الْكِتَابَ بِالْحَقِّ مُصَدِّقًا لِمَا بَيْنَ يَدَيْهِ وَأَنْزَلَ التَّوْرَاةَ وَالْإِنْجِيلَ مِنْ قَبْلُ هُدًى لِلنَّاسِ وَأَنْزَلَ الْفُرْقَانَ / آل عمران 3 -و4

205تَبَارَكَ الَّذِي نَزَّلَ الْفُرْقَانَ عَلَى عَبْدِهِ لِيَكُونَ لِلْعَالَمِينَ نَذِيرًا   سورة الفرقان. الاية1

uniquely, instead of a worshipper of his ego or a worshipper of both Allah and his ego. In this case, all of the prophets who have received a Holy Book are included in the frame of this verse: Mohammad, Jesus, John the Baptist, Moses, David, Abraham.

All the Holy Books revealed from divinity to the prophets to guide people are also included in the frame of the following verses: Torah, Enjil, Quran, Zabour, Sohof é Ebrahim, Sohof é Adam, Sohof é Moses, among others. Verse 53 of the second Surah introduces the Book of Moses (Sohof é Moses) as al-Forghân:

And we gave to Moses the Book (al Ketâb) and al-Forghân having hope for you to be guided.[206] Surah 2, v: 53

Verse 48 of Surah 21 is in accordance with this sentence as well:

We gave to Moses and Aaron al-Forghân and light, and a reminder for the people of trust.[207]

In addition, verse 185 of the second Surah refers to the Quran as al-Forghân:

The month of Ramadan (is the period) in which the Quran was sent down as guidance for people and the evidences of guidance, and al-Forghân.[208] Surah 2, v: 185

Among all the prophets who were receivers of a Holy Book, Abraham was the only one to whom Allah said:

---

[206] و اذ آتينا موسى الكتاب و الفرقان لعلكم تهتدون سورة البقرة الاية 53

[207] و لقد آتينا موسى و هارون الفرقان و ضياء و ذكرا للمتقين سورة الانبياء الايه 48

[208] ـ شهر الرمضان الذى انزل فيه القرآن هدى للناس و بينات من الهدى و الفرقان. البقرة- الاية 185 ـ هُوَ الَّذِى أَنْزَلَ عَلَيْكَ الْكِتَابَ مِنْهُ آيَاتٌ مُحْكَمَاتٌ هُنَّ أُمُّ الْكِتَابِ وَأُخَرُ مُتَشَابِهَاتٌ فَأَمَّا الَّذِينَ فِى قُلُوبِهِمْ زَيْغٌ فَيَتَّبِعُونَ مَا تَشَابَهَ مِنْهُ ابْتِغَاءَ الفِتْنَةِ وَابْتِغَاءَ تَأْوِيلِهِ وَمَا يَعْلَمُ تَأْوِيلَهُ إِلَّا اللَّهُ وَالرَّاسِخُونَ فِى الْعِلْمِ يَقُولُونَ آمَنَّا بِهِ كُلٌّ مِنْ عِنْدِرَبِّنَا وَمَا يَذَّكَّرُ إِلَّا أُولُوا الأَلْبَابِ آل عمران - الاية 7

124

'I give the mission of guiding the whole humanity to you.' And he asked what about my descendants? Allah replied 'my pact does not concern those who are the oppressors'. Surah 2, v: 124[209]

Therefore, Abd is either Abraham, to whom a Book with the quality of al-Forghân was given, or another prophet in the lineage of the descendants of Abraham, whose mission was limitless and timeless. The Quran itself confirms that Mohammad had a mission to read the texts of the preceding Holy Books (al-Forghân), that were written in non-Arabic languages, for those who did not understand any language other than Arabic (namely the Bedouins of the Arabian Peninsula). In line with this, the Quran states:

The Quran is sent to bring guidance to the people living in 'Om ol Ghora va man howlehâ' Surah 42, v: 7 *(for the people in Mecca and the region around it).*[210]

Nowadays, resulting from the recent discoveries of old scrolls and manuscripts, it is known that spiritual communities were living in the region of the Middle East. These recently discovered scrolls were written between 200 BC and 100 AD in the city of Qumran, next to the shore of the Dead Sea, and covered by a pile of folded scrolls inside pots which were stored in eleven caves around this region. These communities preserved the teachings of the ancient prophets and their written documents. Among the documents discovered in Qumran, there are many chapters that correspond

---

209 ـ و اذ ابتلى ابراهيم ربه بكلمات فاتمهن قال انى جاعلك للناس اماما قال و من ذريتى قال لاينال عهدى الظالمين البقرة ـ الاية 124

210 ـ كذلك اوحينا اليك قرآنا عربيا لتنذر أمّ القرى و من حولها سورة الشورى ـ الاية /7 وهذا كتاب انزلناه مبارك مصدق الذى بين يديه و لتنذر ام القرى و من حولها و الذين يومنون بالاخرة يومنون به، و هم على صلاتهم يحافظون. سورةالانعام الاية 92

with the content of the Bible while some other parts cannot be traced to it.[211]

Certain verses in the Quran also testify the division of the content of the Bible into different parts. Indeed, the Quran confirms that the hidden part of the Bible had been written down on the scrolls that were brought deliberately out of the sight of the Jewish community by certain religious authorities.

O you who have believed, indeed many of the scholars and the monks devour the wealth of people unjustly and avert [them] from the way of Allah. And those who hoard gold and silver and spend it not in the way of Allah – give them tidings of a painful punishment. The Day when it will be heated in the fire of Hell and seared therewith will be their foreheads, their flanks, and their backs, [it will be said], 'This is what you hoarded for yourselves, so taste what you used to hoard'. Surah 9, v: 34-35 [212] *Among the Jews (religious authorities) are those who distort words from their [proper] usages and say, 'We hear and disobey' ... O you who were given the Scripture (Jewish people of Medina), believe in what We have sent down [to Mohammad], confirming that which is with you, before We obliterate faces and turn them towards their backs or curse them as We cursed the Sabbath-breakers. And ever is the decree of Allah accomplished. Surah 4, v: 46-47*[213]

The Quran further explains that these separated parts were preserved and protected by people who were sincerely guided and followed the right path. The Quran gives order to Mohammad to follow in the footsteps of this community, and deeply protect the pure teachings of Abraham and the prophets descending from the lineage of Abraham.

---

211 ـ ورمز گزا. النصوص الكاملة لمخطوطات البحر الميت. ترجمه دكتر سهيل زكار. دار قتيبة. چاپ اول. 2006

212 ـ سورة التوبة / البرائة 34-35

213 ـ سورة النساء الايات 46-47

They who believe and do not mix their belief with injustice – those will have security, and they are [rightly] guided. And that was Our [conclusive] argument which We gave Abraham against his people. We raise by degrees whom We will. Indeed, your Lord is Wise and Knowing. And We gave to Abraham, Isaac and Jacob – all [of them] We guided. And Noah, We guided before; and among his descendants, David and Solomon and Job and Joseph and Moses and Aaron. Thus do We reward the doers of good. And Zechariah and John and Jesus and Elias – and all were of the righteous. And Ishmael and Elisha and Jonah and Lot – and all [of them] We preferred over the worlds. And [some] among their fathers and their descendants and their brothers – and We chose them and We guided them to a straight path.

That is the guidance of Allah by which He guides whomever He wills of His servants. But if they had associated others with Allah, then worthless for them would be whatever they were doing. Those are the ones to whom We gave the Scripture and authority and prophethood. But if the disbelievers deny it, then We have entrusted it to a people who are not therein disbelievers. Those are the ones whom Allah has guided, so (oh Mohammad) follow the footstep of their guidance. Say, 'I ask of you for this message no payment. It is not but a reminder for the worlds.' And they did not appraise Allah with true appraisal when they said, 'Allah did not reveal to a human being anything.' Say, 'Who revealed the Scripture that Moses brought as light and guidance to the people?

You [Jews] make it into pages, disclosing [some of] it and concealing much. And you were taught that which you knew not – neither you nor your fathers.' Say, 'Allah [revealed it].' Then leave them in their [empty] discourse, amusing themselves. And this is a Book which We have sent down, blessed and confirming what was before it, that you may warn the Mother of Cities and those around it. Those who believe in the Hereafter believe in it, and they are maintaining their prayers. And who is more unjust than one who invents a lie about Allah or says, 'It has been inspired to me,' while nothing has been inspired to him, and one who says, 'I will reveal [something] like what Allah revealed.' Surah 6, v: 82 - 93[214]

. [214] ـ سورة الانعام الايات 82 - 93

From the description in the Quran, we can conclude that somehow Mohammad, and the community to which Mohammad was related, had a connection with this lineage of the keepers of the scrolls, parchments, manuscripts and books. The discoveries of Qumran revealed the existence of different examples of the Old Testament, the Torah, the Book of Moses, Zabour of David, as well as the books of Isaiah and Jeremy, Daniel, and Habakkuk.

And indeed, among the 'People of the Scripture' (Ahl ol Ketâb) are those who believe in Allah and what was revealed to you and what was revealed to them, [being] humbly submissive to Allah. They do not exchange the verses of Allah for a small price. Those will have their reward with their Lord. Indeed, Allah is swift in account. Surah 3, v: 199[215]

Ahl ol Ketâb, meaning 'the people of the Holy Books' referring to the Bible including both Old and New Testaments of the Jewish and Christian communities respectively, are composed of two groups of people:

1. Those who were misusing the teachings of the prophets for material benefits. The Quran gives the example of the companions of Sabbath to describe this category of Ahl ol Ketab, who are materialists and 'hoard gold and silver.' Surah 9, v: 34. [216]

215ـ سورة آل عمران الاية 199

216 والذين يكنزون الذهب و الفضة و لاينفقونها فى سبيل الله فبشرهم بعذاب اليم سورة التوبة الاية 34

2. Those who were the treasure keepers of the prophetical heritages in each period of time protect the teachings of the spiritual guides and transmit them to the coming generations.

The Quran stresses the fact that the second category of Ahl ol Ketâb were the followers of the teachings of all of the prophets in the lineage of Abraham, and that it is not right to consider them as Jewish or Christian, but instead as the 'followers of the path of Abraham' Mellat é Ebrahim. Surah 22, v: 78.[217]

And who would be averse to the Path of Abraham except one who makes a fool of himself. And We had chosen him in this world, and indeed he, in the Hereafter, will be among the righteous. When his Lord said to him, 'Embark on the path', he said 'I have embarked on the path of Islam towards the Lord of the worlds.' And Abraham instructed his sons [to do the same] and [so did] Jacob, [saying], 'O my sons, indeed Allah has chosen for you this religion, so do not die except while you are Muslims.' Or were you witnesses when death approached Jacob, when he said to his sons, 'What will you worship after me?' They said, 'We will worship your God and the God of your fathers, Abraham and Ishmael and Isaac — one God. And we are Muslims who have embarked on the path towards Him.' That was a nation which has passed on. It will have [the consequence of] what it earned, and you will have what you have earned. And you will not be asked about what they used to do. They say, 'Be Jews or Christians [so] you will be guided.' Say, 'Rather, [we follow] the religion of Abraham, inclining towards truth, and he was not of the polytheists.' Say, [O believers], 'We have believed in Allah and what has been revealed to us and what has been revealed to Abraham and Ishmael and Isaac and Jacob and the Descendants and what was given to Moses and Jesus and what was given to the prophets from their Lord. We make no distinction between any of them, and we are Muslims who have embarked on the path towards to Him.' So if they

---

[217] سورة الحج الايه 78 مِلَّة ابيكُم ابراهيم و هوَ سَمَّاكم المسلمين من قبل

believe in the same as you believe in, then they have been [rightly] guided; but if they turn away, they are only in dissension, and Allah will be sufficient for you against them.

And He is the Hearing, the Knowing. [And say, 'Ours is] the religion of Allah. And who is better than Allah in [ordaining] religion? And we are worshippers of Him.' Say, [O Mohammad], 'Do you argue with us about Allah while He is our Lord and your Lord? For us are our deeds, and for you are your deeds. And we are sincere [in deed and intention] to Him.' Or do you say that Abraham and Ishmael and Isaac and Jacob and the Descendants were Jews or Christians? Say, 'Are you more knowing or is Allah?' And who is more unjust than one who conceals a testimony he has from Allah? And Allah is not unaware of what you do. That is a nation which has passed on. It will have [the consequence of] what it earned, and you will have what you have earned. And you will not be asked about what they used to do.[218] Surah 2, v: 130 - 140.

The Path of Abraham: Mellat é Ebrahim[219] / Islam

The Quran explains more about the path of Abraham in the verse in which it is said:

When the Lord of Abraham told him 'aslem', meaning find the peace in your heart, and he replied I decided to embark on the path of gaining health for my heart, which is the meaning of Islam, and trusted to the Lord of both universe.[220] Surah 2, v: 131.

[It is] the path of your father, Abraham, who named you 'Muslims' before [in former scriptures] and in this [revelation] that the Messenger may be a witness over you and you may be witnesses over the people. So establish prayer and give Zakah and hold fast to Allah. He is your protector; and excellent is the protector, and excellent is the helper.[221] Surah 22, v: 78.

---

218 سورة البقرة الايات 130-140

219 سورة البقرة الاية 135.   Surah 2, v: 135

220 اذ قال له ربه اسلم قال اسلمت لرب العالمين سورة البقرة الاية 131

221 مله ابيكم ابراهيم .هو سماكم المسلمين من قبل و فيهذا ليكون الرسول شهيدا عليكم و تكونوا شهداء على الناس فاقيمواالصلوه و آتوا الزكات و اعتصموا بالله هو موليكم فنعم المولى و نعم النصير سورة الحج الاية 78

In these verses Abraham is introduced as the founder of the path of monotheism, which means to worship the unique Creator and not to be held by the attachment of duality or superstition or polytheism. This path is named by Allah or Abraham, Islam, meaning - 'the path of establishing peace and health in one's heart.' The Lord of Abraham advised him to become Muslim, and he decided to start on the path of healing his heart. Later on he guided people to the same path, which was called by him Islam.

Often 'Islam' is translated as 'submission' or 'obedience' and interpreted as 'blind following'. This is a wrong and misleading translation. The root of the word 'Islam' is 'selm' and 'salâm' which can be translated as 'salvation' or 'peace'. 'Sàlàmà' and 'yaslemo' are verbal forms of 'selm', meaning 'achieve peace of the heart' 'or achieve health of the heart'. 'Tasleem' is the expression which would be translated as 'submission'. The verbs derived from 'Tasleem' are 'sallama' meaning 'he submitted' and 'yossalemo' meaning 'he submits'. The exact translation of 'Islam' or 'Eslam' is 'the path to a healthy heart'. The verb 'aslama' means 'he started the path towards achieving health of the heart' and the verb 'yoslemo' means 'he starts the path towards achieving health of the heart'.

In this passage, the Quran does not use the word 'Din', which is a synonym for the word path, but uses the word 'Mellat', which is a synonym for doctrine instead. At the same time the Quran rejects the affiliation of Abraham to Judaism or Christianity:

Abraham was not Jew or Christian, but Hanif and Muslim. Surah 3, v: 67.[222]

The Quran does not accept the reasoning of Jewish and Christian priests who believe that it is necessary for everybody who wants to join the religion of Abraham to convert either to Judaism or to Christianity, and says that

---

222ماكان ابراهيم يهوديا و لانصرانيا و لكن كان حنيفا مسلما و ماكان من المشركين. سورة آل عمران الاية 67

Abraham lived before Moses and Jesus, so in order to follow the path of Abraham it is necessary to join the school of Abraham – which was the same school in which Moses, Jesus, Isaac, Jacob, and all the other prophets were educated.

They said: Be either Jew or Christian to be guided. (O Mohammad) say: but be the followers of the path of Abraham, Hanif. He was not a polytheist. Surah 2, v: 135.[223]

O People of the Books, why do you argue about Abraham while the Torah and the Gospel were not revealed until after him? Then will you not reason? Here you are – those who have argued about that of which you have [some] knowledge, but why do you argue about that of which you have no knowledge? And Allah knows, while you know not. Abraham was neither a Jew nor a Christian, but he was one inclining towards truth, a Muslim. And he was not of the polytheists. Surah 3, v: 65 to 67.[224]

And who would turn his attachment from the path, mellat, of Abraham except one who makes a fool of himself? Surah 2, v: 130.[225]

Indeed, the most worthy of Abraham among the people are those who followed him [in submission to Allah] and this prophet, and those who believe [in his message]. And Allah is the ally of the believers. Surah 3, v: 84.[226]

It is within the frame of this continuity that the Quran makes a public appeal to the 'people of the Books' to create a large union with each other around one word (which had been uttered before all of the prophets and religious communities by Abraham):

---

[223]و قالوا هودا او نصارا تهتدوا .قل بل مله ابراهيم حنيفا و ماكان من المشركين /البقرة - الاية 135

[224]يَا أَهْلَ الْكِتَابِ لِمَ تُحَاجُّونَ فِي إِبْرَاهِيمَ وَمَا أُنزِلَتِ التَّوْرَاةُ وَالإِنجِيلُ إِلَّا مِن بَعْدِهِ ۚ أَفَلَا تَعْقِلُونَ هَا أَنتُمْ هَٰؤُلَاءِ حَاجَجْتُمْ فِيمَا لَكُمُ بِهِ عِلْمٌ فَلِمَ تُحَاجُّونَ فِيمَا لَيْسَ لَكُم بِهِ عِلْمٌ ۚ وَاللَّهُ يَعْلَمُ وَأَنتُمْ لَا تَعْلَمُونَ . مَا كَانَ إِبْرَاهِيمُ يَهُودِيًّا وَلَا نَصْرَانِيًّا وَلَٰكِن كَانَ حَنِيفًا مُّسْلِمًا وَمَا كَانَ مِنَ الْمُشْرِكِينَ آل عمران 67 -65

[225]و من يرغب عن مله ابراهيم الا من سفه نفسه؟ البقرة- الاية 130

[226]إِنَّ أَوْلَى النَّاسِ بِإِبْرَاهِيمَ لَلَّذِينَ اتَّبَعُوهُ وَهَٰذَا النَّبِيُّ وَالَّذِينَ آمَنُوا ۗ وَاللَّهُ وَلِيُّ الْمُؤْمِنِينَ آل عمران الاية 68 -

Say, 'O People of the Scripture, come to a word that is equitable between us and you – that we will not worship except Allah and not associate anything with Him and not take one another as lords instead of Allah.' But if they turn away, then say, 'Bear witness that we are Muslims.' Surah 3, v: 64.[227]

The same advice about unity between the religions – in the line of Abraham – is often given in the Quran:

Say, [O believers], 'We have believed in Allah and what has been revealed to us and what has been revealed to Abraham and Ishmael and Isaac and Jacob and the Descendants/Asbât – 12 tribes of Israel – and what was given to Moses and Jesus and what was given to the prophets from their Lord. We make no distinction between any of them, and we are Muslims who trust Him.' Surah 2, v: 136.[228]

Say, 'We have believed in Allah and in what was revealed to us and what was revealed to Abraham, Ishmael, Isaac, Jacob, and the Descendants, and in what was given to Moses and Jesus and to the prophets from their Lord. We make no distinction between any of them, and we are Muslims who trust Him.' Surah 3, v: 84.[229]

In the second half of the first century AD, the city of Qumran was invaded by the Roman army and completely destroyed. The inhabitants were composed of Essenes and Sadducean (Zadokites) and they had prepared themselves for this event by writing all of their scriptures on long scrolls (the longest one being about 147.50 metres, which was found in the eighth cave in Qumran), which they hid in pots in the corners of the caves. Before leaving the region forever, they had made copies of the scriptures and took refuge in

---

227 قُلْ يَا أَهْلَ الْكِتَابِ تَعَالَوْا إِلَى كَلِمَةٍ سَوَاءٍ بَيْنَنَا وَبَيْنَكُمْ أَلَّا نَعْبُدَ إِلَّا اللهَ وَلَا نُشْرِكَ بِهِ شَيْئًا وَلَا يَتَّخِذَ بَعْضُنَا بَعْضًا أَرْبَابًا مِّن دُونِ اللهِ ۖ فَإِن تَوَلَّوْا فَقُولُوا اشْهَدُوا بِأَنَّا مُسْلِمُونَ آل عمران الاية 64-

228 قُولُوا " آمَنَّا بِاللهِ وَمَا أُنزِلَ إِلَيْنَا وَمَا أُنزِلَ إِلَى إِبْرَاهِيمَ وَإِسْمَاعِيلَ وَإِسْحَاقَ وَيَعْقُوبَ وَالْأَسْبَاطِ وَمَا أُوتِيَ مُوسَى وَعِيسَى وَمَا أُوتِيَ النَّبِيُّونَ مِنْ رَبِّهِمْ لَا نُفَرِّقُ بَيْنَ أَحَدٍ مِّنْهُمْ وَنَحْنُ لَهُ مُسْلِمُونَ / "البقرة الايه 136/ ؛

229 قُلْ " :آمَنَّا بِاللهِ وَمَا أُنزِلَ عَلَيْنَا وَمَا أُنزِلَ عَلَى إِبْرَاهِيمَ وَإِسْمَاعِيلَ وَإِسْحَاقَ وَيَعْقُوبَ وَالْأَسْبَاطِ وَمَا أُوتِيَ مُوسَى وَعِيسَى وَالنَّبِيُّونَ مِنْ رَبِّهِمْ لَا نُفَرِّقُ بَيْنَ أَحَدٍ مِّنْهُمْ وَنَحْنُ لَهُ مُسْلِمُونَ /آل عمران الايه. 84/

various locations in Jordan, Syria, Mesopotamia, and Cappadocia, inside caves within the mountainous regions. Through further examination, we will see that some kind of continuity exists between the forgotten scriptures of Qumran and the diverse passages of the Quran.

Upon examining the quantity of the scrolls and bronze pages on which all of the major literatures were kept in Qumran, in various languages such as Aramaic, Greek, Hebrew, or Nabatean, it is hard to imagine that the Qumran inhabitants made a complete copy of all of the texts before escaping from the Roman invasion. Instead, they were probably only able to copy an extract of the most essential teachings. This extract could have been written in the frame of a comprehensive and reconstituted ensemble, considered as a Holy Book, and served as the most important reference for the wise sages of the dispersed community, during the migration to the other lands. That Holy Book could have been given different names, such as al-Forghân. This Holy Book could have been composed of various tales of the ancient prophets, and in particular, the rules necessary for being a member of the community of the pure seekers. If this was the case, then that part of this possible Holy Book could be a copy of documents from the group of manuscripts from the Dead Sea (constituting thirty per cent of all the Dead Sea scrolls), which sheds light on the rules and beliefs of an unknown community, which was neither Jewish, nor Christian, nor Sabian, who lived in Qumran and contained the 'Community Rule', the 'War Scroll', the 'Pesher of Habakkuk', and the 'Rule of the Blessing'.[230] As we mentioned before, the last discoveries

---

[230] Abegg, Jr., Martin, Peter Flint, and Eugene Ulrich, *The Dead Sea Scrolls Bible: The Oldest Known Bible Translated for the First Time into English*, San Francisco: Harper, 2002. A part of the ensemble of manuscripts found in the region of Qumran (situated in the northern part of Arabian Peninsula) remains unidentified. The identified part of the scriptures is dividable into at least three categories:

(1) Some forty per cent of them are copies of texts from the Hebrew Bible;

(2) Approximately thirty per cent are texts from the Second Temple Period and which ultimately were not canonised in the Hebrew Bible, such as the Book of Enoch, Jubilees, the Book of Tobit, the Wisdom of Sirach, Psalms 152–155, etc.; and

concerning the Qumran region confirm the coexistence of two groups of monotheist people in that region, namely the Essenes and Zadokites.[231]

About the sincere person: Sadougin in the Quran

In Hebrew, 'Zadokites' is a synonym for Seddyghoun, صدّيقون , a word in the Arabic version of the Quranic jargon, which means 'the sincere persons'. This word is derived from 'sèdgh' صدق which means sincerity. In the Quran Seddygh صدّيق in its plural form Seddyghoun صدّيقون is the qualification of the people who have sincere faith towards Allah and his messengers:

Those who believe in Allah and his messengers, they are Seddyghoun. Surah 57, v: 19.[232]

In Surah 4, 'Seddyghin' صدّيقين are mentioned in the rank of prophets نبيّون, martyrs شهداء , and the righteous صالحين:

And whoever obeys Allah and the Messenger – those will be with the ones upon whom Allah has bestowed favour of the prophets, 'Seddyghin' الصديقين , the martyrs and the righteous. And excellent are those as companions.[233] Surah 4, v: 69

---

(3) The remaining thirty per cent belong to a community different and separate from the traditional Jewish community.

[231] A specific variation on the Qumran–Sectarian theory that has gained much recent popularity is the work of Lawrence H. Schiffman, who proposes that the community was led by a group of Zadokite priests (Sadducees). The most important document in support of this view is the 'Miqsat Ma'ase Ha-Torah' (4QMMT), which cites purity laws (such as the transfer of impurities) identical to those attributed in rabbinic writings to the Sadducees. 4QMMT also reproduces a festival calendar that follows Sadducee principles for the dating of certain festival days. Schiffman, Lawrence H., *Reclaiming the Dead Sea Scrolls: their True Meaning for Judaism and Christianity*, Anchor Bible Reference Library (Doubleday) 1995.

232و الذين امنوا بالله و رسله اولئك هم الصديقون الحديد الايه 19

233 وَمَن يُطِعِ اللَّهَ وَالرَّسُولَ فَأُولَٰئِكَ مَعَ الَّذِينَ أَنْعَمَ اللَّهُ عَلَيْهِم مِّنَ النَّبِيِّينَ وَالصِّدِّيقِينَ وَالشُّهَدَاءِ وَالصَّالِحِينَ وَحَسُنَ أُولَٰئِكَ رَفِيقًا سوره النساء   الآيه 69

135

These verses show that according to the Quran, Seddyghin had been a particular category of faithful monotheists who are not prophets, but are in the rank of the prophets. They preserve the continuity of the teachings of the prophets through the generations. To be more precise, each prophet is a member of the Seddyghin community, but members of this community are not automatically charged with the mission of a prophet. According to the Quran the first Seddigh was Abraham:

Remind in the Book, Abraham who was (both) Seddigh and Nabii (prophet). Surah 19, v: 41.[234]

In the Quran other spiritual personalities who were from the line of Abraham are also cited as Seddigh:

Remind in the Book, Idris who was (both) Seddigh and Nabii (prophet). Surah 19, v: 56.[235]
O Joseph, O Seddigh, explain us about the seven fat cows. Surah 12, v: 46.[236]
His mother (mother of Jesus, i.e. Mary) was Seddigheh. Surah 5, v: 75.[237]

In the first lines of this book, we talked about two sources of the sentences Mohammad preached to the people of Mecca: the *'Pesher of Abraham'* and the *'Pesher of Moses'.*

---

[234]واذكر فى الكتاب ابراهيم إنه كان صديقا نبيا سوره مريم، الايه 41   و امه صديقه سوره المائده الآيه 75

[235]و اذكر فى الكتاب ادريس انه كان صديقا نبيا سوره مريم الآيه 56

[236]يوسف ايها الصديق افتنا فى سبع بقرات سمان سوره يوسف الآيه 46

[237]و امه صديقه سوره المائده الآيه 75

Indeed, this is in the former scriptures, the scriptures of Abraham and Moses.[238]

The Sohof é oula الصحف الاولى, the old Peshers, could be copies and extracts from the parchments and scrolls of Qumran, in the hands of those who transmitted the rules and ceremonies of the Zadokite community up until the time of Mohammad. Amongst the scriptures discovered in Qumran, there existed an ensemble of sentences under the name of 'the Pesher of Moses', which are different and independent from the Torah. This difference between the passages of the Bible and the Pesher of Moses found in Qumran could explain certain discrepancies between the verses of the Quran and the Bible regarding the affair of Moses. The story in the Quran reminds us of the Biblical legends, but appears to originate from an independent source.[239] The 'Pesher of Abraham', however, has not been found amongst the identified manuscripts of Qumran. The absence of this important source can be explained. The 'Book of Rules' alongside the 'Book of War' and all the texts of the unknown community we have been considering are in fact the teachings revealed by Abraham. In the following pages we will examine this hypothesis more closely.

In the texts that followed the appearance of the Quran, we can read these sentences, which remain in the Islamic tradition, from a companion of Mohammad named Abu Zar é Ghaffari.

Ibn é Mardouyeh ابن مردويه on the one hand and al Ajori الآجرى on the other reported what Abu Zar ابوذر غفارى said: *Once I (Abu Zar) asked the prophet the following question: O messenger of Allah! Has something been revealed to you from the content of the 'Peshers of Abraham'? He replied: yes (and He said):*

---

[238] رسولٌ من الله يتلوا عليهم صحفا مطهره فيها كتب قيمه. إن هذا لفى الصحف الاولى صحف ابراهيم و موسى سورةالاعلى 18-19

[239] Fatemeh Hashtroudi, 2011. *The scrolls of the Dead Sea, History and opinions.* (Farsi) The university of the religions and denominations, Qom/ Iran.

He has certainly succeeded who purifies himself. And mentions the name of his Lord and prays. But you prefer the worldly life, While the Hereafter is better and more enduring. Surah 87, v: 14 - 17.[240]

The same révâyàt related to Abu Zar é Ghaffari is also cited by other reporters such as Akrameh, ibn Abbas, and Zahhak. The difference between their interpretation of the révâyàt of Abu Zar is about the content of 'hada' هذا 'this one': where in the Surah it is said 'this is written in the former scriptures, إِنَّ هَذَا لَفِىالصحف الاولى the scripture of Moses and Abraham صُحُفِ ابراهيم و موسى.' For Akrameh عكرمه and ibn Abbas ابن عباس the entire Surah 87 existed in the Pesher of Abraham and for Zahhak ضحاك the entire Quran existed within the Pesher of Abraham.[241]

The Quran not only mentions the Pesher of Abraham as the source of a part of the Quran, but also repeatedly talks about the school of the spiritual education of Abraham. The Quran uses different titles for this constructive school such as Hanif, Islam, or the path of Abraham, where Hanif corresponds with monotheism. Islam means the process of changing the state of the heart from sickness or illness to strength and health. This is because the word 'Islam' is derived from Selm سلم meaning health. The opposite word to Selm سلم is Soghm سُقم, meaning illness.

The tale of Abraham is described in detail in sixty-nine verses of twenty-five Surah of the Quran including al Baghareh, al Imran, an Nesâ, al An'âm, at Towbeh, Houd, Yousef, Ebrahim, al Hejr, an Nahl, Maryam, al Anbia, al Hajj, as Sho'àrâ, al Ankàbout, al Ahzâb, as Sâffât, Sâd, as

---

ـ 240قد افلح من تزكى و ذكر اسم ربه فصلى بل تؤثرون الحياه الدنيا و الاخره خير و ابقى سورة الاعلى- الايات 14تا 17

This revayat is reported in the commentary of *Quran At Tahrir vat Tanvir*, Mohammad Taher Ashour- ibn Ashour/Dar Sahnoun, p. 291

241 The commentary of the Quran by Qartabi. Mohammad ibn Ahmad ah Ansari al Qardabi (from Cordoba), Dar ol Fekr. pp 22-23.

Ashowrâ, az Zokhrof, az Zâriât, an Najm, al Hadid, al Momtaheneh, al A'lâ. In the presentation of the Quran, all of the exact prayers and ceremonies of worship remain amongst the monotheists because of the teachings of Abraham to his followers. Indeed, the Quran introduces Abraham as the best example for the seekers of God's light and God's face. Abraham is the guide for those who travel from non-perfection to perfection, and from darkness to light, and from disease to stable health, and offers a powerful system of immunity for a vaccinated heart. Given the particular place of Abraham in the frame of the didactic method of the Quran, the invisible source of inspiration and revelation to Mohammad orders him to recite and preach the news about Abraham: وَاتْلُ عَلَيْهِمْ نَبَأَ إِبْرَاهِيمَ Surah 56, v: 69.

According to the Quran, Abraham was born in an idol-worshipping family, tribe, and civilisation.[242] After he had tried to find out the reason for

---

[242] وَاتْلُ عَلَيْهِمْ نَبَأَ إِبْرَاهِيمَ إِذْ قَالَ لِأَبِيهِ وَقَوْمِهِ مَا تَعْبُدُونَ قَالُوا نَعْبُدُ أَصْنَامًا فَنَظَلُّ لَهَا عَاكِفِينَ قَالَ هَلْ يَسْمَعُونَكُمْ إِذْ تَدْعُونَ أَوْ يَنْفَعُونَكُمْ أَوْ يَضُرُّونَ قَالُوا بَلْ وَجَدْنَا آبَاءَنَا كَذَلِكَ يَفْعَلُونَ قَالَ أَفَرَأَيْتُمْ مَا كُنْتُمْ تَعْبُدُونَ أَنْتُمْ وَآبَاؤُكُمُ الْأَقْدَمُونَ فَإِنَّهُمْ عَدُوٌّ لِي إِلَّا رَبَّ الْعَالَمِينَ الَّذِي خَلَقَنِي فَهُوَ يَهْدِينِ وَالَّذِي هُوَ يُطْعِمُنِي وَيَسْقِينِ وَإِذَا مَرِضْتُ فَهُوَ يَشْفِينِ وَالَّذِي يُمِيتُنِي ثُمَّ يُحْيِينِ وَالَّذِي أَطْمَعُ أَنْ يَغْفِرَ لِي خَطِيئَتِي يَوْمَ الدِّينِ رَبِّ هَبْ لِي حُكْمًا وَأَلْحِقْنِي بِالصَّالِحِينَ وَاجْعَلْ لِي لِسَانَ صِدْقٍ فِي الْآخِرِينَ وَاجْعَلْنِي مِنْ وَرَثَةِ جَنَّةِ النَّعِيمِ وَاغْفِرْ لِأَبِي إِنَّهُ كَانَ مِنَ الضَّالِّينَ وَلَا تُخْزِنِي يَوْمَ يُبْعَثُونَ يَوْمَ لَا يَنْفَعُ مَالٌ وَلَا بَنُونَ إِلَّا مَنْ أَتَى اللَّهَ بِقَلْبٍ سَلِيمٍ / سُورَةُ الشُّعَرَاءِ . الآيات 69 - 89

وَإِذْ قَالَ إِبْرَاهِيمُ لِأَبِيهِ آزَرَ أَتَتَّخِذُ أَصْنَامًا آلِهَةً إِنِّي أَرَاكَ وَقَوْمَكَ فِي ضَلَالٍ مُبِينٍ وَكَذَلِكَ نُرِي إِبْرَاهِيمَ مَلَكُوتَ السَّمَاوَاتِ وَالْأَرْضِ وَلِيَكُونَ مِنَ الْمُوقِنِينَ فَلَمَّا جَنَّ عَلَيْهِ اللَّيْلُ رَأَى كَوْكَبًا قَالَ هَذَا رَبِّي فَلَمَّا أَفَلَ قَالَ لَا أُحِبُّ الْآفِلِينَ فَلَمَّا رَأَى الْقَمَرَ بَازِغًا قَالَ هَذَا رَبِّي فَلَمَّا أَفَلَ قَالَ لَئِنْ لَمْ يَهْدِنِي رَبِّي لَأَكُونَنَّ مِنَ الْقَوْمِ الضَّالِّينَ فَلَمَّا رَأَى الشَّمْسَ بَازِغَةً قَالَ هَذَا رَبِّي هَذَا أَكْبَرُ فَلَمَّا أَفَلَتْ قَالَ يَا قَوْمِ إِنِّي بَرِيءٌ مِمَّا تُشْرِكُونَ إِنِّي وَجَّهْتُ وَجْهِيَ لِلَّذِي فَطَرَ السَّمَاوَاتِ وَالْأَرْضَ حَنِيفًا وَمَا أَنَا مِنَ الْمُشْرِكِينَ وَحَاجَّهُ قَوْمُهُ قَالَ أَتُحَاجُّونِّي فِي اللَّهِ وَقَدْ هَدَانِ وَلَا أَخَافُ مَا تُشْرِكُونَ بِهِ إِلَّا أَنْ يَشَاءَ رَبِّي شَيْئًا وَسِعَ رَبِّي كُلَّ شَيْءٍ عِلْمًا أَفَلَا تَتَذَكَّرُونَ وَكَيْفَ أَخَافُ مَا أَشْرَكْتُمْ وَلَا تَخَافُونَ أَنَّكُمْ أَشْرَكْتُمْ بِاللَّهِ مَا لَمْ يُنَزِّلْ بِهِ عَلَيْكُمْ سُلْطَانًا فَأَيُّ الْفَرِيقَيْنِ أَحَقُّ بِالْأَمْنِ إِنْ كُنْتُمْ تَعْلَمُونَ الَّذِينَ آمَنُوا وَلَمْ يَلْبِسُوا إِيمَانَهُمْ بِظُلْمٍ أُولَئِكَ لَهُمُ الْأَمْنُ وَهُمْ مُهْتَدُونَ وَتِلْكَ حُجَّتُنَا آتَيْنَاهَا إِبْرَاهِيمَ عَلَى قَوْمِهِ نَرْفَعُ دَرَجَاتٍ مَنْ نَشَاءُ إِنَّ رَبَّكَ حَكِيمٌ عَلِيمٌ وَوَهَبْنَا لَهُ إِسْحَاقَ وَيَعْقُوبَ كُلًّا هَدَيْنَا وَنُوحًا هَدَيْنَا مِنْ قَبْلُ وَمِنْ ذُرِّيَّتِهِ دَاوُودَ وَسُلَيْمَانَ وَأَيُّوبَ وَيُوسُفَ وَمُوسَى وَهَارُونَ وَكَذَلِكَ نَجْزِي الْمُحْسِنِينَ وَزَكَرِيَّا وَيَحْيَى وَعِيسَى وَإِلْيَاسَ كُلٌّ مِنَ الصَّالِحِينَ وَإِسْمَاعِيلَ وَالْيَسَعَ وَيُونُسَ وَلُوطًا وَكُلًّا فَضَّلْنَا عَلَى الْعَالَمِينَ وَمِنْ آبَائِهِمْ وَذُرِّيَّاتِهِمْ وَإِخْوَانِهِمْ وَاجْتَبَيْنَاهُمْ وَهَدَيْنَاهُمْ إِلَى صِرَاطٍ مُسْتَقِيمٍ ذَلِكَ هُدَى اللَّهِ يَهْدِي بِهِ مَنْ يَشَاءُ مِنْ عِبَادِهِ وَلَوْ أَشْرَكُوا لَحَبِطَ عَنْهُمْ مَا كَانُوا يَعْمَلُونَ أُولَئِكَ الَّذِينَ آتَيْنَاهُمُ الْكِتَابَ وَالْحُكْمَ وَالنُّبُوَّةَ فَإِنْ يَكْفُرْ بِهَا هَؤُلَاءِ فَقَدْ وَكَّلْنَا بِهَا قَوْمًا لَيْسُوا بِهَا بِكَافِرِينَ أُولَئِكَ الَّذِينَ هَدَى اللَّهُ فَبِهُدَاهُمُ اقْتَدِهْ قُلْ لَا أَسْأَلُكُمْ عَلَيْهِ أَجْرًا إِنْ هُوَ إِلَّا ذِكْرَى لِلْعَالَمِينَ وَمَا قَدَرُوا اللَّهَ حَقَّ قَدْرِهِ إِذْ قَالُوا مَا أَنْزَلَ اللَّهُ عَلَى بَشَرٍ مِنْ شَيْءٍ قُلْ مَنْ أَنْزَلَ الْكِتَابَ الَّذِي جَاءَ بِهِ مُوسَى نُورًا وَهُدًى لِلنَّاسِ تَجْعَلُونَهُ قَرَاطِيسَ تُبْدُونَهَا وَتُخْفُونَ كَثِيرًا وَعُلِّمْتُمْ مَا لَمْ تَعْلَمُوا أَنْتُمْ وَلَا آبَاؤُكُمْ قُلِ اللَّهُ ثُمَّ ذَرْهُمْ فِي خَوْضِهِمْ يَلْعَبُونَ وَهَذَا كِتَابٌ أَنْزَلْنَاهُ مُبَارَكٌ مُصَدِّقُ الَّذِي بَيْنَ يَدَيْهِ وَلِتُنْذِرَ أُمَّ الْقُرَى وَمَنْ حَوْلَهَا وَالَّذِينَ يُؤْمِنُونَ بِالْآخِرَةِ يُؤْمِنُونَ بِهِ وَهُمْ عَلَى صَلَاتِهِمْ يُحَافِظُونَ وَمَنْ أَظْلَمُ مِمَّنِ افْتَرَى عَلَى اللَّهِ كَذِبًا أَوْ قَالَ أُوحِيَ إِلَيَّ وَلَمْ يُوحَ إِلَيْهِ شَيْءٌ وَمَنْ قَالَ سَأُنْزِلُ مِثْلَ مَا أَنْزَلَ اللَّهُ سُورَةُ الأنعام . الآيات 74-93

139

the idol worship and could not find any answer, he began to reflect deeply about the powerful superstitions and ancestral traditions that could not be explained by his surroundings. After a long analysis of his own inner state he had to admit to himself that his heart was ill as well. From that moment he established a new paradigm in his life. He detached himself from all the idols in his mind first, and then refrained from participating in certain traditional ceremonies of his people, which was against the usual behaviour of the population in his region. Thus he was accused of treason. This enormous revolutionary action was the first sign of chivalry accomplished by Abraham. For this reason the people of that city called him Fàtâ فتى *'spiritual knight'*: ó

They (the people of that city) said we have heard about a Fàtâ, knight who is preaching them, his compatriots, who is called Abraham. Surah 21, v: 60.[243]

After this, the religious authorities brought Abraham before an open court right in the public eye. The tyrant of the land ordered that Abraham be dropped into a large pile of fire, which he survived. After this difficult test, Abraham continued his seeking in order to discover the invisible side of the earth and the skies, and to gain complete conviction about existence and the unity of the Creator of the Universe. During this long inner journey, he contemplated the light emanating from the face of his Lord in the form of a star, moon, and sun, as well as without any form. At the end he reached the ultimate point of perfection and purity.

Afterwards, in order to gain certainty about the resurrection, he asked his Lord to show him how He reconstitutes the fragmented pieces of the bodies of the dead, in order to restore their souls back into them. After that he passed on to a new test, which was to become prepared to sacrifice his

---

[243] Mohammad Jarir Tabari. Tafsir é Tabari/commentary of the Quran/Dar ol Mà âref: p460-461.

سورة الانبياء الاية 60 قَالُوا سَمِعْنَا فَتًى يَذْكُرُهُمْ يُقَالُ لَهُ إِبْرَاهِيمُ

own son by his own hand. After travelling all of these intricate steps on the gradual ladder of substantial evolution, he received the honourable title of Imam (leader) and was bestowed with the mission of introducing the best model of spiritual growth to the people, in order to guide whole generations of mankind to unity, monotheism, and perfection. As such, Abraham is introduced as the best model of a spiritual knight, a spiritual chevalier, for the whole of humanity.

And We had certainly given Abraham his growth – maturity[244] before, and We were of him well-Knowing. When he said to his father and his people, 'What are these statues to which you are devoted?' They said, 'We found our fathers worshippers of them.' He said, 'You were certainly, you and your fathers, in manifest error.' They said, 'Have you come to us with truth, or are you of those who jest?' He said, '[No], rather, your Lord is the Lord of the heavens and the earth who created them, and I, to that, am of those who testify. And [I swear] by Allah, I will surely plan against your idols after you have turned and gone away.' So he made them into fragments, except a large one among them, that they might return to it [and question]. They said, 'Who has done this to our gods? Indeed, he is of the wrongdoers.'

They said, 'We heard a young man mention them who is called Abraham.' They said, 'Then bring him before the eyes of the people that they may testify.' They said, 'Have you done this to our Gods, O Abraham?' He said, 'Rather, this – the largest of them did it, so ask them, if they should [be able to] speak.' So they returned to [blaming] themselves and said [to each other], 'Indeed, you are the wrongdoers.' Then they reversed themselves, [saying], 'You have already known that these do not speak!' He said, 'Then do you worship instead of Allah that which does not benefit you at all or harm you? Uff (curse) to you and to what you worship instead of Allah. Then will you not use reason?' They said, 'Burn him and support your gods – if you are to act.' Allah said, 'O fire, be coolness and safety upon Abraham.' And they intended for him harm, but We made

---

[244] Rushd means growing up to reach maturity. The evolution of an infant bird from the stage of non-being inside an egg to the stage of a majestic white eagle is the example of Rushd.

them the greatest losers. And We delivered him and Lot to the land which We had blessed for the worlds. Surah 21, v: 51 - 71.[245]

Abraham received the divine order to travel from his native land to a place called Pharan in order to establish a part of his family in that land.[246]

But God said to Abraham, ...13 As for the son of the slave woman, I will make a nation of him also, because he is your offspring. 14 So Abraham rose early in the morning, and took bread and a skin of water, and gave it to Hagar, putting it on her shoulder, along with the child, and sent her away. And she departed, and wandered about in the wilderness of Beer-sheba. 15 When the water in the skin was gone, she cast the child under one of the bushes. 16 Then she went and sat down opposite him a good way off, about the distance of a bowshot; for she said, 'Do not let me look on the death of the child.' And as she sat opposite him, she lifted up her voice and wept. 17 And God heard the voice of the boy; and the Angel of God called to Hagar from sky, and said to her, What troubles you, Hagar? Do not be afraid; for God has heard the voice of the boy where he is. 18 Come, lift up the boy and hold him fast with your hand, for I will make

---

[245] وَلَقَدْ آتَيْنَا إِبْرَاهِيمَ رُشْدَهُ مِن قَبْلُ وَكُنَّا بِهِ عَالِمِينَ إِذْ قَالَ لِأَبِيهِ وَقَوْمِهِ مَا هَذِهِ التَّمَاثِيلُ الَّتِي أَنتُمْ لَهَا عَاكِفُونَ قَالُوا وَجَدْنَا آبَاءَنَا لَهَا عَابِدِينَ قَالَ لَقَدْ كُنتُمْ أَنتُمْ وَآبَاؤُكُمْ فِي ضَلَالٍ مُبِينٍ قَالُوا أَجِئْتَنَا بِالْحَقِّ أَمْ أَنتَ مِنَ اللَّاعِبِينَ قَالَ بَل رَّبُّكُمْ رَبُّ السَّمَاوَاتِ وَالْأَرْضِ الَّذِي فَطَرَهُنَّ وَأَنَا عَلَى ذَلِكُم مِّنَ الشَّاهِدِينَ وَتَاللَّهِ لَأَكِيدَنَّ أَصْنَامَكُم بَعْدَ أَن تُوَلُّوا مُدْبِرِينَ فَجَعَلَهُمْ جُذَاذًا إِلَّا كَبِيرًا لَّهُمْ لَعَلَّهُمْ إِلَيْهِ يَرْجِعُونَ قَالُوا مَن فَعَلَ هَذَا بِآلِهَتِنَا إِنَّهُ لَمِنَ الظَّالِمِينَ قَالُوا سَمِعْنَا فَتًى يَذْكُرُهُمْ يُقَالُ لَهُ إِبْرَاهِيمُ قَالُوا فَأْتُوا بِهِ عَلَى أَعْيُنِ النَّاسِ لَعَلَّهُمْ يَشْهَدُونَ قَالُوا أَأَنتَ فَعَلْتَ هَذَا بِآلِهَتِنَا يَا إِبْرَاهِيمُ قَالَ بَلْ فَعَلَهُ كَبِيرُهُمْ هَذَا فَاسْأَلُوهُمْ إِن كَانُوا يَنطِقُونَ فَرَجَعُوا إِلَى أَنفُسِهِمْ فَقَالُوا إِنَّكُمْ أَنتُمُ الظَّالِمُونَ ثُمَّ نُكِسُوا عَلَى رُءُوسِهِمْ لَقَدْ عَلِمْتَ مَا هَؤُلَاءِ يَنطِقُونَ قَالَ أَفَتَعْبُدُونَ مِن دُونِ اللَّهِ مَا لَا يَنفَعُكُمْ شَيْئًا وَلَا يَضُرُّكُمْ أُفٍّ لَّكُمْ وَلِمَا تَعْبُدُونَ مِن دُونِ اللَّهِ أَفَلَا تَعْقِلُونَ قَالُوا حَرِّقُوهُ وَانصُرُوا آلِهَتَكُمْ إِن كُنتُمْ فَاعِلِينَ قُلْنَا يَا نَارُ كُونِي بَرْدًا وَسَلَامًا عَلَى إِبْرَاهِيمَ وَأَرَادُوا بِهِ كَيْدًا فَجَعَلْنَاهُمُ الْأَخْسَرِينَ وَنَجَّيْنَاهُ وَلُوطًا إِلَى الْأَرْضِ الَّتِي بَارَكْنَا فِيهَا لِلْعَالَمِينَ وَوَهَبْنَا لَهُ إِسْحَاقَ وَيَعْقُوبَ نَافِلَةً وَكُلًّا جَعَلْنَا صَالِحِينَ وَجَعَلْنَاهُمْ أَئِمَّةً يَهْدُونَ بِأَمْرِنَا وَأَوْحَيْنَا إِلَيْهِمْ فِعْلَ الْخَيْرَاتِ وَإِقَامَ الصَّلَاةِ وَإِيتَاءَ الزَّكَاةِ وَكَانُوا لَنَا عَابِدِينَ سورة الانبياء الايات 51-73

وَإِذْ قَالَ إِبْرَاهِيمُ رَبِّ اجْعَلْ هَذَا الْبَلَدَ آمِنًا وَاجْنُبْنِي وَبَنِيَّ أَن نَّعْبُدَ الْأَصْنَامَ رَبِّ إِنَّهُنَّ أَضْلَلْنَ كَثِيرًا مِّنَ النَّاسِ فَمَن تَبِعَنِي فَإِنَّهُ مِنِّي وَمَنْ عَصَانِي فَإِنَّكَ غَفُورٌ رَّحِيمٌ رَّبَّنَا إِنِّي أَسْكَنتُ مِن ذُرِّيَّتِي بِوَادٍ غَيْرِ ذِي زَرْعٍ عِندَ بَيْتِكَ الْمُحَرَّمِ رَبَّنَا لِيُقِيمُوا الصَّلَاةَ فَاجْعَلْ أَفْئِدَةً مِّنَ النَّاسِ تَهْوِي إِلَيْهِمْ وَارْزُقْهُم مِّنَ الثَّمَرَاتِ لَعَلَّهُمْ يَشْكُرُونَ رَبَّنَا إِنَّكَ تَعْلَمُ مَا نُخْفِي وَمَا نُعْلِنُ وَمَا يَخْفَى عَلَى اللَّهِ مِن شَيْءٍ فِي الْأَرْضِ وَلَا فِي السَّمَاءِ الْحَمْدُ لِلَّهِ الَّذِي وَهَبَ لِي عَلَى الْكِبَرِ إِسْمَاعِيلَ وَإِسْحَاقَ إِنَّ رَبِّي لَسَمِيعُ الدُّعَاءِ رَبِّ اجْعَلْنِي مُقِيمَ الصَّلَاةِ وَمِن ذُرِّيَّتِي رَبَّنَا وَتَقَبَّلْ دُعَاءِ رَبَّنَا اغْفِرْ لِي وَلِوَالِدَيَّ وَلِلْمُؤْمِنِينَ يَوْمَ يَقُومُ الْحِسَابُ ابراهيم41 35

- [246] و خدا با آن پسر میبود و او نمو کرده ساکن صحرا شد و در تیراندازی مهارت یافت و در صحرای فاران ساکن شد و مادرش زنی از مصر برایش گرفت. عهدعتیق /سفر پیدایش /باب بیست و یک، آیه های 22-21

a great nation of him.' 19 Then God opened her eyes, and she saw a well of water. She went, and filled the skin with water, and gave the boy a drink. 20 God was with the boy, and he grew up; he lived in the wilderness, and became an expert with the bow. 21 He lived in the wilderness of **Pharan***; and his mother brought a wife for him from the land of Egypt.*[247]

Some years later Abraham repaired and rebuilt the prayer sanctuary of Adam and Seth in company of his grown up son Ishmael as the central point of prayer for everybody all around the land of Pharan.

Indeed, the first House [of worship] established for mankind was that at Bakkah – blessed and a guidance for the worlds. In it are clear signs [such as] the standing place of Abraham. And whoever enters it shall be safe. And [due] to Allah from the people is a pilgrimage to the House – for whoever is able to find thereto a way. But whoever disbelieves, then indeed, Allah is free from need of the worlds. Surah 3, v: 96.

And [mention, O Mohammad], when Abraham was tried by his Lord with commands and he fulfilled them. [Allah] said, 'Indeed, I will make you a leader for the people.' [Abraham] said, 'And of my descendants?' [Allah] said, 'My covenant does not include the wrongdoers.'[248] *And [mention] when We made the House a place of return for the people and [a place of] security. And take, [O believers], from the standing place of Abraham a place of prayer. And We charged Abraham and Ishmael, [saying], 'Purify My House for those who perform Tawaf and those who are staying [there] for worship and those who bow and prostrate [in prayer].' And [mention] when Abraham said, 'My Lord, make this a secure city and provide its people with fruits - whoever of them believes in Allah and the Last Day.' [Allah] said. 'And whoever disbelieves, I will grant him enjoyment for a little; then I will force him to the punishment of the Fire, and wretched is the destination.' And [mention] when Abraham was raising the*

---

[247] Genesis, Chapter 21, verses 10 to 21.

[248]و اذ ابتلى ابراهيم ربه بكلمات فأتمهن قال انى جاعلك للناس اماما قال و من ذريتى قال لاينال عهدى الظالمين.
سورة البقرة الاية124

143

foundations of the House and [with him] Ishmael, [saying], 'Our Lord, accept [this] from us. Indeed You are the Hearing, the Knowing. Our Lord, and make us Muslims [in submission] to You and from our descendants a Muslim nation [in submission] to You. And show us our rites and accept our repentance. Indeed, You are the Accepting of repentance, the Merciful. **Our Lord, and send among them a messenger from themselves who will recite to them Your verses and teach them the Book and wisdom and purify them.** *Indeed, You are the Exalted in Might, the Wise.'* Surah 2, v: 124 - 129.[249]

God revealed to Abraham the complete rules of chivalry in order to build the foundation of an exemplary society, based on fraternity between individuals and obedience towards the Creator. The rules revealed included the ensemble of the ceremonial prayers, the style of meditation and seclusion and the remembering of the name of God in the heart, the daily prayers in the morning, noon, evening, and night, the incantations and the sentences for the practice of the daily prayers, ablution, the direction for praying, doing pilgrimage and offering animal sacrifice, fasting, giving an amount and taxes for Allah, and distributing wealth between people in society to help poor individuals, to mention only a few of the ethical principles of chivalry.

Say, 'Allah has told the truth. So follow the path of Abraham, 'Hanif' – inclining towards truth, and he was not of the polytheists.' Surah 3, v: 95.

---

249 وَإِذْ جَعَلْنَا الْبَيْتَ مَثَابَةً لِلنَّاسِ وَأَمْناً وَاتَّخِذُواْ مِن مَّقَامِ إِبْرَاهِيمَ مُصَلًّى وَعَهِدْنَا إِلَى إِبْرَاهِيمَ وَإِسْمَاعِيلَ أَن طَهِّرَا بَيْتِيَ لِلطَّائِفِينَ وَالْعَاكِفِينَ وَالرُّكَّعِ السُّجُودِ وَإِذْ قَالَ إِبْرَاهِيمُ رَبِّ اجْعَلْ هَذَا بَلَداً آمِناً وَارْزُقْ أَهْلَهُ مِنَ الثَّمَرَاتِ مَنْ آمَنَ مِنْهُم بِاللَّهِ وَالْيَوْمِ الآخِرِ قَالَ وَمَن كَفَرَ فَأُمَتِّعُهُ قَلِيلاً ثُمَّ أَضْطَرُّهُ إِلَى عَذَابِ النَّارِ وَبِئْسَ الْمَصِيرُ. وَإِذْ يَرْفَعُ إِبْرَاهِيمُ الْقَوَاعِدَ مِنَ الْبَيْتِ وَإِسْمَاعِيلُ رَبَّنَا تَقَبَّلْ مِنَّا إِنَّكَ أَنتَ السَّمِيعُ الْعَلِيمُ. رَبَّنَا وَاجْعَلْنَا مُسْلِمَيْنِ لَكَ وَمِن ذُرِّيَّتِنَا أُمَّةً مُّسْلِمَةً لَّكَ وَأَرِنَا مَنَاسِكَنَا وَتُبْ عَلَيْنَا إِنَّكَ أَنتَ التَّوَّابُ الرَّحِيمُ. رَبَّنَا وَابْعَثْ فِيهِمْ رَسُولاً مِّنْهُمْ يَتْلُو عَلَيْهِمْ آيَاتِكَ وَيُعَلِّمُهُمُ الْكِتَابَ وَالْحِكْمَةَ وَيُزَكِّيهِمْ إِنَّكَ أَنتَ الْعَزِيزُ الْحَكِيمُ. سورة البقرة الايات 125-129

The monastery of Bosra: Bàhirâ

There are sixty-nine verses in the Quran about the spiritual life of Abraham and the details about his path, preceding Judaism, Christianity, and every other sacred spiritual school in the footsteps of Noah, Seth, and Adam. Verse 73 of Surah 21 (Anbia – Prophets) explains very clearly the continuity of the path of Abraham, beyond time and place, all the way up to the time of Mohammad, by the followers of the tradition of Abraham. The Quran introduces the keepers of the Abrahamic tradition as the divine leaders of humanity that are under heavenly guidance and a constant supra-sensorial relationship as a historical evolution:

And We gave him (Abraham) Isaac and Jacob in addition, and all [of them] We made righteous. And We made them leaders[250] who 'keep constantly guiding[251] by Our command. And We inspired to them the doing of good deeds, establishment of prayer, and giving of zakah; and they were worshippers of Us.' Surah 21, v: 72, 73[252]

According to these verses, the Quran confirms without any doubt that the tradition of Abraham was transmitted by the tradition keepers, Seddyghin الصديقين and Nabiyoun النبيون, throughout centuries and millennia. This continuous transition from generation to generation continued until the time of the teachers of the school to which Mohammad and his family were related. As we will explain in further chapters, this school was situated in Bosra بُصرا which lies in the southern region of Shâm

---

[250] Àemméh means leaders; it is the plural form of émâm (imām). The first individual introduced in the Quran being honoured by the title of émâm is Abraham; and after him those who keep alive the tradition of Abraham are also émams to the end of time.

[251] Vahdoun is a verb in the present form. It means to keep giving guidance. Therefore, the action of these leaders never stops, but goes on continuously and constantly. These leaders keep giving guidance throughout the following generations.

252و وهبنا له اسحاق و يعقوب نافله .و كلا جعلنا صالحين .و جعلناهم ائمه يهدون بامرنا .و اوحينا اليهم فعل الخيرات و اقام الصلاة و ايتاء الزكوة .و كانوا لنا عابدين   سورة الانبياء . الايات 73- 72

145

شام in Syria and the northern part of the Arabian Peninsula. The sages who managed the community of monotheists around this hilltop monastery in the suburb of a city named Bosra بُصرا had the title of Bàhirâ بَحیرا. Ibn Husham mentioned in his book *Sirat ol Nabaviyeh* that Salmân Farsi[253] escaped from Iran and went to Shâm (Syria) to study the true teachings of Jesus with the wise men, named Bàhirâs. The family of Mohammad, including his uncle Abu Tâlib ابوطالب, his father Abdollah عبدالله, his mother Fatimah فاطمهء یمنی and other Hânif حنیف of the region of Mecca such as Waraka ibn Nowfel and the circle related to him, Khadijeh and Sâlem, often visited this monastery. The language of the inhabitants of that region was a dialect of Aramaic آرامی, named Syriac سریانی. The spiritual seekers who were related to this sacred centre were literate and educated people, capable of reading and reciting the verses and the sentences of their Holy Book which was named Qeryànà, قریانا.[254]

In the Quran, verse 4 from the Surah 'Ebrahim' states:

---

[253] Salmân Farsi was one of the companions of Mohammad.

[254] Contextual evidence for the original meaning of 'Quran': The very word qur'ân is not attested in any Arabic sources before the appearance of the Quran itself. This supports the strong linguistic probability that the use of this word for the new revelations of Mohammad would only have been intelligible to the Arabs at that time if analogous words were prominent in contemporary Christian or Jewish use. Before and after Mohammad's time, the Syriac cognate term qeryànà, 'lection, 'reading' was used by Syriac-speaking Christians (presumably borrowed by Arabic-speaking Christians) as well as for oral and liturgical readings from holy writings (=lectio, anagnosis) and for the passage of the scripture that was read aloud (=lectio, perioché, anagnosma, etc). John Bowman in particular has rightly stressed the strong parallels in liturgical terminology and usage between Eastern Christian liturgical use of a lectionary, or ktàbà d'qeryànà, and what we can reconstruct of liturgical use of the qur'ânic revelations from the Qur'ân itself. Also of likely relevance is the additional parallel in both Muslim use of qur'ân and Syriac use of qeryànà to Rabbinic and later Jewish use of the Hebrew cognates qeri'à miqrà' as terms denoting the act of scripture reading and the passage read aloud, respectively. Miqrà' is used also as a Talmudic term for the whole Bible, one that 'serves to underline both vocal manner of study and the central role that the public reading of the Scriptures played in the liturgy of the Jews.' In *Beyond the Written Word: Oral aspects of scripture in the history of religion'*, William A. Graham; 1987, University of Cambridge, p. 90.

And We did not send any messenger except speaking in the language of his people to state clearly for them. Surah 14, v: 4.[255]

We can conclude that the first phase of the mission of Mohammad in the line of Abraham was to preach to his contemporary people in Mecca and to teach them the heritage of Abraham and the other spiritual masters in his lineage. In order to accomplish this task, Mohammad had to recite aloud the sentences of the Pesher of Abraham صُحُفِ ابراهيم that were originally written in the Syriac-Aramaic language, the language of the inhabitants of the Bàhirâ monastery,[256] but in a clear Arabic version for those people, who did not understand any language other than Arabic.

Ha, Meem.[This is] a revelation from the Entirely Merciful, the Especially Merciful, A Book whose verses have been detailed, an Arabic Quran for a people who know. Surah 41, v: 1 to 3.[257]

Indeed, those who disbelieve in the message after it has come to them... And indeed, it is a mighty Book. Falsehood cannot approach it from before it or from behind it; [it is] a revelation from a [Lord who is] Wise and Praiseworthy. Nothing is said to you, [O Mohammad], except what was already said to the messengers before you. Indeed, your Lord is a possessor of forgiveness and a possessor of painful penalty. And if We had made it a non-Arabic Quran, they would have said, 'Why are its verses not explained in detail [in our language]? Is it a foreign [recitation] and an Arab [messenger]?' Say, 'It is, for those who believe, a guidance and cure.' Surah 41, v: 41 - 44.[258]

ـ 255و ما ارسلنا من رسول الا بلسان قومه ليبين لهم سورة ابراهيم الآيه 4

[256] According to the Old Testament Abraham lived about 1890 years BC. He was native of Mesopotamia where the major portion of the inhabitants spoke the Aramaic language.

ـ 257حأء ميم تنزيل من الرحمن الرحيم كتاب فصلت آياته قرآناعربيا لقوم يعلمون سورة فصلت . الايات 1- 3

ـ 258ان الذين كفروا بالذكر لما جائهم و انه لكتاب عزيز .لايأتيه الباطل من بين يديه و لا من خلفه تنزيل من حكيم حميد .مايقال لك الاماقد قيل للرسل من قبلك ان ربك لذومغفره و ذوعقاب اليم و لوجعلناه قرآنا عجميا لقالوا لولافصلت آياته أ أعجميّ و عربيّ قل هوللذين آمنوا هدى وشفاءٌ ..سورة فصلت . الايات 41-44

Therefore, the content of the sentences of a Holy Book preceding the Quran were exposed to the Arabic-speaking people in the frame of their maternal language, but it could have been introduced in any other language as well. The Quran does not argue about language as an important matter and instead shows it merely as an instrument of communication, nothing more. This principle is explained in more detail in the other verses:

And indeed, the Quran is the revelation of the Lord of the worlds. The Trustworthy Spirit has brought it down. Upon your heart, [O Mohammad], that you may be of the warners – In a clear Arabic language. And indeed, it is also written in the old Psalms/scriptures. **And has it not been a sign to them (who have doubt about its origin) that it is known/recognised by the scholars of the Children of Israel? And even if We had revealed it to one among the non-Arabs/ A'jami . And he had recited it to them [perfectly], they would [still] not have been believers in it.** Surah 26, v: 192 - 199.[259]

These verses give a final conclusion about the Quran itself. Some of the sentences of the Quran were also written in the Zobor é awalin, the old scriptures, and the best evidence for this fact is that the scholars of the Israelite people knew and recognised these sentences. These known verses written in the old Psalms, known by the Jewish scholars, were revealed and taught to Mohammad in Arabic in order to be preached by him to the people around him. It is important to note that if those sentences had been revealed to a non-Arabic-speaking man, people certainly would have not believed him if he had preached to them. These old Psalms could have been named Qeryànà in Syriac speech. In other words, these verses do not negate the pre-existence of the Quran in an A'Jami (non-Arabic) language before its appearance in the Arabic version. Instead, the verses stress the fact that

---

[259]و انه لتنزيل رب العالمين نزل به الروح الامين على قلبك لتكون من المنذرين بلسان عربى مبين و انه لفى زبر الاولين. **ام لم يكن لهم آية ان يعلمه علماء بنى اسرائيل؟ و لو نزلناه على بعض الاعجمين فقراه عليهم ماكانوا به مومنين** سورة الشعراء. الايات 192-199

the Quran was transmitted to Mohammad from scriptures in non-Arabic language to Arabic by the way of revelation.

We have explained that the Quran divides both Jewish and Christian scholars into two categories: the righteous ones, and the materialistic ones. In these sentences, the Quran confirms once again that Mohammad is a preacher of a book that the scholars of 'the people of the Holy Books' know perfectly, yet in a non-Arabic language. It shows at the same time that those scholars who attested the validity of the Arabic sentences recited aloud by Mohammad, must have known both the original language of the Psalms as well as the Arabic language used by Mohammad, and that they must therefore have been bilingual.

In the time of Mohammad, some other followers of Abraham lived on the Arabian Peninsula and testified the validity and the preciseness of the teachings of Abraham in the Arabic version revealed from the mouth of Mohammad. These followers were named Hanif as well.[260] The Honafa were educated individuals who knew how to read the old scriptures in different languages including Syriac, Aramaic, Hebrew, Greco-Latin, and so forth. They were monotheists and followers of the tradition of Abraham and Abrahams' descendants (Seddyghin and Nabyioun) and made up a minority in Mecca. The majority of the people living in Mecca and in the regions around Mecca were polytheist Bedouins. These people were idol worshippers who changed the Kabah, the house of Allah, into a house of idols.

They did not pay attention to the appeal of the Honafa when they wanted to guide them to the path of monotheism. They believed that they were doing things the right way, in accordance with the tradition of their parents and their ancestors. Furthermore, they believed that they were living and respecting the tradition of Abraham. Yet, when the Hanif wanted

---

[260] We will talk more about the community of Hanif in Mecca preceding the birth of Mohammad son of Abdollah and the development of his path.

to preach the book of Abraham and the books of the other masters to them, the idol worshippers closed their ears with their fingers and replied with the pretext:

We don't understand what you would like to tell us, because we don't understand this non-Arabic language. (It is the result of the sentances 196 to 199 of the Surah 26 – "as Sho'ara"/ Poets/).

The originial scripture: Zobor é Oula

According to the Quran, a part of the content of the Book revealed to Mohammad was already written in a non-Arabic language on a number of pages, and certain people already knew it very well. At one time, this original scripture is introduced as Zobor é Oula and at another time Sohof é Oula, among other titles. This book must have been composed of different chapters in the style of the Bible, starting with the creation of the universe all the way up to the last events, which happened before Mohammad's public announcement of his mission. All of this content was transmitted into the Quran of Mohammad and explained in detail by him to the people during his preachings. This section of the Book of Mohammad constitutes its main part, and foundation, which is also referred to as 'Om ol Ketab'.

Alif, Lam, Meem. Allah – there is no deity except Him, the Ever-Living, the Sustainer of existence. **He has sent down upon you, the Book in truth, confirming what was before it. And He revealed the Torah and the Gospel before, as guidance for the people. And He revealed the Forghân.** Surah 3, v: 1 - 4.

It is He who has sent down to you, [O Mohammad], the Book; in it are verses [that are] precise – they are the foundation of the Book – and others unspecific. As for those in whose hearts is deviation [from truth], they will follow that of it which is unspecific, seeking discord and seeking an interpretation [suitable to them]. And no one knows its [true] interpretation except Allah. But those firm in knowledge say, 'We believe in it. All [of it] is from our Lord.' And no one will be reminded except those of understanding. [Who say], 'Our Lord, let not our hearts deviate after You have guided us and grant us from Yourself mercy. Indeed, You are the Bestower.' Surah 3, v: 7- 8.

نَزَّلَ عليک الكتابَ بالحق مُصدِّقاً لمابين يديه وانزل التورية والانجيل من قبل هُدىً للناس و انزلالفُرقَان. سورةآل عمران. الايات 3-4

However, the Book of Mohammad is not limited to this frame. Mohammad preaches and the disbelievers criticise him. The reaction of these non-believers is also recorded in the Book of Mohammad (the Quran) as well as Mohammad's replies to the critiques. In the case of the critiques, the verses are composed of two sides, namely the position of the disbelievers and the position of Mohammad. The Quran precisely explains the position of the adversaries of Mohammad and afterwards mentions the orders given to Mohammad on what specifically to reply to these adversaries. In this case the words: 'Say to them...' are addressed to Mohammad. The non-believers are divided into multiple categories such as idol worshippers, polytheists, dualists, materialists, atheists, and the Jewish and Christian priests. As such, they pose diverse questions to Mohammad to evaluate his knowledge. Their questions and their positions are explained in the Quran.

Finally, the Quran of Mohammad accords partially with the Holy Books which existed before the Quran, but the Quran contains more detail than those preceding books as it also describes the circumstances of the life and mission of Mohammad.

About book called Qeryànà

As we will explain in the following chapters, the version of the Holy Book revealed to Mohammad, which was written in a non-Arabic language, contained different chapters in the style of the Bible. But its particularity was its orientation towards the events which had taken place in the history of the Arabian Peninsula: namely, the events of the vanished civilisations and the people who had dominated that area for a while, and also their punishment due to their tyrannical attitude towards people and their disobedience towards their cosmic Lord. Qeryànà could originate from the word 'ghar'à' meaning 'reading' and from 'gara'a' meaning 'to join the various pieces of a puzzle to each other'. Certain verses of the Quran mention the fact that the original book was a complete scripture, but that it had been revealed to Mohammad little by little and passage by passage, separated by intervals, to be recited to the people step by step. The divine Lord separated the whole book into multiple fragments in order to care for its recomposition so it could be written down in the form of a complete book.

And [it is] a Quran which We have separated [by intervals] that you might recite it to the people over a prolonged period. And We have sent it down gradually. Surah 17, v: 106.

وَقُرآناً فَرَقناهُ لِتَقرَأَهُ عَلَى النَّاس عَلى مُكثٍ وَ نَزَّلناهتَنزيلاً . سورة الاسراء. الاية 106

Fàràghà (to separate) and ghàrà'à (to join together) are two opposite actions, which complete each other. The Quran is separated by intervals to be read and recited slowly and gradually, and finally to be composed in its initial form. In the verses of the Quran, this usage is introduced from the vocabulary of 'qorân' in parallel with another aspect of this vocabulary 'qor'ân'.

Recite the Quran with measured recitation. Indeed, We will cast upon you a heavy word. Surah 73, v: 4 - 5.

وَ رَتّل القرانَ تَرتيلاً . اِذّا سَنُلقى عَلَيكَ قولاً ثَقيلاً . سورة المزمل. الايات 4-5

And, [O Mohammad], do not hasten with [recitation of] the Quran before its revelation is completed to you, and say, 'My Lord, increase me in knowledge.' Surah 20, v: 114.

ولاتَعجَل بِالقُران مِن قبل أن يُقضى اليكَ وحيُهُ وقُل رَبِّ زِدنى عِلماً سورة طه. الاية 114

Move not your tongue with it, [O Mohammad], to hasten with recitation of the Quran. Indeed, it is up to Us its collection and its recomposition, jam' và qorân. So when We have recomposed it, then follow its recitation. Then upon Us is its clarification [to you]. Surah 75, v: 16 - 19.

لاتُحرّك بِهِ لِسانَك لِتَعجَلَ بِهِ. اِنَّ علينا جَمعَهُ وقُرانَهُ. فاذا قَراناهُ فاتَّبِع قُرانَهُ ثُمّ اِنَّ علينا بيانَهُ. سورة القيمة. 16-19.

We will read again (the verses of the book upon you) in order not to forget it, except what Allah would like (you not to remember.) Surah 87, v: 6 -7.

سَنُقرِئُكَ فلا تنسى. الاماشاء اللهُ اِنَّهُ يعلمُ الجَهرَ ومايَخفى. سورة الاعلى. الايات 6-7

In these verses, the word 'Quran' is employed for two meanings: recitation and recomposition. Quran means to join two or multiple things together in one place, like the moment in the early morning where night and day join each other; it also means reading and reciting aloud a Holy Book. The monks and the Gnostic people living in the region of Bosra and Syria sang and recited early in the morning, and at the other times of prayer, certain incantations from a Holy Book which was named Qeryànà. The monks and Gnostic people followed a strict discipline in order to respect these times of prayer.[261] The times of the daily prayers are mentioned in the Book of Mohammad as well:

---

[261] Aiin Ghara'àt va ketabat dar sireh é nabavi, *The style of reciting and writing in the way of the Prophet*, Mohsen Rajabi Ghodsi - edition: Bustan é ketab: Iran 2014.

Establish prayer at the decline of the sun [from its meridian] until the darkness of the night and [also] the Quran of dawn. Indeed, the recitation of dawn is ever witnessed. And from [part of] the night, pray with it as additional [worship] for you; it is expected that your Lord will resurrect you to a praised station. Surah 17, v: 78, 79.

اقم الصلوة لِدُلُوكِ الشَّمس الى غَسَقِ الليل و قرانَ الفجر. اِنَّ قران الفجر كانَ مشهوداً. و من الليل فتهَجّد بِهِنافلةً لكَ عسى آنيبعَذَكَ ربُّكَ مقاماً محموداً. سورة الاسراء. الايات 78-79

The book of Qeryànà could have been written in different alphabet, as used in Syria and before that, in Qumran, including the Aramaic-Syriac. The oldest version of the scripture of the Quran ever found is written in Hijazi, a style that appears to originate from Jazm, and Musnad.

The relationship between the Qeryànà and the Quran

The word Qeryànà, in the style of Syriac-speaking people, is not mentioned in the Quran. However, the Quran, in the scripture of Mohammad, is sometimes referred to as the name of his Book, and sometimes as the name of a Holy Book which existed before the Book of Mohammad, and had been sent down to Mohammad in order to be recited by him to the people. We will see this point in more detail by referring to the following verses of the Quran.

Say, 'Allah is witness between me and you. And this Quran was revealed to me that I may warn you thereby and whomever it reaches... Those to whom We have given the Scripture, al Ketab, Book recognise it as they recognise their [own] sons. Those who will lose themselves [in the Hereafter] do not believe. And who is more unjust than one who invents about Allah a lie or denies His verses? Indeed, the wrongdoers will not succeed.' Surah 6, v: 19 - 21.

قل الله شهيدٌ بينى و بينكم و اوحَى اليَّ هذاالقران لِأنذِرَكم به وَمَن بَلَغَ اِئِذَكُم لَتَشهدون اَنَّ مع الله الهةً أخرى قل لاَشهَد. قل اِنَّما هُوَ الهٌ واحدٌ و اِننى بريٌ مماتشركون. الذين آتيناهم الكتاب

يعرفونه كمايعرفون ابنائهم. الذين خسروااانفسَهم فهم لايومنون. ومَن اظلم ممن افترى على الله كذباً او كذَّبَ باياتهِ اِنَّه لايُفلح الظالمون. سورة الانعام. 19-21

So if you are in doubt, about that which We have revealed to you, then **ask those who have been reciting the Scripture before you**. *The truth has certainly come to you from your Lord, so never be among the doubters.* Surah 10, v: 94.

فان كنتَ فى شكٍ ممااانزلنااليكَ **فاسئل الذين يقروٰن الكتابَ من قبلك**. لقدجائك الحقُ من ربک. فلاتكونن من الممترين. سورة يونس. الاية 94

Here, the sentence talks about an existing book named Quran, known very clearly and precisely by the righteous people of the Holy Books, which has been revealed to Mohammad to warn the wrongdoers about the consequences of their actions. Those people, who recited and read the book before Mohammad, can convince him by their testimony and are able to wash any doubt from his mind about the preciseness of the sentences that he learns by revelation.

And We have certainly given you, [O Mohammad], seven of the often repeated [verses] and the great Quran. Surah 15, v: 87.[262]

We relate to you, [O Mohammad], the best of stories in what We have revealed to you of this Quran although you were, before it, among the unaware. Surah 12, v: 3.

نحن نقص عليک احسن القصص بمااوحينااليک هذاالقران و ان كنت من قبله لمن الغافلين سورة يوسف الايه3

And [it is] a Quran which We have separated [by intervals] that you might recite it to the people over a prolonged period. And We have sent it down gradually. Say, "Believe in it or do not believe. Indeed, those who were given knowledge before it - when it is recited to them, they fall upon their faces in prostration, And they say, "Exalted is

---

our Lord! Indeed, the promise of our Lord has been fulfilled." And they fall upon their faces weeping, and the Qur'an increases them in humble submission. Surah 17, v: 106-109.

وقرانافرقناه لتقراهُ على الناس على مكثٍ ونزلناهتنزيلاً. قل آمنوا به او لاتومنوا ان **الذين اوتواالعلم من قبله اذا يُتلى عليهم يَخرّون للاذقان سُجّدا**. ويقولون سبحان ربنا ان كان وعدُربنالمفعولا. ويَخرّون للاذقان يبكون ويزيدُهمخشوعاً. سوره الاسراء الايات 106-109

Then I swear by the setting of the stars, And indeed, it is an oath – if you could know – [most] great. Indeed, it is a noble Quran. In a Register well-protected; none touch it except the purified. [It is] a revelation from the Lord of the worlds. Surah 56, v: 75 - 80.

فلاقسم بمواقع النجوم و انه لقسم لوتعلمون عظيم انه لقرانٌ كريم فى كتاب مكنون. لايمسُّه الاالمطهرون تنزيل من رب العالمين. سورة الواقعة. الايات 75-80

The Most Merciful. Who Taught the Quran, Surah 55, v: 1-2.

الرحمن. عَلم القرآن. سورة الرحمن. الايات 1-2

In this verse, instead of saying, 'revealing the Quran' it says 'teaching the Quran'. The Quran is introduced as an existing book which was taught to Mohammad who, before learning it, was unaware of it:

Alif, Lam, Ra. These are the verses of the clear Book. Indeed, We have sent it down as an Arabic Quran that you might understand. We relate to you, [O Mohammad], the best of stories in what We have revealed to you of this Quran although you were, before it, among the unaware. Surah 12, v: 1 - 3.

الر. تلک آيات الكتاب المبين. انانزلناه قرانا عربيا لعلكم تعقلون. نحن نقصُّ عليک احسن القصص بمااوحينا اليک هذاالقران و ان كنت من قبله لمن الغافلين. سورة يوسف. الايات 1-3

In the Surah named Borouj, the Quran is revealed as a book inscribed on a preserved slate (Lowh):

But this is an honoured Quran [Inscribed] in a Preserved Slate. Surah 85, v: 21, 22.

بل هو قران مجيد. فى لوح محفوظ. سورة البروج. الايات 21-22

There are some complementary verses about the existence of two books named Quran: one before Mohammad and the other one existing during and after the revelation to Mohammad. The difference between them is that while the first book is not written in Arabic, the second one is:

And thus We have sent it down as an Arabic Quran and have diversified therein the warnings that perhaps they will avoid [sin] or it would cause them remembrance. Surah 20, v: 113.

وكذلك انزلناه قراناعربيا وصرفنافيه من الوعيد لعلهم يتقون اويُحدِثُ لهم ذكرا. سورة طه. الايه 113

كتاب فصلت آياتُهُ قراناعربيا لقوم يعلمون. سورة فصلت. الآية 3

And thus We have revealed to you an Arabic Quran that you may warn the Mother of Cities [Mecca] and those around it and warn of the Day of Assembly, about which there is no doubt. A party will be in Paradise and a party in the Blaze. Surah 42, v: 7.

وكذلك اوحينااليك قراناعربيالتنذر ام القرى و من حولها وتنذر يوم الجمع لاريب فيه فريق فى الجنة وفريق فى السعير. سورة الشورى. الايه 7

Ha - Mim. By the clear Book, الكتاب المبين *that indeed, We have made it (the mentioned 'clear Book') a Quran in Arabic version that you might understand. And indeed it (the mentioned 'clear Book') is, in the Mother of the Book (Umm-ol-Ketab) with Us, exalted and full of wisdom.* Surah 43, v: 2-4.

حم.والكتاب المبين. اناجعلناه قراناعربياالعلكم تعقلون. وانه فى ام الكتاب لدينالعلىٌّ حكيم. سورة
الزخرف. 1-4

Here, this fact is clearly stated: The original version of the 'clear Book' الكتاب المبين exists in the frame of 'Omm ol Ketab'[263] آم الكتاب, a global

---

[263] Michael Baigent. Richard Leigh: *The Complete Dead Sea Scrolls in English*: Seventh Edition (Penguin Classics). 2012.

Black, Matthew (1969), *The Scrolls and Christianity*, London: S.P.C.K.

Burrows, Millar (1951), *The Dead Sea Scrolls*, American School of Oriental Research.

Campebell, Johnathan (1998), *Dead Sea Scrolls, the Complete Story*, Ulysses Press Berke.

Collin, John Josef (1997), *Seers, Sibyls and sages in Hellenistic-Roman Judaism*, Leiden: The Netherlands.

Graystone, Geoffrey (1956), *The Dead Sea Scrolls and the Originality of Christ*, New York: Sheed & ward.

Jull, A. J. T. and others (1995), 'Radiocarbon Dating of scrolls and Linen Fragments from the Judean Desert', Radiocarbon 37.

Licht, Jacob & Feredrick Fyvie Bruce (1971), 'Dead Sea Scrolls', in: The Encyclopaedia Judaica, vol. 5.

Moore Cross Jr., Frank (1958), *The Ancient Library of Qumran and Modern Biblical Studies*, Doubleday, Garden City.

Rowley, H. H. (1964), *The Dead Sea Scrolls and The New Testament*, London: S.P.C.K.

Schiffman, Lawrence H. (2005), 'Dead Sea Scrolls', in: The Encyclopaedia of Religion, Mirca Eliade (ed.) second edition, MacMillan Publ, vol. 4.

Sommer, A. Dupont (1952), *The Dead Sea Scrolls*, tr. E. Margaret Rowley, Basil Blackwell Publ.

The Book of the Divisions of Times into Jubilees and Weeks found in ten copies, written in Hebrew scripture and found in caves 1, 2, and 4 is in co-relationship with the book of 'Honouh' written in Aramaic scripture, in correspondence with the Manichaean literature.

In cave 1, the Pesher (interpretation) of the book of Habakkuk was found.

Also in cave 1 the Book of War was found. It is about the prediction of a war in the end of times, which will last forty years and will end in the victory of the generation of light over the generation of darkness. People will rejoice and rebuild the Temple of Jerusalem.

book, or mother of scriptures, and it has been put into Arabic so as to be accessible for Arabic-speaking people to understand and think about its contents.

To conclude this part of the discussion, one could state that there is evidence for an amalgam of the two scriptures, given that in all of the cited verses there are two Holy Books referred to by one name: Quran. The first book is the original one (أُمُّ الكتاب), while the second book referred to is the Arabic one. The Quran also states that the original could not have had any usage in the region of the Arabian Peninsula because the majority of the nomadic Bedouins in this region were illiterate, driven by superstition and ignorance, and did not know A'Jami اعجمى, meaning any non-Arabic language. However, the Quran does not give any precise information about the language of the original book. It only states that the Jewish scholars knew it very well, as well as they knew their own sons, and were therefore able to testify to the similarity between the Quran of Mohammad and the original book. Yet this does not mean that the original book must have been written in Hebrew. Instead, it is possible to imagine that those scholars to whom the Quran refers knew multiple languages.

Fatemeh Hashtroudi, 2011, *The scrolls of the Dead Sea, History and opinions.* (Farsi) The university of the religions and denominations. Qom/Iran.

Section Three

The sources of Islam

Figure 14 - Fragment of a scroll ascribed to Habakkuk.
(Prophet Habakkuk lived in around the seventh century BC)

Previously in this book, we have dug a long tunnel to the undiscovered corners of history, back to the time of the existence of the city of Qumran, where scrolls that had been written between about 400 BC and 300 AD were found. The group and individuals who had been living in Qumran travelled to other regions and carried with them their monotheistic ancestral traditions. This community was the millenary people of the Books (Ah-lol-Ketab).

Before the time of Jesus, these people expected the apparition of God's light in the form of a Saviour. They joined Jesus and formed a new community around him that became the first generation of the Christian community. From the early period of Christianity we can see two different versions interpreting the teachings of Jesus: the version of Barnabas[264] and the version of Paul.[265] After the time of Jesus this discrepancy between the two parts of Christianity[266] had a major impact on a very important part of the scriptures of the Dead Sea. According to certain scholars and researchers on this matter, the 'wicked priest' mentioned in the post-Jesus literature of Qumran corresponds with Paul.[267]

---

[264] Barnabas was one of the prominent Christian disciples in Jerusalem. According to Acts 4:36 Barnabas was a Cypriot Jew. Named an apostle (Acts 14:14), he and Paul the Apostle undertook missionary journeys together and defended Gentile converts against the Judaizers. He is traditionally identified as the founder of the Cypriot Orthodox Church. The feast day of Barnabas is celebrated on June 11. Barnabas' story appears in the Acts of the Apostles, and Paul mentions him in some of his epistles. Clement of Alexandria and some scholars have ascribed the Epistle of Barnabas to him, but his authorship is disputed. *Barnabas*, Cross, F. L.,ed. The Oxford Dictionary of the Christian church. New York: Oxford University Press. 2005.

[265] Paul the Apostle (Paulos; 5 –67 AD), originally known as Saul of Tarsus (Hebrew; Greek: Saulos Tarseus), was an apostle (though not one of the Twelve Apostles) who taught the Gospel of Christ to the first-century world. He is generally considered one of the most important figures of the Apostolic Age. In the mid-30s to the mid-50s, he founded several churches in Asia Minor and Europe. Paul used his status as both a Jewish and a Roman citizen as an advantage in his ministry to both Jewish and Roman audiences. According to writings in the New Testament Paul, who was originally called Saul, was dedicated to the persecution of the early disciples of Jesus in the area of Jerusalem. In the narrative of the book of Acts, while Saul was travelling on the road from Jerusalem to Damascus on a mission to 'bring them which were there bound unto Jerusalem', the resurrected Jesus appeared to him in a great light. He was struck blind, but after three days his sight was restored by Ananias of Damascus, and Paul began to preach that Jesus of Nazareth is the Jewish Messiah and the Son of God. Approximately half of the book of Acts deals with Paul's life and works.

'Saint Paul, the Apostle, original name Saul of Tarsus', from Encyclopaedia Britannica Online Academic Edition. Global.britannica.com. Retrieved July 2014.

[266] In essence the difference can be claimed as such: Barnabas was a seeker who was interested in following the spiritual path described by Jesus in practice, whereas Paul was a theologian (Mottekalem) who created a new religion attributed to Jesus. While we cannot find Barnabas in the canonical scriptures of Irenaeus of Lyon, Paul's letters are a part of the New Testament. By this Paul's ideas became a base for Christianity as it was later established by Constantine the Great.

[267] Ritual laws Acts of Torah 4QMMT

The struggle inside the new Christian community left some traces in the scrolls of the Dead Sea and let certain researchers such as Eisenman think 'The Wicked Priest could be

During the last years of the second Christian century, Irenaeus of Lyon[268] officialised four Gospels as the canonical gospels and ordered the destruction of every other gospel, which he referred to as Apocryphal and Gnostic. In the first half of the third century AD, a new prophet, Mâr Mâni Hayya son of Pâtàk, was born in Ctesiphon in 216 AD [269] and twenty years later proclaimed himself as the expected Paracletus Fàrghàlitous – فرقليطوس موعود predicted by Jesus – and the 'Seal of the Prophets' خاتم النبيين. A considerable number of people in the Persian Empire, as well as in the Roman Empire, in China, and in Africa, converted to his religion within a very short period of time. This included the spiritually wise people who had

---

a surname of Paulus, and 'The teacher of the righteousness could be a surname of the brother of Jesus.

بنا به نظریه مطرح شده در کتابی که به تازگی انتشار یافته، "یعقوب عادل" در "مصحف حبقوق نبی""آیزنمن" باور دارد که "معلم رستگاری"('James the Just' in the Habakkuk Pesher) عنوانی بوده است که به "برادر عیسی" که مخالف او بوده اطلاق می‌شده، و "مرد دروغگو (The man of the Lie) عنوانی برای اشاره به پولس بوده، و "کاهن بدکار" (The Wicked Priest) لقب "حدّان دوم" به شمار میرفته است. دانشمند آلمانی، کارستن تید (Carsten Thiede)در مبحث نسخه‌های انجیل اولیه مطرح می‌کند که شناسایی Q57 به عنوان انجیل مرقس از سوی کالاگان مستلزم بررسی کامل گمانه‌زنی‌های جدید درباره انشای اناجیل است.

The Dawn of Qumran: The Sectarian Torah and the Teacher of Righteousness by Ben Zion Wacholder.

Robert Eisenman believed that the scrolls were written by a small group of the Sedoughit/ Zadokin sect.

The 'Letter of the teacher of Righteousness to the Wicked Priest' found in the cave QMMT4.

Barbara Thiering. 'Jesus & the Riddle of the Dead Sea Scrolls'. Article published by Sidney University about the struggle between the righteous teacher and the man of lie.

Fatemeh Hashtroudi. 2011, *The scrolls of the Dead Sea. History and Opinions.* (Farsi) The University of the Religions and Denominations. Qom/Iran.

[268] *Irenaeus of Lyons. Identifying Christianity.* John Behr. Christian Theology in Context. Oxford University Press. 2013.

[269] Ctesiphon was the capital city of the Parthian and Sassanian Empires (247 BC-224 AD and 224-651 respectively). It was one of the great cities of late ancient Mesopotamia. Its most conspicuous structure remaining today is the great archway of Ctesiphon. Kurz, Otto (1941). 'The Date of the Ṭāq i Kisrā'. The Journal of the Royal Asiatic Society of Great Britain and Ireland. (New Series) 73 (1): 37–41.

been awaiting the apparition of an eschatological Saviour to close the apocalyptical period of the end of time, the 'people of the Books' whose ascendants lived in Qumran. Mâni wrote multiple books in multiple languages including Aramaic. His two main books were the Pure Evangelium انجیل پاک ی and Zabour, which were introduced by him as the exact version of the teachings of Jesus. He did not wish to be considered as the founder of a new religion, but rather the assembler of the main old religions such as Zoroastrianism, Christianity, and Buddhism. He was full of love and admiration for Jesus and wrote some hymns and poetry to express his devotion to Jesus. In the first half of the fourth century AD a new version of Christianity was officialised in the Roman Empire by Constantine.

In the second half of the fourth century, under the guidance of a priest named Augustine,[270] the religious governmental authority in the Byzantine Empire became very strict and began to impose pressure upon the followers of Mâni, also known as Manicheans. Several times the people of this Gnostic community were discovered and after confessing their real faith, they were condemned to be burned alive. The latest example of a community who were burned alive in such a manner is the Cathars in Europe.[271] So, as a precaution, the Manicheans dissolved and dispersed

---

[270] Augustine of Hippo (born 13 November 354; died 28 August 430), also known as Saint Augustine or Saint Austin, was an early Christian theologian and philosopher whose writings influenced the development of Western Christianity and Western philosophy. Among his most important works are *City of God* and *Confessions*. In his early years, he was heavily influenced by Manichaeism. After his baptism and conversion to Christianity in 387, Augustine developed his own approach to philosophy and theology, accommodating a variety of methods and perspectives. Believing that the grace of Christ was indispensable to human freedom, he helped formulate the doctrine of original sin and made seminal contributions to the development of just war theory. Oxford English Dictionary. March 2011. Oxford University Press. Retrieved 25 May 2011.

[271] *The Cathars, Heresy and Authority in Medieval Europe*, ed. Edward Peters, University of Pennsylvania Press, 1980.

within the Christian society, trying to hide their documents as well as their faith.

Meanwhile, they distanced themselves from the centres of the cities and went to the mountainous regions, around the agglomerations, to build up their sanctuaries and temples. One of the main condensations of these hidden Manichean communities was established in the southern region of Syria. This so-called Christian community kept copies of the treasure of the path of Abraham (Mellat é Ebrahim ملة ابراهيم), as well as all of the prophets who came after him, all the way up to Mâni and his successors. They continued to write down, in addition to their ancestral scriptures, the events of each generation. In the manner of their masters, they also expected the apparition of a new eschatological Saviour' (Mo'oud é Akher oz Zàmân موعود آخر الزمان) to change the balance that existed in society and to remove the roots of injustice.

Abraham was introduced to 'the children of Adam'[272] (Bani Adam آدم بنى) as the best example of an accomplished monotheist, a spiritual knight, who built a temple of worship in a land called 'Pharan'[273] to centralise the orientation of all monotheists of the world in one direction. This act has been seen as very important by the followers of the teachings of Abraham, throughout the centuries. Pharan is located in the middle of the Arabian Peninsula. The Manicheans and the New- Manicheans were interested in

---

[272] Mankind in general; the entire humanity; all human beings to the end of time.

[273] 'Pharan' as a word does not exist in the jargon of the Quran. This word exists in the Old Testament, and in the Pesher of Habakkuk. According to the Old Testament Abraham placed his son Ishmael and his wife Hajar in that land (Pharan) where he became a grown man, and got married to an Egyptian girl and raised a big family. According to the Quran it was in that place (Pharan) that Abraham, assisted by his son Esmael (Ishmael), constructed a sanctuary to worship the unique Creator of the universe, under the divine inspiration (Vahi). According to Ibn Husham it was some generations after the death of Ishmael, that the land (Pharan) was disrespected by an invader tribe called 'Jorham'. Hence, Pharan became a forgotten place. Ibn Husham. Ibid. Farsi version. Vol. 1, pp.71to 76.

that place, particularly in the last fifty years of the Sassanid period and after the conquest of Yemen by the followers of Mazdak.[274]

The Quran's view on Mani Farghalit-Baraghlites[275]

The Quran does not contain any direct reference to the term Mâni, and does not mention his name among the names of the other prophets. However, Prophet Mâni does have a role in the Quran. The Quran's explanations about Mâni[276] are totally different from those of Abraham, Moses, Jesus, and so forth in the following way:

It is written in the Book revealed to Mohammad that Jesus introduced himself as a prophet, and predicted the arrival of another prophet after him named 'Ahmad'.

And [mention] when Jesus, the son of Mary, said, 'O children of Israel, indeed I am the messenger of Allah to you confirming what came before me of the Torah and bringing good tidings of a messenger to come after me, whose name is Ahmad.' But when he came to them with clear evidences, they said, 'This is obvious magic.' Surah 61, v: 6. [277]

---

[274] Ibn Husham. Ibid. Farsi version. Vol. 1, pp.42 to 49.

[275] Ibn Husham. Ibid. Vol. 1, p. 140: 'In Roman (Greek) language al-Baraghlites البرقليطس'

[276] Mani (in Middle Persian Mani and Syriac *Mānī*, Latin *Manes*; also *Manichaeus*, from Syriac *Mānī Hayyā* 'Living Mani', 216–276 AD), of Iranian origin, was the prophet and the founder of Manichaeism, a Gnostic religion of late antiquity which was once widespread. Mani was born in 216 AD in or near Seleucia-Ctesiphon in Parthian Babylonia – at the time still part of the Parthian dynasty in the Persian Empire. Six of his major works were written in 'Syriac Aramaic', and the seventh, dedicated to the king of the Sassanid Empire, Shapur I, was written in Middle Persian, his native language. He died by being hanged on 2 March 276 AD in Gundeshapur گندی شاپور, under the Sassanid Empire.

[277]ـ مبشرا برسول یاتی من بعدی اسمه احمد سوره الصف آیه 6

Al-Bédâyàt vàn-Nahaiàt. Esmaiil ibn Omar ibn Dàméshghi al-Qorashi. Edition: Dâr ol Alàm ol Kotob. 2003. Chapter SSàbàb ol Arab elà Ismail ibn Ebrahim. P.100-110; Al Bàd' vàt Tàrikh. Al-Motàhhàr ibn Tàhir al-Mughadàssi. Vol. III. Chapter 10.

It is certain that Jesus would not have used the word of 'Ahmad', because he never spoke Arabic, but rather the equivalent in his own maternal language of Aramaic. In his book *as-Sirat-on Nabavyieh* Abu Mohammad Abdul ibn Husham al Basri writes of the opinion of the Muslims about their understanding and commentary concerning the word of Ahmad. He writes the following:

Jesus wrote in his Gospel revealed to him from Allah the description of Rasoul ollah (Mohammad) according to what 'Yohannas ol Havary' (The Apostle John) ... it is certain the word will be accomplished as it will be in 'an-Nâmous', they (the wrongdoers and disbelievers) hated me by wrongness, when 'al-Monhâmànnâ' المنحمثّا who will be sent by Ràbb (Lord), and the Holy Spirit, he will be my witness, and you as well.

Ibn Husham mentioned this addition from Ibn Eshâgh: *Al Monàhémnâ* المنحمثّا *in Syriac language means Mohammad* محمد *, and in Roman language means al-Baraghelites* البرقليطس .[278]

In the cited paragraph ibn Husham does not talk about the word Ahmad احمد used in the Quran, but Mohammad محمد . On the other hand, the word Baraghelites البرقليطس is the Arabic- Aramaic-Syriac pronunciation of the Greek word 'Paracletus' پاراكلتوس , used in the Gospel of St John. In other words, the Quran talks about the prediction of Jesus regarding the arrival of a person with whom the Holy Spirit makes company, whose name is Ahmad (and not Mohammad). Ibn Husham mixes up Ahmad احمد and Mohammad محمد (which are two separate names). This confirms that the Muslim commentators did not have any exact knowledge of the equivalent

---

[278] Ibn Husham. Ibid. Arabic version. Vol. 1, p. 140.

of Ahmad in the jargon of the Quran and its correspondence in Aramaic (the language of Jesus).[279]

In addition, in the other languages that Jesus was said to have spoken, such as Greek, it is Paracletous, پاراکلتوس , and in Hebrew it is Manhamnâ منحمنّا. The Muslim interpreters and reporters state that in the Gospel of St John the prediction of Jesus about a prophet after him was mentioned under the name 'Monhaménnâ'.[280] Monhaménnâ منحمنا in Aramaic corresponds with the word 'Menakhem' المناخم in Hebrew, and with 'Paracletous' پاراکلتوس in Greek, a synonym of Ahmad in Arabic according to the Quran. This prediction about the apparition of a divine person is cited in all the Gospels. It is said that after the departure of Jesus his apostles gathered and the Holy Spirit came down into their circle according to the prediction of Jesus. The fact, that the apostles kept contact with the invisible and angelic world, is mentioned in the Quran. In other words, for the Christian people the prediction of Jesus was realised after his departure, and this file was closed.

But for certain other people this prediction of Jesus became synonymous with the announcement of a new prophet. According to the Quran the prophet of Islam is named Mohammad, and not Ahmad. Mohammad does not correspond either with Monhaménnâ منحمنا , or with Menakhem مناحم , nor with Farghalit فرقلیطوس , nor with Paracletus پاراکلتوس . Therefore, we should accept that when the Quran mentions Jesus's prediction about the coming prophet under this particular name, it

---

- [279]ذكر عيسى ابن مريم لمبعث النبى .قال ابن اسحاق :فيما بلغنى -عما كان وضع عيسى ابن مريم فيما جائه من الله فى الانجيل لاهل الانجيل من صفة رسول الله مما أثبتَ يُحَتّس الحوارىُ لهم حين نسخ لهم الانجيل عن عهد عيسى ابن مريم عليه السلام فى رسول الله اليهم انه قال ..." :لكن لابدَّ من أن تتم الكلمة التى فى الناموس، إنهم ابغضونى مجانا اى باطلا .فلو قد جاء المُنحَمنّا هذا الذى يرسله الله اليكم من عند الرب و روح القدس هذا الذى من عندالرب خرج فهو شهيد على و انتم ايضا "...و المنحمنا بالسريانيه محمد و هو بالروميه البرقليطس.

Ibn Husham. Ibid. Arabic version. Vol. 1, p. 140.

[280] Ibn Husham. Ibid. Arabic version. Vol. 1, p. 140. 'Al-Baraghelites' is an Arabic adaptation of the Roman word 'Fargelitus'.

does not mean Mohammad, but another prophet. The question is, which prophet? According to history the only prophet in the whole history of prophets who proclaimed himself as Pharghalitous فرقليطوس is Mani, who lived after Jesus and before Mohammad.

We respect him so dearly, Farghalitous Mani.[281]

Farghalitous! You are generated from Jesus. You appeared in Peace. Ô Mâni.[282]

Even though the Quran states clearly that both the Old and New Testaments predict the arrival of the Prophet of Islam, speculation about his name is just an invention of those who interpreted the Quran in the post-Islamic period.

Consequentially, the Quran talks about Mani from the mouth of Jesus. One of the main books of Mani, written originally in Syriac, is 'the Evangelion' (good news – Béshâràt البشارة) or according to the jargon of the Quran 'Enjil'[283] الانجيل . The main mission of Mani was to purify the Evangelion of Jesus from each incorrect addition. So when the Quran refers to the Evangelion (Enjil) it does not mean the book of Jesus only, but the book of Jesus according to the version of Mani.

The name of the other Book of Mani about Jesus is Zabour زبور which was written in the style of the Psalm of David. The Quran also refers to the Zabour زبور of David and to other Zabours as well, and reminds us that

---

281 Zabour, p.220.

282 Zabour, p.227.

283 The Evangelion (Syriac, Greek, Coptic = 'good news'/بشارت). Also known as the *Gospel of Mani*. Quotations from the first chapter were brought in Arabic by ابن النديم Ibn al-Nadim, who lived in Baghdad at a time when there were still Manicheans living there, in his book الفهرست the 'Fihrist' (written in 938 AD), a catalogue of all written books known to him.

the source of a part of the Quran are the Zabours لفى زُبُر الاولى (including the Zabour of Mani).[284]

One of the important signs of the existence of a tangible relationship between the heritage of Mani and Manichean literature on one hand, and the Quran on the other hand, is the title of 'the Seal of the Prophets' النبيين خاتم which was invented and used for the first time by Mani in his book of Shapourgân شاپورگان , and re-employed a second time in the Quran to signify Mohammad. The Quran does not explain why Mohammad has been given this title, whereas Mani explains in detail the reason for the usage and the meaning of this title himself, which means the 'gatherer of the heritages of three prophets before him such as Jesus عيسى , Buddha بودا and Zoroaster زرتشت '.

From these facts we understand that the members of the Qumran community left their city for Syria around the end of the second century AD, before the apparition of Mani and Manichaeism, which was in the first half of the third century AD. They were awaiting the appearance of the Farghalit فرقليطوس in accordance with the prediction of Jesus.[285] Therefore, after the apparition of Mani at least a part of their community converted to his religion. The continuity of the Qumran stream to the teachings of Mani is founded on a solid historical basis. One of the pieces of evidence is the book of Giants كتاب غولها , which is a part of the teachings of Mani and has an important place in Manichean literature. The original fragments of this

---

[284] In 1969 in Upper Egypt a Greek parchment codex dating to 400 AD was discovered. It is now designated *Codex Manichaicus Coloniensis* because it is conserved at the University of Cologne. It combines a hagiographic account of Mani's career and spiritual development with information about Mani's religious teachings, and contains fragments of his writings.

Abul Gasem Ebrahimpour 1375. Ed: Fekré Rouz, translated from Charles Allberry 'A Manichaean Psalm', p.220.

[285] 'We respect him so dearly', Farghalit Mani, Zabour, page 220. 'Oh Farghalit, you are generated from Jesus. You appeared in peace O Mani.' Zabour, page 227.

book were discovered amongst the pre-Manichean scriptures at Qumran.[286] Another document related to the Qumran community that was used by the Manichean people was the Book of Enoch.

Actually, after the genocide of the Manichean followers in Persia during the Sassanid period, by order of the highest religious authority Hirbad Kartir هیربد کرتیر , the remaining part of the Manichean community of Persia went in two opposite directions: to China in the east and to Rome in the west. In the Chinese territory Manichaeism became the official religion for a period of eighty years. In the Roman Empire as well, Manichaeism found a very good place amongst the different social layers. After the introduction of the new version of Christianity in the fourth century, during the period of Constantine, Manichaeism lost its place and the followers of this religion fell under the persecution of the religious state. So in order to survive this difficult situation they tried to give the impression that they had converted to the official version of Roman Christianity and hid themselves amongst the followers of the principle of the Trinity. However, in the second half of the fourth century, Augustine the Patriarch decreed that people who were suspected of being related to Manichaeism should be interrogated by experts of the Church and confess their true faith during a strenuous session of inquisition, in order to clarify whether or not they had really converted to Christianity. Subsequently, a great number of the hidden followers of Mani were tortured and killed. Some of them escaped from the cities and agglomerations, migrating towards the mountains and deserts, far from the inquisitive people, and continued pretending to be Christians, but without accepting the principle of the Trinity and the crucifixion of Jesus. The faraway deserts and mountainous regions around Mecca were full of caves and offered a good refuge to the non-Christian and non-Zoroastrian people who had escaped

---

[286] A copy of this Manichaean document was discovered in the region of Turpan in China as well, in accordance with the migration of the Manichaean community to China.

from the inquisitors to places where they could stay and await the arrival of an eschatological Saviour. These people, such as the monks living in the monasteries on the hills, avoided using the name of Mani.

Following this period, the Manichean literature joined the group of teachings of the migrated people of the Qumran community. They had chosen the lifestyle of monks, living in caves and mountains, and proclaimed themselves to be Christians. Their world vision spread to the monastery of Bosra, situated in the south of Syria and north of the Arabian Peninsula, to which the family of Mohammad was related. Some literature relating to the apostle Thomas (who by tradition went to India and was also venerated in Syria), such as portions of the Syriac 'the Acts of Thomas', and 'the Psalms of Thomas', were preserved by the Manichean community in Syria. The Gospel of Thomas was also attributed to Manichaeism by the early Church fathers. When the Quran talks about the righteous Christian community, it means those who do not accept the principle of the Trinity.

(O Mohammad) and keep yourself patient in company of those who call upon their Lord in the morning and the evening, seeking His countenance. And let not your eyes pass beyond them, desiring adornments of the worldly life, and do not obey one whose heart We have made heedless of Our remembrance and who follows his desire and whose affair is ever [in] neglect. And say: 'The truth is from your Lord, so whoever wills — let him believe; and whoever wills — let him disbelieve.' Surah 18, v: 28, 29.[287]

287- ۷وَاصْبِرْ نَفْسَكَ مَعَ الَّذِينَ يَدْعُونَ رَبَّهُم بِالْغَدَاةِ وَالْعَشِيِّ يُرِيدُونَ وَجْهَهُ وَلَا تَعْدُ عَيْنَاكَ عَنْهُمْ تُرِيدُ زِينَةَ الْحَيَاةِ الدُّنْيَا وَلَا تُطِعْ مَنْ أَغْفَلْنَا قَلْبَهُ عَن ذِكْرِنَا وَاتَّبَعَ هَوَاهُ وَكَانَ أَمْرُهُ فُرُطًا وَقُلِ الْحَقُّ مِن رَّبِّكُمْ فَمَن شَاء فَلْيُؤْمِن وَمَن شَاء فَلْيَكْفُرْ إِنَّا أَعْتَدْنَا لِلظَّالِمِينَ نَارًا أَحَاطَ بِهِمْ سُرَادِقُهَا وَإِن يَسْتَغِيثُوا يُغَاثُوا بِمَاء كَالْمُهْلِ يَشْوِي الْوُجُوهَ بِئْسَ الشَّرَابُ وَسَاءتْ مُرْتَفَقًا إِنَّ الَّذِينَ آمَنُوا وَعَمِلُوا الصَّالِحَاتِ إِنَّا لَا نُضِيعُ أَجْرَ مَنْ أَحْسَنَ عَمَلًا سورة الكهف. الآيات 28-30

The Christians in the Quran

The Quran distinguishes four categories of Christians[288] and refers to the existence of a group of monotheists and Gnostics, very close to the companions of Mohammad, knowledgeable about the heritage of the spiritual masters. The Quran does not call this group Christian, but rather 'those who call themselves Christian'. The Quran says that they are the closest people to Mohammad and his people. There is another citation in the Quran about the Gnostic monks who totally abandon the affairs of this world because of their love for the divinity.

We have already sent Our messengers with clear evidences and sent down with them the Scripture and the balance that the people may maintain [their affairs] in justice. And We sent down iron, wherein is great military might and benefits for the people, and so that Allah may make evident those who support Him and His messengers unseen. Indeed, Allah is Powerful and Exalted in Might. And We have already sent Noah and Abraham and placed in their descendants prophethood and scripture; and among them is he who is guided, but many of them are defiantly disobedient. Then We sent following their footsteps Our messengers and followed [them] with Jesus, the son of Mary, and gave him the Gospel. And We placed in the hearts of those who followed him compassion and mercy and monasticism, which they innovated; We did not prescribe it for them except [that they did so] seeking the approval of Allah. But they did not observe it with due observance. So We gave the ones who believed among them their reward, but many of them are defiantly disobedient. Surah 57, v: 26- 27.[289]

---

[288] Surah 3, v: 53 to 54, the Apostles and the followers of Jesus who were **monotheist**. Surah 57, v: 26 to 27, the **Gnostic monks** who broke their pact with themselves and became disobedient.   Surah 5, v: 82 to 85, **Gnostic monks** who called themselves Christians and amongst the closest to Allah. Surah 5, v: 72 to 73, those who believe in the Trinity. The Quran calls them "no- believers" (**polytheist**).

لقد كفر والذين قالوا ان الله هوالمسيح بن مريم ... لقدكفر الذين قالوا ان الله ثالث ثلاثه. سورة المانده. الايات 72-73

[289]ولقد أرسلنا نوحا وإبراهيم وجعلنا في ذريتهما النبوة والكتاب فمنهم مهتد وكثير منهم فاسقون. ثم قفينا على

The part of the verse citing '*and they did not respect their pact as it should have been respected*' (مارعوها حق رعايته) recalls the case of those who were, for a part of their lives, on the path of Mâni, and followers of the Gnostic lifestyle, but after a while broke their pact and turned to another way. It also refers to certain patriarchs such as the priest Augustin.

And you (O Mohammad) will find the nearest of them in affection to the believers those who say, 'We are Christians.' That is because among them are Gnosis and monks/ghessis القسيس and Rohban الرهبان and because they are not arrogant. And when they hear what has been revealed to the Messenger, you see their eyes overflowing with tears because of what they have recognised of the truth. They say, 'Our Lord, we have believed, so register us among the witnesses. And why should we not believe in Allah and what has come to us of the truth? And we aspire that our Lord will admit us [to Paradise] with the righteous people.' So Allah rewarded them for what they said with gardens [in Paradise] beneath which rivers flow, wherein they abide eternally. And that is the reward of doers of good. Surah 5, v: 82 - 85.[290]

آثارهم برسلنا .و قفينا بعيسى ابن مريم وآتيناه الإنجيل وجعلنا في قلوب الذين اتبعوه رأفة ورحمة؛ ورهبانية ابتدعوها /ما كتبناها عليهم /إلا ابتغاء رضوان الله .فما رعوها حق رعايتها. فآتينا الذين آمنوا منهم أجرهم. وكثير منهم فاسقون   سورة الحديد الايات 26-27

290 - و لتجدن اقربهم موده للذين آمنوا الذين قالوا انا نصارا .ذلك بان منهم قسيسين و رهبانا و انهم لايستكبرون. واذا سمعوا ماانزل الى الرسول ترى اعينهم تفيض من الدمع مما عرفوا من الحق يقولون ربنا آمنا فاكتبنا مع الشاهدين. و مالنا لانومن بالله و ماجائنا من الحق و نطمع ان يُدخلنا ربُنا مع القوم الصالحين سوره المائده الآيه 82- 85

There is an important saying/revayat regarding the reason that the Gnostic people were committed to a monastic life in the hills and mountains.

Prophet Mohammad said to ibn Mas'oud: 'O ibn Mas'oud. Did you know that the people of Israel were divided into seventy-two groups and between them only three groups will reach to the safe state? After Jesus, son of Mary, it was the first group who stood up against the tyrants and oppressors and appealed others to the path of Allah and the religion of Jesus and fought against the tyrants and were killed, and persisted on their resistance and escaped to God; the second group were those who came following Jesus and appealed others to the path of Jesus and Allah. But they were not in good military power, so they lost the battle and were killed by the tyrants and were burnt in the fire, but persisted upon their objective and finished to escape to God. The third group did not have the force to

174

The Quran does not talk about the belief of the Gnostics, but it states that there are a lot of similarities between their faith and the teachings of Mohammad. The position of Mohammad and the Quran towards the 'truth' regarding the crucifixion is shared between those people and Mohammad. This is the world vision of the Manicheans as well.

O People of the Scripture, there has come to you Our Messenger to make clear to you [the religion] after a period [of suspension] of messengers, lest you say, 'There came not to us any bringer of good tidings or a warner.' But there has come to you a bringer of good tidings and a warner. And Allah is over all things competent. Surah 5, v: 19.[291]

---

fight against the tyrants, and did not have the force to make an uprising against the tyrant in benefit of the equality in the society. So they escaped to the mountains and became the monastic and the worshippers, and these are those whose state is mentioned in the Quran: *And We placed in the hearts of those who followed him compassion and mercy and monasticism which they innovated; We did not prescribe it for them except [that they did so] seeking the approval of Allah.'*

According to this revayat monasticism and Gnosticism appeared between the followers of the path of Jesus once they were persecuted and pushed into the fire. It reminds us of the case of the companions of Okhdoud before Islam and the Cathars after Islam, both of them Manicheans 'introducing themselves' as Christians!

وقد قال ابن أبي حاتم: حدثنا إسحاق بن أبي حمزة أبو يعقوب الرازي ، حدثنا السندي بن عبدويه ، حدثنا بكير بن معروف ، عن مقاتل بن حيان ، عن القاسم بن عبد الرحمن بن عبد الله بن مسعود ، عن أبيه ، عن جده عبدالله ابن مسعود قال: قال لي رسول الله ـ صلى الله عليه وسلم " : يا ابن مسعود . "قلت :لبيك يا رسول الله ، قال " : هل علمت أن بني إسرائيل افترقوا على ثنتين وسبعين فرقة ؟ لم ينج منها إلا ثلاث فرق ، قامت بين الملوك والجبابرة بعد عيسى ابن مريم ، عليه السلام ، فدعت إلى دين الله ودين عيسى ابن مريم ، فقاتلت الجبابرة فقتلت فصبرت ونجت ، ثم قامت طائفة أخرى لم يكن لها قوة بالقتال ، فقامت بين الملوك والجبابرة فدعوا إلى دين الله ودين عيسى ابن مريم ، فقتلت وقطعت بالمناشير وحرقت بالنيران ، فصبرت ونجت .ثم قامت طائفة أخرى لم يكن لها قوة بالقتال ولم تطق القيام بالقسط ، فلحقت بالجبال فتعبدت وترهبت ، وهم الذين ذكرهم الله ، عز وجل : "ورهبانية ابتدعوها ما كتبناها عليهم ."

تفسير ابن كثير /إسماعيل بن عمر بن كثير القرشي الدمشقي /دار طيبة /سنة النشر 1422هـ: 2002/ م

ـ 291 يا أهل الكتاب قد جاءكم رسولنا يبين لكم على فترة من الرسل أن تقولوا ما جاءنا من بشير ولا نذير فقد جاءكم بشير ونذير والله على كل شيء قدير. سوره المائده الايه 19

واختلفوا في مدة الفترة بين عيسى عليه السلام ومحمد صلى الله عليه وسلم ، قال أبو عثمان النهدي :بستمائة سنة ، وقال قتادة :خمسمائة وستون سنة ، وقال معمر والكلبي ، خمسمائة وأربعون سنة وسميت فترة لأن الرسل كانت تترى بعد موسى عليه السلام من غير انقطاع إلى زمن عيسى عليه السلام ، ولم يكن بعد عيسى عليه السلام سوى رسولنا صلى الله عليه وسلم . أن تقولوا (كيلا تقولوا ،)ما جاءنا من بشير ولا نذير فقد جاءكم بشير ونذير والله على كل شيء قدير   تفسير البغوي /صفحه / 35تفسير البغوي .الحسين بن مسعود البغوي /دار طيبة

The place of the Apostles in the Quran

The Quran introduces the Apostles of Jesus as righteous monotheists, in order to give a clear example of chivalry to the companions of Mohammad.

This is what We recite to you, [O Mohammad], of [Our] verses and the precise [and wise] message. Surah 3, v: 58.[292]

But when Jesus felt [persistence in] disbelief from them, he said, 'Who are my supporters for [the cause of] Allah?' The disciples said, 'We are supporters for Allah. We have believed in Allah and testify that we are Muslims [submitting to Him]. Our Lord, we have believed in what You revealed and have followed the messenger Jesus, so register us among the witnesses [to truth].' And the disbelievers planned, but Allah planned. And Allah is the best of planners. Surah 3, v: 52 - 54.[293]

O you who have believed, be supporters of Allah, as when Jesus, the son of Mary, said to the disciples, 'Who are my supporters for Allah?' The disciples said, 'We are supporters of Allah.' And a faction of the Children of Israel believed and a faction

---

Mà'àlim ot Tanzil fi Tafsir ol Quran. At Tafsir ol Bàghàvi. Hoseyin ibn Mas'oud al Baghavi. 510 H. edition: Dar ot Taybah. 8 vols. 1997. Beyrout. Dâr ol Ehyâ ot Torâth ol Aràbi.

According to certain reporters and interpreters of the Quran there was no prophet between Jesus and Mohammad. But in this verse there is no sign of Jesus, so this period of suspension is between Mani and Mohammad, but those Muslims did not know anything about a prophet named Mani. But 'fetrat o men ar rosol' means the emptiness of any prophet in the Arabian Peninsula, speaking in Arabic for the Bedouins, as it is cited in the Surah Yasin: '(O Mohammad you are sent) to preach those for whom any preacher never was sent.' The people who were living in the mountains were called 'Sufis' by people of that region, because they covered their bodies with sheepskin. Mà'alim ot Tanzil Fi Tafsir ol Quran. Tafsir Baghani - Al Hoseyn ibn Mas'oud al Bagani, 510 Hegira Ed: Dar ot Taybah, 8. Volumes - 1997 Beyrout. Dar Èhyâ ot Torath ol Arabi.

[292]ذلک نتلوه علیک من الایات و الذکر الحکیم سوره آل عمران آیه 58

[293]فلما احس عیسی منهم الکفر قال من انصاری الی الله قال الحواریون نحن انصار الله آمنا بالله و اشهد باننا مسلمون .ربنا آمنا بما انزلت و اتبعنا الرسول فاکتبنا مع الشاهدین .و مکروا و مکرالله و الله خیر الماکرین .سوره آل عمران -آیه 52 تا 54

disbelieved. So We supported those who believed against their enemy, and they became dominant. Surah 61, v: 14.[294]

The Quran precisely states that after the departure of Jesus the gate of divine revelation Vàhi (وحی) was not closed and the apostles remained in contact with the invisible world.

And [remember] when I inspired to the disciples, 'Believe in Me and in My messenger Jesus.' They said, 'We have believed, so bear witness that indeed we are Muslims [in submission to Allah].' [And remember] when the disciples said, 'O Jesus, Son of Mary, can your Lord send down to us a table [spread with food] from the heaven? [Jesus] said, 'Fear Allah, if you should be believers.' Surah 5, v: 111,112.[295]

The Quran gives an example of 'the companions of the village' (اصحاب القریه) to which three Apostles of Jesus had been sent, which corresponds with the journey of Barnabas, Paul, and Lazarus to Cyprus.

And present to them an example: 'the people of the village'; when the messengers came to it, When We sent to them two but they denied them, so We strengthened them with a third. And they said: 'Indeed, we are messengers to you.' They said: 'You are not but human beings like us, and the Most Merciful has not revealed a thing. You are only telling lies.' They said: 'Our Lord knows that we are messengers to you, and we are not responsible except for clear notification.' They said: 'Indeed, we consider you a bad omen. If you do not desist, we will surely stone you, and there will surely touch you, from us, a

---

[294] ـ يا ايهاالذين آمنوا كونوا انصار الله كمال قال عيسى ابن مريم للحواريين من انصارى الى الله قال الحواريون نحن انصار الله فآمنت طائفة من بنى اسرائيل و كفرت طائفة فايّدنا الذين آمنوا على عدوهم فاصبحوا ظاهرين سوره الصف ـآيه 14

[295] و اذ اوحيت الى الحواريين أن آمنوا بى و برسولى قالوا آمنا و اشهد باننا مسلمون. اذ قال الحواريون يا عيسى بن مريم هل يستطيع ربك أن يُنَزِل علينا مائده من السماء قال اتقوا الله إن كنتم مومنين سوره المائده الايات 111- 112

painful punishment.' They said: 'Your omen is with yourselves. Is it because you were reminded? Rather, you are a transgressing people.'

And there came from the farthest end of the city a man, running. He said: 'O my people, follow the messengers. Follow those who do not ask of you [any] payment, and they are [rightly] guided. And why should I not worship He who created me and to whom you will be returned? Should I take other than Him [false] deities [while], if the Most Merciful intends for me some adversity, their intercession will not avail me at all, nor can they save me? Indeed, I would then be in manifest error. Indeed, I have believed in your Lord, so listen to me.' It was said: 'Enter Paradise.' He said: 'I wish my people could know of how my Lord has forgiven me and placed me among the honoured.' And We did not send down upon his people after him any soldiers from the heaven, nor would We have done so. It was not but one shout, and immediately they were extinguished. How regretful for the servants. There did not come to them any messenger except that they used to ridicule him. Surah 36, v: 13 - 30.[296]

---

[296]و اضرب لهم مثلا" :اصحاب القريه"؛ اذ جائه المرسلون اذ ارسلنا اليهم اثنين فكذبوهما فعززنا بثالث فقالوا انا اليكم مرسلين ...سوره يس الايات 13- 30

Kawan and Quran

Figure 15 - A page from the Cologne Mani-Codex, in Greek

The canon of Mani included six works originally written in Syriac, and one in Persian called the *Shabuhragan* شاپورگان . While none of his books have survived in their complete form, there are numerous fragments and quotations from them, including a long Syriac quotation from one of his works, as well as a large amount of material in Middle Persian, Coptic, and numerous other languages. Examples of surviving portions of his works include: the *Shabuhragan*[297](Middle Persian), the Book of Giants (numerous fragments in many languages), the *Fundamental Epistle* (quoted at length by Saint Augustine), a number of fragments of his *Living Gospel* (or *Great Gospel*), a Syriac excerpt quoted by Theodore Bar Konai, and his *Letter to Edessa* contained in the Mani-Codex of Cologne, Germany. Mani also wrote the book *Arzhang* ارژنگ, a Holy Book of Manichaeism. It contained many

---

[297] Shabuhragan. One of the books written by Mani (216-274/7 AD), founder of the Manichaean religion, in which he summarized his teachings systematically. Encyclopaedia Iranica

drawings and paintings to express and explain Manichaeism regarding creation and the history of the world.[298]

There are certain paragraphs in the Quran and in the books of Prophet Mani[299] that give the impression to the reader that they stem from 'one unique source'. That is because the same sentences have been revealed twice, in two different languages, to two different persons, with about four centuries between them, namely Mani and Mohammad. The following is a brief example about the principle of 'Raj'at رجعت :[300]

Sweet place of rest, oh garden! May you be a sweet place of rest for me. Return to me, remain in me. May we be of one accord through your beneficence.[301]

---

[298] The Book of Giants (Ketâb Goulân) is titled Kawan as well. Larry Clark. 1982: 197, cited from the collection of the treatise called 'Emerging from Darkness', studies in the recovery of Manichaean sources edited by Paul Mirecki and Jason BeDuhn, edition Brill 1996. G. Haloun and W.B. Henning: 'The compendium of the doctrines and styles of the teachings of Mani, the Buddha of light'. Asia Major 3, 1953.

[299] L. Koenen. 'Manichaean Apocalypticism at the crossroads of Iranian, Egyptian, Jewish and Christian thought', in Codex Manichaeicus Coloniensis. Ed: L. Cirillo and A. Roselli. Cosenza 1986: Manichaean eschatology, teachings about the final days, provided information on what happened during and after the death of a single human being and also on what would happen before and at the end of this world. These two aspects were, however, less discernible than in other religions such as Christianity and Zoroastrianism. Teachings about the transmigration of the soul, peculiar in Manichaeism, linked the fates of the unredeemed majority of individuals after death with the judgment at the end of time.

For Mani and his community, the foundation of cosmic eschatology was the expectation of the impending end of the world. He considered himself as having been sent 'in this last generation' (Polotsky and Böhlig, p. 179; cf. Stroumsa, 1981, p. 169 and n. 28), and the progressive degeneration of mankind was interpreted by him as an omen of the end. The author of the Coptic homily 'Of the great war' (Polotsky, 1934, pp. 7-42) believed that under the dominion of the great king the Manichaean church would be led by an apostle who had actually known Mani. A. V. W. Jackson's contrary hypothesis, that the Manicheans had prophesied Mani's return at the end of time, remains unconfirmed; the text that he cited (Middle Pers. S 8) refers, as does its title, *Aryâmân*, to the Second Coming of Christ (Jackson, 1930, p. 182).

[300] Verbally this word means to return back. However, in the jargon of the Quran Raj'at signifies the return of the soul to accomplish a mission, or to return back to his Rabb. We are for Allah and we return back to Him. انا لله و انا اليه الراجعون (Surah 2, v: 156).

[301] The Hymn on Body-and-Soul. A Manichaean liturgical hymn in Parthian. Abu Reyhan al Biruni. Atharol Bagieh an el Gorounel Khalieh. The chronology of Ancient Nations.

To the righteous it will be said, 'O reassured soul, Return to your Lord, well-pleased and pleasing to Him, And enter among My righteous servants. And enter My Garden.' Surah 89, v: 27 - 30.[302]

The most important similarity between certain sentences and paragraphs of the content of the Quran and the content of the teachings of Mani is regarding 'the principle of Kawan'.[303] The Book of the Giants (Ketab é Gholân) is titled 'Kawan' as well.[304]

The Book of the Two Principles, Dw Bwn[305], دو بُن analyses the pre-existence of one unique Creator 'Ahura Mazda'(God), before creation who brought out of nothingness the whole universe and all of the ephemeral

---

Trans. 1984 Minerva Verlag. Al Birouni writes about body and soul according to Mani's teachings.

[302] ـ يا ايتها النفس المطئنه ارجعى الى ربک راضيه مرضيه فادخلى فى عبادى و ادخلى جنتى سوره و الفجر ـ آيات 27 تا 30

[303] The principle of the synthesis, which is a result of the opposition between thesis and anti-thesis, is named Koan. One of the books of Mani was consecrated totally to this problem and was titled Koan.

[304] Larry Clark. 1982, p. 197, cited from the collection of the treatises called 'Emerging from Darkness', studies in the recovery of Manichaean Sources. Edition Brill- 1996. G. Haloun and W.B. Henning. 'The Compendium of the Doctrines and styles of the Teachings of Mani, the Budha of Light'. Edition: Asia Major 3. 1953.

[305] DW BWN. DW in the language of Mani means 'two'. BWN means foundation. DW BWN means two foundations similar to a twin tower model. In the cosmology of Mani Ormuzd, which is an equivalent of Jehowa-Allah, the unique Creator created the whole universe and placed the creation entirely upon these two invisible pillars that are polar to each other. This represents the principle of constant negation of thesis and anti-thesis generated by itself and this perpetual interaction between these two forces propels the endless evolution of all beings, which resolves in the synthesis of the antagonistic forces. The end of the universe happens when the Creator removes these two pillars and the universe collapses into nothingness. The souls of the righteous people enter into heaven, the less righteous people pass through a labyrinth towards perfection, whereas the wrongdoers join each other in the sphere named hell.

beings categorised on the basis of duality, according to the principle of the eternal battle between antagonist forces of light and darkness.[306]

Alif, Lam, Meem, Ra. These are the verses of the Book; and what has been revealed to you from your Lord is the truth, but most of the people do not believe. It is Allah who erected the skies without pillars that you can see; then He established Himself above the Throne and made subject the sun and the moon, each running its course for a specified term. He arranges each matter; He details the signs that you may, of the meeting with your Lord, be certain. And it is He who spread the earth and placed therein firmly set mountains and rivers; and from all of the fruits He made therein two mates; He causes the night to cover the day. Indeed in that are signs for a people who give thought. And within the land are neighbouring plots and gardens of grapevines and crops and palm trees, growing several from a root or otherwise, watered with one water; but We make some of them exceed others in quality of fruit. Indeed in that are signs for a people who reason. Surah 13, v: 1 - 4.

The universe is based on two principles that resemble two pillars which are opposite to each other and which are negating and replacing each other

---

[306] The book, published by Le Coq (1911) and identified with the Chinese *Traité* (Chavannes and Pelliot, 1913), has now been identified as a part of the Turkish version of the Parthian 'Sermon of the Light-Nous' (Klimkeit and Schmidt-Glintzer, 1984). '*dw bwn*' was used sometimes for *Šābuhragān*. The title 'Book of the Two Principles' is cited in Chinese sources as having been presented to the Empress Wu by a Mihr-Ormezd (Hutter, 1992, p. 146), but it is not known which book is meant. The title 'Book of the Two Principles and the Three Epochs' could also mean the 'Compendium of the doctrines and styles of the teaching of Mani, the Buddha of Light', because both formulas are often mentioned in it. Also mentioned is a so-called 'Table of the Great Two Principles', presumably the *Ardahang* – whatever it was. The *Šābuhragān* is not mentioned in the 'Compendium of the doctrines and styles of the teaching of Mani'. The list there seems to be dependent on a Western source (Haloun and Henning, 1953, pp. 204-11). The use of 'two principles' in the Chinese title, which originally (as Middle Persian *dw bwn*) indicated the eschatological chapters of *Šābuhragān*, may show the further development of this term. It represents the name of the religion itself in the Eastern world. Thus one cannot conclude that every book bearing this title in later times contains translations from, or paraphrases of, *Šābuhragān*.

eternally, and it is the inner force of the propulsion that runs the universe on the road of its continual evolution. This can be interpreted in the same way as day and night, darkness and light, wrong or right.[307]

---

[307] Zabur é Mâni. Abul Gâsim Ebrâhimpoor Téhran 1357. Edition: 'Fékr é Rouz' translated from Charles.R.C. Allberry. 'A Manichaean Psalm', p. 2200, Zabur é Mâni. Abul Gâsim Ebrâhimpoor Téhran. 1388. Edition Ostoureh. D.N. MacKenzie. 'Mani's Shabuhragan I'. Bosas 1979 II. 1980. A. Afshar Shirazi. Motoun é Arabi va Farsi dar bâryé Mâni và Mânàviyat. Tehran 1335. J.P.Asmussen. Manichaean Literature. Persian heritage series 22. Delmar. N.Y. 1975. M. Boyce. A Catalogue of the Iranian Manuscripts in Manichaean Script in the German Turfan collection. Institut Fur orientforcung. Berlin. 1960. M. Boyce. A Reader in Manichaean Middle Persian and Parthian: Texts with notes. Acta Iranica 9. Leiden. Tehran. Liège. 1975.

The Chronology of Ancient Nations. English version of the Arabic Text of the Athar-ul-Bakiya of Al-Biruni. Or 'Vestige of the Past'. 390 H. 1000 AD. C. Edward Sachau. London. 1879 edition, 1984. Minerva Verlag. Al-Biruni writes about body and soul according to the teachings of Mâni.

Mâné' Mohammad Mâné'. Al-Amâkèn ol Athârieh fi Shebh é Jazirà tol Arabieh. Edition: Vekâlàt Bé Néjât lil Alàm. 1978. Arabis. Ahmad as Sab'i. Târikh é Makkeh. Translated to Farsi. www. Hadj.ir/Booksl/1818.htm. Qusay and his generations after him, pp. 56-58 About Mâni's Books: Ibn Nàdim in his book al-Fihrist. The book of Mme Boyce, the book of Professor MacKenzie, Arthur Christiansen 'Iran in the Sassanid Period; Mani'. 215/6-276 AD Al-Byruni. 'The Vestiges of the Past', édition London 1879 p. 189-190: In the beginning of his book called Shabuhragan; which he composed for Shabpur b. Ardeshir he says: 'Wisdom and deeds have always from time to time been brought to mankind by the messengers of God. So in one age they have been brought by the messenger called Buddha, to India; in another by Zâradusht to Persia, in another by Jesus to the West. Thereupon this revelation has come down, this prophethood in this last age through me, Mâni, the messenger of God of truth to Babylonia'. In his Gospel, which he arranged according to the twenty-two letters of the alphabet, he says that he is Paraclete announced by Messiah, and that he is the 'Seal of the Prophets.'

و فى نهايه عمر دنيا ...يضع الملاكان مثنى ملاک اللذان يحمل السماء و الارض احمالها فتقع و ينقص کل شىء و تشتعل النيران من وسط هذاالاضطراب و تمتد فتحرق العالم کله .بعد الموت يدخل الصديقون الجنه و لکن المومنون الذين هم اقل درجه و الذين لم يخلصوا انفسهم من الماده يحيون من جديد فى الدنيا فى حالا متفاوته حسب سلوکهم .اما المجرمون فيذهبون الى جهنم .ص 178او يفصل بين الجنه و النار جدار لايمکن عبوره و يقام جدار لايعبر بين العالمين و تسعد مملکه النور بسلام ابدى179 .

قال الماني انى جئت من بلاد بابل لابلغ دعوتى للناس کافه و لقدعلّم مانى اتباعه انه فى يوم القيمه ستحرق الارض و ان المومنين الحقيقين سيذهبون الى الجنه و ان المجرمين الى جهنم172 .

All praise is due to Allah who created earth and skies, and posed, Jà'alà, (them on two pillars) the darkness and light. Surah 6, v: 1.[308]

A sign of the opposite forces in the universe is the fact the day is taken over by the night and people find themselves in the darkness. Surah 36, v: 37.[309]

In the layer of human beings, in society and in social reports, the world vision of the people is divided into two categories and for each category there are certain followers: the companions of light and the companions of darkness.

Say, 'Is the blind who does not see inside of darkness in the equal level to the seeing? Or is darkness equivalent to light?' Surah 13, v: 16.

Indeed the sightless and the insightful are not equal, and darkness and light are not equal. Surah 35, v: 19-20.

The oppressors and the violators of human rights are the companions of darkness, and the spiritual chevaliers are the companions of light. The oppressors are looking to establish their own tyrannical system and the spiritual chevaliers defend the defenceless people in front of them. Allah is guiding the companions of light towards light.

Allah is the ally of those who believe. He brings them out from darkness into the light. And those who disbelieve – their allies are Tâghout. They take them out of the light into darkness. Those are the companions of the Fire; they will abide eternally therein. Surah 2, v: 257.

The reason for sending Holy Books and raising apostles and prophets is to give guidance to the companions of light in their continual battle against the unjust systems.

---

[308]الحمدلله الذى خلق السموات و الارض و جعل الظلمات و النور سوره الانعام الايه اول

[309]و آيه لهم الليل نسلخ منه النهار فاذا هم مظلمون سوره يس آيه 37

The book (Quran) that we sent to you to conduct people out of darkness towards light. Surah 14, v: 1.

Allah is the Light of the skies and the earth. *The example of His light is like a niche within which is a lamp, the lamp is within glass, the glass as if it were a pearly [white] star lit from [the oil of] a blessed olive tree, neither of the east nor of the west, whose oil would almost glow even if untouched by fire. Light upon light. Allah guides to His light whom He wills. And Allah presents examples for the people, and Allah is Knowing of all things.* Surah 24, v: 35.

اللَّهُ نُورُ السَّمَاوَاتِ وَالأَرْضِ مَثَلُ نُورِهِ كَمِشْكَاةٍ فِيهَا مِصْبَاحٌ الْمِصْبَاحُ فِي زُجَاجَةٍ الزُّجَاجَةُ كَأَنَّهَا كَوْكَبٌ دُرِّيٌّ يُوقَدُ مِنْ شَجَرَةٍ مُبَارَكَةٍ زَيْتُونَةٍ لا شَرْقِيَّةٍ وَلاغَرْبِيَّةٍ يَكَادُ زَيْتُهَا يُضِيءُ وَلَوْلَمْ تَمْسَسْهُ نَارٌ نُورٌ عَلَى نُورٍ يَهْدِي اللَّهُ لِنُورِهِ مَنْ يَشَاءُ وَيَضْرِبُ اللَّهُ الأَمْثَالَ لِلنَّاسِ وَاللَّهُ بِكُلِّ شَيْءٍ عَلِيمٌ . سورة النور. الايه 35

[Such niches are] in houses which Allah has ordered to be raised and that His name be mentioned therein; exalting Him within them in the morning and the evenings. [Are] men whom neither commerce nor sale distracts from the remembrance of Allah and performance of prayer and giving of zakah. They fear a Day in which the hearts and eyes will [fearfully] turn about -That Allah may reward them [according to] the best of what they did and increase them from His bounty. And Allah gives provision to whom He wills without account.

But those who disbelieved - their deeds are like a "Sarab"/ mirage سراب[310] / in a lowland which a thirsty one thinks is water until, when he comes to it, he finds it is nothing but finds Allah before Him, and He will pay him in full his due; and Allah is swift in account.Or [they are] like darknesses within an unfathomable sea which is covered by waves, upon which are waves, over which are clouds - darknesses, some of them upon others. When one puts out his hand [therein], he can hardly see it. And he to whom Allah has not granted light - for him there is no light. Surah 24, v: 36 - 40

---

[310] This word is a Persian word. Ab means water, Sarab means illusion of water in desert.

In the Quran, as in the Zabour and the other books, we read verses about the will of the Lord to give the final victory to the oppressed people by the hand of the knights.

And We have already written in the book of Psalms after the previous mention that the land of Paradise is inherited by my righteous servants. Surah 21, v: 105.

ولقد كتبنا فى الزبور من بعد الذكر انّ الارض يرثها عبادى الصالحون سورة الانبياء الايه
105

So if Jesus predicted the arrival of a new prophet after him it was about a person whose title was Pharghalitous فرقليطوس , and this was Mani. But it does not mean that the arrival of Mohammad was not predicted. It was stated many centuries before Jesus in the text of the Pesher of Habakkuk, as the promised Saviour of Pharan.

The Pesher of Habakkuk

Figure 16 - Tomb and coffin of Habakkuk in his sanctuary in Touisercan, Iran.

Habakkuk 33 - A prayer of the prophet Habakkuk according to Shigionoth.

² O Lord, I have heard of your renown, and I stand in awe, O Lord, of your work.

In our own time revive it; in our own time make it known; in wrath may you remember mercy.

³ God came from Teman, the Holy One from Mount **Pharan.**

Selah

His glory covered the heavens, and the earth was full of his praise.

⁴ The brightness was like the sun; rays came forth from his hand, where his power lay hidden.

⁵ Before him went pestilence, and plague followed close behind.

⁶ He stopped and shook the earth; he looked and made the nations tremble.

The eternal mountains were shattered; along his ancient pathways the everlasting hills sank low.

⁷ I saw the tents of Cushan under affliction; the tent-curtains of the land of Midian trembled.

⁸ Was your wrath against the rivers, O Lord? Or your anger against the rivers, or your rage against the sea, when you drove your horses, your chariots to victory?³¹¹

---

³¹¹ http://www.catholic.org/bible/book.php?id=42&bible_chapter=3 1 A prayer of the prophet Habakkuk; tone as for dirges.

2 Yahweh, I have heard of your renown; your work, Yahweh, inspires me with dread. Make

From what we have examined so far it is clear that quotes about Mani, and about the world vision of Mani and Manichaeism, exist in the Quran, and the people of the pact of knighthood according to the teachings of Jesus and Mani were living in a period where they expected the apparition of a new promised and prophesied person: the Saviour of Pharan, Mohammad.

Chivalry: the destiny of the spiritual knights according to the Quran

We have already sent Our messengers with clear evidences and sent down with them the Scripture and the balance that the people may maintain [their affairs] in justice. And We sent down iron, wherein is great military might and benefits for the people, and so that Allah may make evident those who support Him and His messengers unseen. Indeed, Allah is Powerful and Exalted in Might. Surah 57, v: 25.[312]

Considering the fact that the message of Mohammad to his audience was based on the repetition of the words of a pre-existing book (called Sohof e Abraham, Surah 87, v: 18-19), then the content of that book should

---

it live again in our time, make it known in our time; in wrath remember mercy.

3 Eloah comes from Teman, and the Holy One from Mount Paran. His majesty covers the heavens, and his glory fills the earth.

4 His brightness is like the day, rays flash from his hands that is where his power lies hidden.

5 Pestilence goes before him and plague follows close behind.

6 When he stands up, he makes the earth tremble, with his glance he makes the nations quake. And the eternal mountains are dislodged, the everlasting hills sink down, his pathway from of old.

7 I saw the tents of Cushan in trouble, the tent-curtains of Midian shuddering.

8 Yahweh, are you enraged with the rivers, are you angry with the sea, that you should mount your chargers, your rescuing chariots?

[312]لقد أرسلنا رسلنا بالبينات وأنزلنا معهم الكتاب والميزان ليقوم الناس بالقسط وأنزلنا الحديد فيه بأس شديد ومنافع للناس وليعلم الله من ينصره ورسله بالغيب إن الله قوي عزيز سورة الحديد . الآية 25

be understood through certain verses of the Quran as well. And indeed, in the Quran, Abraham is introduced from the framework of the Bible as the founder of the school of *fotowwat* – chivalry.[313] According to the Quran, every single action undertaken by Abraham is rooted in the path of chivalry. The Quran stresses that Abraham was one of the followers of the tradition of Noah. The school of Abraham, Mellat é Abraham, consists of a particular method of education based on the values of monotheism, known as Hanif, which explains that by becoming a chevalier, the pupil reaches the ultimate stage of perfection as a human being.

Indeed, Abraham was a [comprehensive] leader, devoutly obedient to Allah, inclining towards truth, and he was not of those who associate others with Allah. [He was] grateful for His favours. Allah chose him and guided him to a straight path. And We gave him good in this world, and indeed, in the Hereafter he will be among the righteous. Then We revealed to you, [O Mohammad], to follow the religion of Abraham, inclining towards truth; and he was not of those who associate with Allah. Surah 16, v: 120 - 123.[314]

The Quran deeply emphasizes the values of knighthood and altruism; altruism and respect for human rights is the most important pillar of social education in the path of Abraham. The best example of chivalry seen in the Quran is the feast of Abraham, when upon seeing three wanderers in the middle of the desert, he prepares a big feast and receives these unknown tourists as welcome guests, inviting them under his tent, offering them

---

313واتل عليهم نبأ إبراهيم... /سورة الشعراء 69-82 قد كانت لكم أسوة حسنة في إبراهيم والذين معه إذ قالوا لقومهم إنا برأء منكم ومما تعبدون من دون الله كفرنا بكم وبدا بيننا وبينكم العداوة والبغضاء أبدا حتى تؤمنوا بالله وحده . سورة الممتحنة، الايه 4 ؛ وإذ قال إبراهيم لأبيه وقومه إنني براء مما تعبدون إلا الذي فطرني فإنه سيهدين وجعلها كلمة باقية في عقبه لعلهم يرجعون الزخرف 26to28

314ان ابراهيم كان امه قانتا لله حنيفا و لم يك من المشركين شاكرا لانعمه اجتباه و هداه الى صراط مستقيم .و آتيناه فى الدنيا حسنه و انه فى الاخره لمن الصالحين ثم اوحينا اليك أن اتبع مله ابراهيم حنيفا و ما كان من المشركين سوره النحل. الايات 15-18

food, drink, and hospitality without asking for any reward, and without asking them any questions regarding their beliefs or world vision. Mellat é Ebrahim is the school of spiritual chivalry and, according to the Quran, Abraham is the perfect example of this school, and he is a complete Ummah, Community.[315] Interestingly, what is said about Abraham in the Quran corresponds only partially with the story of Abraham in the Bible.

The Quran emphasises the behaviour of Abraham; he wanted to break down the wild superstitious behaviours, customs, and traditions of the despots, who had no respect for human values and human beings in general, in particular none towards people who were not related to any tribe, and orphans, prisoners, and defenceless poor people, who the tyrants forced to become their slaves. They had no respect towards women and killed newborn girls, and they also lent money with interest to force poor people into financial breakdown in order to own them as their slaves.

The Quran reminds us that the destiny and turn of the universe does not follow a positive and easy path according to the will of the knights. Many knights were burned alive in fire pits by tyrants or lost their lives under a hail of stones from their oppressors, while other groups of knights were forced to leave their respective lands and migrate to other territories, or to hide themselves in caves and in the mountains, or wander in the deserts to find refuge.[316] Abraham himself was arrested, tortured and thrown into a mountain of fire when he was living in Uruk. Later on he

---

[315] The Quran describes Abraham as a homogene community أمّة قانتة , meaning he was following one goal and was a holistic person living in unity with the Creator. Together with his followers who had the same lifestyle he constituted a community oriented towards the same goal. In this case, community has nothing to do with the structure of society, where people follow different intentions. Quran, Surah 16, v: 120: *He was a comprehensive Ummah, devotedly obedient to Allah, a Hanif, inclining towards truth and he wasn't of those who associate others with Allah.* Al Bedayat van Nahayat, Esmail ibn Omar ibn Dameshehi al Qarshi. Edition Dar Alàm al Kotob 2003. Chapter sasab ol Arab ela Ismail ibn Ebrahim, pp. 100-110. al Bad' vat Tarikh, al Mottahar ibn Taher Almogadasi, Vol III, chapter 10.

316ـ التَّائِبُونَ العَابِدُونَ الحَامِدُونَ السَّائِحُونَ الرَّاكِعُونَ السَّاجِدُونَ الآمِرُونَ بِالمَعْرُوفِ وَالنَّاهُونَ عَنِ الْمُنكِرِ وَالْحَافِظُونَ لِحُدُودِ اللهِ وَبَشِّرِ الْمُؤْمِنِينَ. سورة التوبة. الاية 112

migrated to the land of Kan'an, to Egypt, to the desert of Arabia, and to Mesopotamia.[317] The Quran gives us numerous evidence to demonstrate the truly horrible treatment suffered by the 'people of the pact of knighthood' who, simply because of their beliefs and faith, were pushed alive into fires at the hands of the agents of the religious governmental authorities, as was the case for the companions of Okhdoud.[318] Those who escaped that genocide went to Ephesus in Cappadocia and hid themselves silently in caves for a period of 300 years, and avoided the city people.[319] The Quran shows at the same time that the members of the circle of chivalry did not change their values and remained faithful to their pact of knighthood until the end of their lives; they expected, during their lives, the apparition of the promised Saviour of God. From the Quran we can see

---

[317] According to some evidence Abraham is also supposed to have visited a part of the region of Mesopotamia situated today in the west of Iran called Nahavand نهاوند or Nouh Avand نوح آوند. The name Nouh Avànd was changed centuries ago to Nàhàvànd. In this region there is a mountainous area named Judi. People of this region are named Judaki. Judi is the name of the mountain on which the Ark of Noah stopped after moving on the waves of water (The Quran, Surah 11, v: 44). According to the old texts and the Holy Books the new generations of mankind restarted their spread throughout the globe from the point on which the Ark of Noah settled. This is the second birthplace of humanity. The first place is the region in which Adam and Eve descended from Eden. For Muslims this point is situated in Mecca, in the region named Bakkah. In Mecca and in Judi there are sanctuaries related to Abraham. In both places the mountains are shaped in a form similar to an egg. In Kabah the place related to Abraham is named Magham éEbrahim, and in Judi the sanctuary is named Emam zadeh Ebrahim. Maybe in this very old place, the Shiites buried the body of one of the children of the Emams whose name was Ebrahim, to keep its sacred aspect, by giving to it an Islamic colour.

[318] Surah 85, v: 1 - 10

والسماء ذات البروج . واليوم الموعود . وشاهد ومشهود . قتل أصحاب الأخدود . النار ذات الوقود . إذ هم عليها قعود . وهم على ما يفعلون بالمؤمنين شهود . وما نقموا منهم إلا أن يؤمنوا بالله العزيز الحميد . الذي له ملك السماوات والأرض والله على كل شيء شهيد . إن الذين فتنوا المؤمنين والمؤمنات ثم لم يتوبوا فلهم عذاب جهنم ولهم عذاب الحريق . سورة البروج. الايات 1-10

[319] Surah 18, v: 9 - 26, *and they remained in their cave for three hundred years and exceeded by nine.*

و لبثوا فى كهفهم ثلاث مائه سنين و ازدادوا تسعا سورة الكهف ـ الايه 25

that in the eyes of the knights, the power of the oppressors was ephemeral, and the period of their supremacy would be short.

The Quran gives the example of the companions of the cave in relation to the companions of Okhdoud in order to explain why certain people left their cities and their social relationships to build sanctuaries at the top of hills, and consecrated their lives to seeking the pearl of ultimate truth inside themselves. The Quran explains that certain periods in history occur during which, the knights are forced to abandon their worldly affairs and become monks and Gnostics. In a revayat, it is reported that Mohammad was very respectful to this category of monks and confirms that they went to the mountains because they were in danger of being arrested and burned alive.[320]

Two main confrontational nations on the borders of Arabia

During the time of the rise of Islam on the Arabian Peninsula, the most important part of the Arabian territory fell under the domination of the Sassanid Dynasty, which spread from Yemen in the southern part of the Peninsula to Hira in its eastern corner. In the north of the Peninsula was the Ghassanid Imarat, an ally of the Byzantine Empire.[321] The Imarat of

---

320ـ وقد قال ابن أبي حاتم :حدثنا إسحاق بن أبي حمزة أبو يعقوب الرازي ، حدثنا السندي بن عبدويه ، حدثنا بكير بن معروف ، عن مقاتل بن حيان ، عن القاسم بن عبد الرحمن بن عبد الله بن مسعود ، عن أبيه ، عن جده عبدالله ابن مسعود قال :قال لي رسول الله صلى الله عليه وسلم " :يا ابن مسعود . "قلت :لبيك يا رسول الله ، قال " :هل علمت أن بني إسرائيل افترقوا على ثنتين وسبعين فرقة ؟ لم ينج منها إلا ثلاث فرق ، قامت بين الملوك والجبابرة بعد عيسى ابن مريم ، عليه السلام ، فدعت إلى دين الله ودين عيسى ابن مريم ، فقاتلت الجبابرة فقتلت فصبرت ونجت ، ثم قامت طائفة أخرى لم يكن لها قوة بالقتال ، فقامت بين الملوك والجبابرة فدعوا إلى دين الله ودين عيسى ابن مريم ، فقتلت وقطعت بالمناشير وحرقت بالنيران ، فصبرت ونجت ثم قامت طائفة أخرى لم يكن لها قوة بالقتال ولم تطق القيام بالقسط ، فلحقت بالجبال فتعبدت وترهبت ، وهم الذين ذكرهم الله ، عز وجل : "ورهبانية ابتدعوها ما كتبناها عليهم ."

تفسير ابن كثير /إسماعيل بن عمر بن كثير القرشي الدمشقي /دار طيبة /سنة النشر1422 :هـ2002 / م

321 Al-Hira الحيرة was a significant city in pre-Islamic Arab history. Hira was a refuge land for the adepts of Manicheanism or Mazdakism. Originally a military encampment, in the fifth and sixth centuries AD, it later became the capital of the Lakhmids. The Arabs were

Ghassanid and the Kingdom of Lakhmid of Hira had been fighting each other for many years. Mecca was situated in the middle of the territories of these two belligerent nations.

In 570 AD Abraha, an Ethiopian military chief, invaded Yemen by the encouragement of the Byzantine Emperor[322] and passed along Mecca, to join the land of Ghassanian, a Byzantine ally,[323] in order to occupy the whole Arabian Peninsula, thereby creating a very powerful front against the Sassanid Empire.[324] But Abrahehfailed in his plan, and Yemen and the south of Arabia, fell under the domination of the Sassanid King Anoushiravan.[325]

---

migrating into the near east of Mesopotamia from the ninth century BC. In the third century AD parts of southern Mesopotamia had a substantial Arab population. Under the Sassanid Empire, southern Mesopotamia was sometimes called Arabaya. The first historical Arab kingdom outside Arabia, Hīra (fourth to seventh centuries), in southern part of Iraq, was a vassal of the Sassanids to stop the invasion of the nomadic tribes from the Arabian Peninsula. The Lakhmid rulers of Hīra were recognized by Shapur II (337-358 AD). The Sassanid Emperor Bahram V ساسانى گور بهرام won the throne with support of Monzar-I, المنذر الاول Lakhmid Prince of Hīra, in 420 AD. These historical events show that the Arabian king of Hīra and the Persian Sassanid Empire were very much interlinked culturally and politically.

تاریخ یعقوبی، ج1 ، ترجمه فارسی. صفحه 245.

[322] Iustinianus Augustus, 483-565 AD

[323] Byzantium was an ancient Greek colony on the site that later became Constantinople, and later still Istanbul. Byzantium was colonized by Greek colonists from Megara in 657 AD. http://en.wikipedia.org/wiki/Byzantium

[324] at-Tarikh ol-Makkeh. Ahmad Soba'i. Farsi translation, p.59. Al-Mo'jam ol-Modon vàl Ghabâél ol-Yàmàniieh. Ebrahim Ahmad al Moghafi. Edition: al-Mànshourat Dâr ol-Hekmat. Sàn'â, 1985. At-Târikh ol Arab fil-Asr el-Jâhelieh. Dr Seyed Abdul Aziz ibn Salim. Edition: Dâr ol-Nehzat el-Arabiyah, 1978. Al-Hey'at ol-Ammeh les-Syahat val-Athir-Athâr ol-Oxodus. Edition: al-Esdâr ol Héy'àt ol-Ammeh lel-Athâr, 2007.

[325] Ibn Husham. Ibid. Farsi version. Vol. 1, pp. 29 to 48.

The interest of the Kings of Hira in poetry

The Kings of Hira were, in general, educated people who acknowledged the need for poets. One of the Kings of Hira was from the family of Umra'ol Qays امرو القیس who was himself a famous poet of his time. It is said that certain people gathered the poetry of the famous poets and wrote it down on scrolls. As mentioned previously, in the 'time of Ignorance', during the period of the pilgrimage, they brought these scrolls to Mecca to hang from the walls of the Kabah in order to recite them in a poetry competition.

We will not enter into any debate about the historical validity of these types of sayings concerning Mo'allaghat é sab'eh معلقات سبعه and ash'ar ol jaheliyat اشعارالجاهلیه, but emphasise the fact that according to the Quran the Bedouins of the Arabian Peninsula, and particularly the inhabitants of Mecca, had an enormous admiration for the art of poetry and recitation. In the Quran, words such as she'r شعر meaning poetry, shâ'er شاعر meaning poet, and sho'àrâ' شُعراء meaning poets, are used to confirm the importance of this art as a commonly held opinion of the people of that time. The existence of rhythms and rhymes in the structures of the first recited verses of the Quran in Mecca gave the impression to certain members of the tribe of Quraysh, familiar with the art of poetry, that those verses were indeed poetry. This caused them to evaluate Mohammad as a poet, who had a genius faculty for captivating the audience with his recitation and the beauty of his compositions, intended to completely push them away from their existing idolatrous beliefs.

Indeed they, when it was said to them, 'There is no deity but Allah,' were arrogant. And were saying, 'Are we to leave our Gods for a mad poet?' Surah 37, v: 35-37.[326]

---

[326]ویقولون أننا لتارکوا آلهتنا لشاعر مجنون. سورة الصافات. الایه 37

So remind [O Mohammad], for you are not, by the favour of your Lord, a soothsayer or a madman. Or do they say [of you], 'A poet for whom we await a misfortune of time?' Surah 52, v: 29, 30.[327]

But they say, '[The revelation is but] a mixture of false dreams; rather, he has invented it; rather, he is a poet. So let him bring us a sign آيه, *miracle, just as the previous [messengers] were sent [with miracles].'* Surah 21, v: 5.[328]

The non-believers thought that Mohammad, as a poet, was captivated by his own poetry and therefore believed that those sentences were inspired from an invisible source.

And when you mention your Lord alone in the Quran, they turn back in aversion. We are most knowing of how they listen to it when they listen to you and [of] when they are in private conversation, when the wrongdoers say: 'You follow not but a man affected by magic (of self-fascination).' Surah 17, v: 46-47.[329]

The Quran rejects this opinion and explains that the verses recited by Mohammad are not poetry, but reminders (AZ Zikr الذكر). The Quran further mentions in Surah 36, v: 69[330] that Mohammad is not a poet (Surah 69, v: 41)[331] and adds: *And the poets – the deviators follow them. Do you not see that in every valley they roam? And that they say what they do not do? Except those [poets] who believe and do righteous deeds and remember Allah often and defend [the*

327ام يقولون شاعر نتربص به ريب المنون سوره الطور الايه 30

328بل قالوا اضغاث احلام بل افتراه بل هو شاعر سورة الانبياء الايه 5

329و اذا ذكرت ربك فى القرآن وحده ،ولّوا على ادبارهم نفورا .نحن اعلم بما يستمعون به اذ يستمعون اليك و اذهم نجوى اذ يقول الظالمون إن تتبعون الا رجلا مسحورا سورة الاسراء الايات 46- 47

330و ما علمناه الشعر و ماينبغى له ان هو الا ذكر و قرآن مبين سوره يس آيه 69

331و ما هو بقول شاعر قليلا ما تومنون سوره الحاقه آيه 41

Muslims] after they were wronged. And those who have wronged are going to know to what [kind of] return they will be returned. Surah 26, v: 224-227.[332]

Preparing the ground for the arrival of the predicted Saviour

Allah has written, 'I will surely overcome, I and My messengers.' Indeed, Allah is Powerful and Exalted in Might. You will not find a people who believe in Allah and the Last Day having affection for those who oppose Allah and His Messenger, even if they were their fathers or their sons or their brothers or their family-tribe عشيره kindred. Those He has decreed within their hearts faith and supported them with spirit from Him. And We will admit them to gardens beneath which rivers flow, wherein they abide eternally. Allah is pleased with them, and they are pleased with Him – those are the party of Allah. Unquestionably, the party of Allah – they are the successful. Surah 58, v: 21,22.[333]

The righteous people were actually awaiting the apparition of their promised Saviour. They knew that God would not change the destiny of a people, if they did not change their destiny themselves.[334] This means that the change should start from within the people who expect the change, and not from the outside. It was therefore necessary for them to prepare the ground. It was because of this that in the period from 380 to 420 AD (about 175 years before Hegira) the community of the righteous in Syria carried out actions in order to prepare the ground for the apparition of the Saviour.

Mani predicts the end of history and the apparition of the paradigm for a new history (in his book of Shabuhragan) as follows. He also

---

332الشعراء يتبعهم الغاوون الم تر انهم فى كل واد يهيمون وأنهم يقولون مالايفعلون الاالذين آمنوا وعملوا الصالحات سوره الشعراء آيه 224

333 كتب الله لأغلبن أنا و رسلى ان الله قوى عزيز سوره المجادله آيه 21و 22

334 ان الله لايغير مابقوم حتى يغيروا ما بانفسهم . سوره الرعد آيه 11 -

elaborates on the struggle between darkness and light as mentioned in Quran (see above):

The end of the world will be presaged by the Great War, a time of conflict and bitterness and waning faith, since by then most of the Light will have been drawn out of the world. There will follow the Second coming of Jesus, who will establish his judgement-seat and separate the righteous from the sinners. Thereafter the gods supporting the cosmos will abandon their tasks, the skies and earths will collapse, and the Great Fire will break out, in which the last particles of Light will be freed and will ascend to the New Paradise as the Last God. Matter will be imprisoned, and the prison will be sealed with a great stone, and finally the New Paradise will be joined again to the Paradise of Light, and its inhabitants, gods and the redeemed will behold once more the face of the Father of Greatness, hidden from them since the struggle began.[335]

---

[335] Boyce's 'Introduction' (Reader8) mentioned by D.N. MacKenzie, Mani's Sâbuhrgân page 503. The close relationship between the eschatological part of the *Šābuhragān* and the Coptic homily 'The Sermon on the Great War' makes it likely that the author of the homily knew and used the *Šābuhragān*. But there remains the problem about whether Kustaios used the Middle Persian version or a Syriac version of it, as P. Alfaric (1919, p. 49) and C. Colpe (1954, pp. 132-33) supposed, or another text of similar content. (Pedersen, 1993, pp. 149-52). Likewise, there is no record and no proof for whether *Šābuhragān* was translated into Syriac later on or translated into Arabic directly from Middle Persian (Colpe, 1954, pp. 123-24, 132). L. Koenen (1986) relates the apocalyptic sources of the *Šābuhragān* to Jewish-Christian and Egyptian ideas. The biographical details in the introduction of *Kephalaia* and the Cologne Mani Codex do not necessarily derive from *Šābuhragān* (Sundermann, 1986a, pp. 83-85). L. Koenen's opinion must be rejected. Obviously he was not aware of the cosmology of the Sabein and their literature concerning the subject such as Ganz-e rabb in Aramaic, similar to the cosmology of Mani.

The travel of Rabieh from Syria to Mecca[336]

About 170 years before the birth of Mohammad, a man named Rabieh came from Syria to Mecca.[337] In Mecca, he married a woman called Fatimah, who originated from Yemen, and whose first husband, Kolâb, had passed away one year previously, leaving two children. One of the children was named Zeyd. After marrying Fatimah, Rabieh brought his wife and Zeyd to Syria. From then on, Zeyd was called by a new name – Qusay. Qusay spent about twenty years in that region, which was the centre of the cultural schools in which the Gnostics and monks were living. These cultural centres were connected to a spiritual centre in Bosra which was under the stewardship of the old righteous seekers, surnamed Bahirâ.[338]

The main teachings of those masters were about the end of the apocalyptical period and the imminent apparition of the divine Saviour, or the new return of Christ. According to the predictions of Habakkuk حبقوق , the place from which the eschatological Saviour was expected to emanate was situated in Pharan فاران , located in Ta'éf الطائف , in the middle of the mountainous region called Bakkah بكة on the Arabian Peninsula[339]. Etymologically Bakkah and Pharan are both related to the source of water or spring.[340] In Pharan there was a spiritual organisation, the centre of which

---

[336] The tale concerning the event of Qusay: Ibn Husham. Ibid Farsi version. Vol. 1, pp. 77 to 92.

[337] Mâne'Mohammad Mânè. Al Àmâken ol Atharieh fi Shebh é Jazirà tol Arabieh. Ed: Vekalat Béenajat Lila'lam 1987. Arabis. Ahmad As Saba'i: Tarikh é Makkeh, translated into Persian. Qusay and his generations after him. pp 56-58.

[338] Ibn Husham. Ibid. Farsi version, pp. 115-117.

[339] Ibn Husham is citing the opinion of an expert called Abu Obaydeh about the place of Bakkah. According to him Bakkah is situated on the lower part of the city of Mecca in the valley of the mountain of Abu Qobays جبل ابوقبیس . There is place in which there is enough water for the thirsty camels. Ibn Husham. Ibid. Farsi version. Vol. 1, p. 71.

[340]اذ الشريب اخذته أكة - فخلّه حتى ييک بيگة

When the camels are very thirsty, let them make crowd around Bakkah. This is a poem cited by ibn Husham from the Period of Ignorance. Ibid. vol. 1, Farsi version, p.71.

was based in a monastery in Bosra, in Syria. Zeyd (Qusay) and Rabieh were affiliated to this organisation.

Zeyd (Qusay) returned to Arabia, to his native place in the region of Mecca. Between 390 and 450 AD, people in that region moved constantly around the mountains and desert. The first plan of the 'millenary people of the organisation of Bosra' was to prepare the ground for the apparition of the promised Saviour (موعود آخرالزمان). They bestowed on Zeyd (Qusay) a mission, to stabilize the wandering tribes in the frame of a city (bàlàd). In order to create a city in the middle of the desert they needed to create a water pool. Zeyd (Qusay) engaged some well-makers and, within a short period of time, they extracted water and filled the pool in Bakkah. Besides this water pool, Zeyd engaged a second team to build a wooden building in a cubic form, called Kabah.

Figure 17 - A coin with the name of Oto Fradat.
A regional King of the province of Pars, Iran.

He called the cubic building the 'House of Allah' and dedicated the construction to the unique Creator of the universe.[341] After a short period,

---

[341] The Cubic House made by Zeyd dedicated to God could have been inspired by the building called Kabah Zartosht کعبه زرتشت, in Shiraz in Iran. The Ka'ba-ye Zartosht (alt: Kaba-ye Zardusht, Kaba-ye Zardosht, Persian کعبه زرتشت), meaning the 'Cube of Zoroaster', is a fifth century B.C.E. Achaemenid-era tower-like construction at Naqsh-e Rustam, an archaeological site just north-west of Persepolis, Iran. The name Ka'ba-ye

the caravans of the traders, who were on the path of the silver road between Africa and Asia Minor, passing from Syria to Arabia towards Yemen and Africa (and vice-versa), directed their camels and horses to this new 'water centre' in the middle of the desert. Mecca became an important transit-trading centre, and Zeyd (Qusay) built five other wells in the same region and established rules and laws, as a result of which the visitors and traders staying in Mecca had to pay tax as a donation for the Lord of the house of Allah, who offered them water, hospitality, and security for their affairs. The Bedouins from the centre of Arabia also went to Mecca and set up their tents in order to reside in that place. Zeyd (Qusay) proposed that the group of Bedouins willing to stay in Mecca should settle their tents around the four corners of the house of Allah. Some years later, those tents were replaced with houses. Beside the Kabah, Zeyd (Qusay) created a gathering house called Dar on Nàdouh (دارالندوة) , in which men older than forty years from the tribes residing in Mecca were able to participate and debate about the important decisions to be made. The intention was to solve any problem between the inhabitants of Mecca, as well as to declare war and peace with other tribes, and generally discuss any general issue. Zeyd (Qusay) was a monotheist and a follower of the path of Abraham. He began to teach the inhabitants of Mecca the tradition of Abraham. He reconstituted the method of

---

Zartosht probably dates to the fourteenth century, when many pre-Islamic sites were identified with figures and events of the Quran or the Shāhnāme. The structure, which is a copy of a sister building at Pasargadae, was built either by Darius I (521-486 BC) when he moved to Persepolis, by Artaxerxes II (404-358 BC) or Artaxerxes III (358-338 BC). The building at Pasargadae is a few decades older. The wall surrounding the tower dates to Sassanid times.

This Cubic House was used by the Persian monotheists in the pre-Islamic period as the central orientation point for prayer. A coin with the name of Oto Fradat, a regional King of the province of Pars, Iran, in the Solukide time, shows the ceremony of prayer in the direction of the Cubic House. This place has existed from 550 BC until today in Persepolis, Shiraz, Iran, built up by Darius the Great, the second Achaemenid king, 2,500 years ago.

Abraham, such as the ritual of daily prayers, ablution, and pilgrimage, and so on.

However, problems started to occur in Mecca from the moment the Bedouins of Adnan origin entered the city and stayed there. These people were not monotheists, but idol worshippers. They were so attached to their idols that when they settled in Mecca, they positioned their idols all around the Kabah, and even inside of the house of Allah. They began to blend the method of Abraham, based on monotheism (Hanif), with their idolatry by pretending that they considered the idols their own intermediaries between themselves and the Lord of the House of Kabah. This mixture created a significant problem in the history of Mecca. In addition, by settling in Mecca the tribe imported all the customs and folklore in which they believed, including: a lack of respect for women; gender inequality; the killing of newborn girls by burying them just after their birth; lending money with interest; lack of respect for the equality between 'the children of Adam' (Bàni - Âdàm - بنى آدم), practising slavery; beheading people; fighting against other tribes to confirm their courage and the authenticity of their origins; having pride in their ancestors; believing in the magical-mysterious power of stones and wood; disbelieving in life after death and disbelieving in the resurrection and return of the soul and spirit; and considering angels to be the daughters of Allah (the Lord of the House of Kabah). This ensemble of behaviour was referred to as 'Ignorance' (al-Jâheliyàt- الجاهلية).

The followers of Qusay's rules were named Hanif, monotheists. They performed their daily ritual prayer in the direction of the Kabah, the House of Allah. But within a short while, this house lost its place of unity, and became an idol centre instead. Worshipping in the direction of the Kabah became harder and harder as praying towards the Kabah became a prayer in the direction of the idols. As such, the house of Allah was transformed to Dar-ol-Asnam (دارُالاصنام).[342]

Qusay had four sons, but distributed all the main responsibilities of the management of the city of Mecca to one of his children – Abd od Dâr (عبدالدار).[343] Abd od Dâr took on various responsibilities such as Hejâbat (الحجابة covering the Kabah once a year), Seghâyat (السقاية serving water to the pilgrims), Sedânat (السدانة keeping the Kabah-key) and leadership of Dâr on Nàdouh (دار الندوه the central gathering place reserved for Arab men older than forty years).[344]

In the time of Qusay, the Kabah became a very important point on the transit road of the traders. It brought to the family of Qusay a considerable amount of money, and the descendants of Qusay consequently became rich and wealthy traders. Yet according to the rules of Qusay, they had to distribute their wealth between all the people of that region. During the years after the death of Qusay, his children started to work with new collaborators, rich traders who did not believe in the tradition of Abraham, and they themselves became uninterested in monotheism and moved towards idolatry.

Mecca after Qusay

After Qusay, Mecca was managed according to the rules of Qusay. The city was divided into four sub-divisions, each part handled by a group of the Quraysh tribe. The leader of Mecca was Abd od Dar, son of Qusay. When Abd od Dar passed away the children of his brother, Abd Manaf, decided to take certain positions out of the hands of the children of Abd od Dar. The children of Abd Manaf were Abd do Shams, Hashem,

---

[342] 'Dar ol Asnam' means house of idolatry.

[343] Ibn Husham. Ibid; Farsi version; Vol.1, p.85; his other sons were called Abdol Ozza (عبدالعزی), Abd é Mànâf (عبدمناف), Abd (عبد).

[344] Ibn Husham. Ibid.

Motalleb, and Nowfel. From this moment onwards the tribe of Quraysh lost its unity and fell into the trap of internal conflict over power and position. Hashem, the son of Abd Manaf, took responsibility for giving water and food to the pilgrims of Mecca. Hashem was the first person to create a new rule for the Quraysh tribe, which was to make two journeys per year during Easter and winter times towards Yemen and Syria; this was called 'Rehlat o Shetâ' vàs Sayf' (رحلة الشتاء و الصيف). He passed away during one of his travels to Syria and left his responsibilities to his younger brother Motalleb. Motalleb went to Syria, bringing with him the son of his brother Hashem. This child was named Abdul-Motalleb. After the death of Motalleb in Yemen, Abdul- Motalleb, son of Hashem, took on the responsibilities of serving the pilgrims.[345]

In the time of Abdul-Motalleb, Mecca had become the centre of ignorance, with a system of slavery in the hands of the powerful chiefs of the bands and clans, who were idol worshippers and disbelievers of the invisible world. At the same time, a great number of Manichean and Mazdakites escaped from Persia and Byzantine lands and travelled to Arabia to take refuge in the mountains and caves. Because they were not related to any tribes of that region, they ended up being captured by the tribes and forced into slavery.

In 550 AD, one of the sons of Abdul-Motalleb called Zobeyr (زبير) gathered together the chiefs of the Quraysh in the house of a man of Mecca called Abdollah Jad'ân (عبدالله جدعان), and made a solid pact between them to preserve the rights of defenceless people such as the refugees, prisoners, poor people, and orphans. This pact was named 'Half ol Fodoul' (حلف الفضول).[346] The children of Abdul-Motalleb, with their respective families, spent their time between Mecca, Yemen, and Syria.

---

[345] Ibn Husham. Ibid. Farsi version.: pp. 85- 99

[346] Ibn Husham. Ibid. pp.88-89 Before the birth of Mohammad (570 AD), the Hanifs of Mecca, believing in the Kabah and the Lord of the cubic house, began to orient their

The birth of Prophet Mohammad

Abdollah and Ameneh, the mother and father of Mohammad, together with Abu Talib, the father of Ali and the uncle of Prophet Mohammad, travelled very often to Syria.

The parents of Mohammad were travelling back from Syria to Mecca fifty-three years before Hegira.[347] During this travel, Abdollah (father of Mohammad) passed away before seeing the birth of his son,[348] so Mohammad was fatherless after he was born.[349] As previously mentioned, Ameneh, the mother of Mohammad, sent him to a Bedouin tribe living in the middle of the desert, named Bani Sa'd, to stay with a wet nurse called Halimeh as Sa'dieh (حليمة السعدية)[350] for a period of three years, which was then extended by two more years. This long period of five years was an opportunity for young Mohammad to learn the true and pure Arabic. After the return of Mohammad to Mecca, the members of the Hanif community and the spiritual wise men of Mecca, who were connected to the monastery of Bosra, took care of him in order to prepare him and

---

attention during daily prayers towards Jerusalem, in order to avoid bowing to the idols placed inside of the house.

[347] Ibn Husham. Ibid- Arabic version. Vol.I p.97/ Farsi version. P.104-105: "when Ameneh-Mohammad's mother- was pregnant of him, saw in vision a powerful light emanated from her womb in which she perceived the Palaces of Bosra in Syria". This vision- dream confirms the relationship of Mohammad-family to the school-temple of Bosra under management of the spiritual-masters named Bahira.

[348] Ibn Husham-Ibid- Arabic version. Vol.I p.97

ولد رسول الله يوم الاثنين لاثنتى عشره ليله خلت من شهر ربيع الاول .عام الفيل

[349] Ibn Husham-Ibid- Arabic version. Vol.I p.97

ثم يلبث عبدالله ابن عبدالمطلب ابو رسول الله أن هلك و ام رسول الله حامل به

[350] Ibn Husham. Ibid. Farsi version. Vol 1. P.106

develop his extrasensorial perception to receive guidance for his divine historical mission by way of inner vibrations.[351]

Vàhi: revelation and extrasensorial telecommunication

Thus He reveals, yoohi, to you as (He did) to those before you. Surah 42, v: 3.

كذلك يوحى اليک و الى الذين من قبلک. سورة الشورى. الايه 3

In the commentary on this verse, regarding the manner of Vàhi (revelation to the prophets), ibn Kathir states:

'…Aisheh (the last wife of Mohammad) reported: "A companion of the Prophet Mohammad called Harith ibn Husham posed a question to Mohammad about how he gets the revelations, Vàhi. The Prophet replied: 'sometimes it comes to me such as the vibration of the bell, salsala tol Jaras. It is hard for me to bear it because it makes me warm by fever and sweating. (Aisha attests and confirmed that during the cold days, when he received the revelation, his forehead was covered in sweat due to a fever). And sometimes the angels talk to me in the shape of a man.' In another version of the same report it is said: 'The angel comes and takes form in my sight and communicates to me and I am filled by it'. (yà'tini al-màlàk fà yàtàmathàlà li và yokàlémoni; yàtini almàlàk ràjolan fàyokàlémoni)."'[352]

This saying of Harith ibn Husham reported by Aisha is mentioned by a considerable number of reporters whose names are cited by ibn Kathir.

---

[351] Ibn Husham, ibid, Farsi version, p.85. Al Harith ibn Abdol Ozza ibn Rifà'ah ibn Màlàn ibn Nasereh ibn Fassieh ibn Nasr ibn Sàid ibn Bakr ibn Hawazen. The milk brother of Mohammad was called Abdollah ibn Hàrith.

[352] Tafsir ol Gartabi. Commentary of Quran. Mohammad ibn Ahmad al Ansari al Ghartabi. Ed: Dar ol Fekr; p.51. Tafsir é Ibn Kathir Commentary of Quran. Ismail ibn Omar é Kathir Dameshghi. Dar ot Tayybeh. 2002, p.187.

Allah chooses from the angel's messengers and from the people (to bring the message to the prophet to communicate to the people). Surah 22, v: 75.

الله يصطفى من الملئكة رسلا و من الناس... سورة الحج. الايه 75

And it is not for any human being that Allah should speak to him. Except by revelation, Vahi: either from behind a partition or He sends a 'messenger' to reveal; by His permission, what He wills. Surah 42, v: 51.

And thus we have revealed to you an inspiration (Rouh) of our command; (while) you did not know what is the Book or (what is) faith. But we have made it a light by which We guide whom We will of our servants. And you guide to a straight path. Surah 42, v: 52.[353]

A direct conversation with Allah is therefore not possible. Instead, the communication is done through a curtain that separates the visible and invisible sides (shahadàt – ghayb; molk and malakout) from each other, or by apparition in the human form of an angel who delivers the divine message. However, the voice of the angel is not audible to the ears. Instead, Vàhi, (revelation) originates from a kind of inner vibration, which is called nédâ. Allah bestows men and angels as messengers of telecommunication by Vàhi, meaning through an inner vibration referred to as nédâ ol khafeyy (نداء الخفىّ), the divine message to the prophets.

By attentively studying the Quran, we certainly understand that Mohammad accomplished the various steps of his mission through an inner guidance. By 'inner guidance' we mean a non-audible voice, namely nédâ. This inner voice, nédâ, constantly instructed Mohammad as he set out the methods and strategy of his actions and reactions in front of his assorted audiences. The inner voice, nédâ, is an important factor in the missions of prophets and spiritual masters. The Quran often stresses the

---

[353] Ibn Kathir explains that Rouh in this place corresponds with the Quran. Tafsir Ibn Kathir. P. 217.

importance of this. Prophets and spiritual masters are among the people whose supra-sensorial perceptions are developed, due to which they can hear the inner voice, nédâ, just as they can perceive the sphere of non-concrete forms. The tales of the prophets in the frame of the Quran give us a multitude of examples about this particular sense. Through talking about the lives of different prophets, the Quran reminds us that during a period of seclusion, in a corner in front of a Mehrab, an individual is able to awaken his natural capacity of telepathy by practising certain spiritual exercises, and step by step opens the sensory capabilities of his non-material body (known as the astral body) in order to capture the non-audible voices. We read in the story of Moses that, whilst walking on the mountain, he perceived a light emanating from a bush which was on fire, and when he approached it he heard a voice talking to him.

In this story, the Quran uses the word nédâ (نداء) and not sédâ (صدا), the meaning of which will be described in the following sentences:

But when he came to it, he – by receiving a 'nédâ' – was called – noudià – from the right side of the valley in a blessed spot – from the tree, 'O Moses, indeed I am Allah, Lord of the worlds.' Surah 28, v: 30.

When he called to his Lord *a private supplication. Surah 19, v: 3. When he (Zakharia) communicated with his Rabb by using an 'inner vibration' (nédâ àn khàfeyyâ) – without any propagation of sound.*

اذ نادى ربه نداء خفيا. سوره مريم. الايه 3

Therefore, Vàhi signifies telecommunication via inner vibration, nédâ, without any sonority or perceivable sound.

So the angels communicated with him via 'inner vibration', nâdàt- nâdâ (فنادته *الملائكة), while he (Zakaria) was standing in prayer in the chamber:*

(O Zakaria) Indeed, Allah gives you good tidings of John, confirming a word from Allah and [who will be] honourable, abstaining [from women], and a prophet from among the righteous. Surah 3, v: 39.

In the Quran, Vàhi, revelation, is a very wide topic.

And your 'Ràbb' communicated by revelation (Vàhi) to the bees (the following messages): 'Take for yourself among the mountains, houses, and among the trees and [in] that which they construct. Then eat from all the fruits and follow the ways that your Ràbb laid down [for you].' Surah 16, v: 68-69.[354]

And We communicated by revelation (Vàhi) to the mother of Moses (the following message): 'Suckle him; but when you fear for him, cast him into the river and do not fear and do not grieve. Indeed, We will return him to you and will make him [one] of the messengers.' Surah 28, v: 7.[355]

And indeed, the Quran is 'what is sent gradually', تنزيل *(tanzil) by 'Ràbb-ol-Alàmin'* ربُّ العالَمين *(the Lord of the worlds). The Trustworthy Spirit has brought it down. Upon your heart, (hence such as 'neda', non-audible to ears) [O Mohammad], that you may be of the warners. In a clear Arabic language. And indeed, it is [mentioned] in the scriptures of former people. And has it not been a sign to them that it is recognised by the scholars of the Children of Israel? And even if We had revealed it to one among the foreigners. And he had recited it to them [perfectly], they would [still] not have been believers in it. Thus have We inserted disbelief into the hearts of the criminals.* Surah 26, v: 192 - 200.[356]

That is from what your Ràbb has communicated to you [O Mohammad] by revelation (Aowhâ اوحى *) of wisdom.* Surah 17, v: 39.[357]

---

354 و اوحى ربک الى النحل أن اتخذى من الجبال بيوتاً و من الشجر و مما يَعرشون .ثم كُلى من كل الثمرات فاسلكى سبلَ ربکِ .سوره النحل آيه هاى 68 و 69

- 355و أوحينا الى امّ موسى أن أرضعيه فاذا خفت عليه فألقيه فى اليَم و لاتخافى ولاتحزنى إنا رآدّوه اليک و جاعلوه من المرسلين .سوره القصص آيه 7

- 356و إنه لتنزيل رب العالمين نزل به الروح الامين على قلبک لتكون من المنذرين بلسان عربى مبين و إنه لفى زبر الاولين اولم يكن لهم آية أن يعلمه علماء بنى اسرائيل ولونزلناه على بعض الاعجمين فقرأه عليهم ماكانوا به مومنين كذلک سلكناه فى قلوب المجرمين سوره الشعراء . الايات 193- 200

- 357ذلک مما اوحى اليک ربک من الحكمة سوره الأسراء ــآيه 39

And this Quran was communicated to me (by revelation أوحَى) that I may warn you thereby and whomever it reaches... Those to whom We have given the 'Scripture' (Bible) recognise it (the Quran) as they recognise their [own] sons. Surah 6, v: 19, 20.[358]

Our understanding is that Vàhi does not relate to the source that communicates the message, but the method of communication. Vàhi signifies 'to communicate without the usage of any words.' It can be accomplished by sending inner vibrations into the heart of the receiver, or by making gesticulations and bodily expressions before the eyes of the people to whom the message would be communicated, as mentioned in the affair of Zachariah when he communicated his orders to the people in front of the gate of the temple.

So he – Zachariah – came out to his people from the prayer chamber and signalled to them (fa Aowhâ elayhim فاوحى اليهم) to exalt [Allah] in the morning and afternoon. Surah 19, v: 11.[359]

On the other hand, communication without the use of words is not confined to Allah or the prophets and saints, as even wrongdoers pass messages amongst themselves via this method.

And indeed do the devils communicate by revelation (youhoun/ليوحون) to their allies among men to dispute with you. Surah 6, v: 121.[360]

In conclusion, Vâhi, or telecommunication, is not necessarily the source of the discovery of hidden and unknown works. A written text or the content of an existing book can be communicated, sentence by

---

[358] و أوحَى الَّى هذا القرآن لانذركم به ...الذين آتيناهم الكتاب يعرفونه كما يعرفون ابنائهم .سوره الانعام الايات 19 و 20

[359] فخرج على قومه من المحراب فاوحى اليهم ان سبحوا بكره و عشيا سوره مريم .الايه 11

[360] - وإنَّ الشَّيَاطينَ لَيُوحُونَ اِلَىٰٓ اُولِيائِهِمْ لِيُجَادِلُوكُمْ سوره الانعام الايه 121

sentence, line by line and chapter by chapter, between a 'message-sender' and a 'message-receiver' just by telepathy and without the use of any words. This style of transition of the message only refers to the technique of communication. It is said clearly in the Quran that the people of the Book (followers of the Bible, Torah, and Gospel) know the Quran, which is communicated to Mohammad by Vâhi, as they know their own children.[361]

Nédâ is communicable from one man to another man, or from a man to non-material beings. In the tale of Zachariah for instance, it is said that in the corner of his Mehrab he was talking by inner voice, nédâ, to his divine Lord.

When the inner voice emanates from an outer source, such as another man or a non-material being, such as an angel, then the action is introduced as Vâhi وحى. Through Vâhi, the Lord guides insects, such as bees, to go far from their hive in order to collect pollen and return safely back to their colony. Another example in the Quran: an ordinary person such as the mother of Moses received Vâhi from her Lord to act according to a hidden strategy in response to Pharaoh's plan. According to the Quran, besides this general aspect of Vâhi, which relates to the awakened sixth sense of all living beings, including mankind, there is a particular type of Vâhi, which is exclusively consecrated for developed spiritual masters, such as the messengers of God, the apostles, and the wise men,

---

[361] Surah 26, v: 193 - 200. Sédâ صدا is when the air molecules vibrate. Consequently, in an empty space sédâ cannot exist due to the lack of a physical means for carrying the vibrations. Another particularity of sédâ صدا is the fact that the sound waves cause vibrations in the air and in the sensitive auditory canals of the ears. As a result, when the outer voice, sédâ صدا, is propagated, everybody is able to hear it. On the contrary, the inner voice touches the inner ear, and it is only audible to the person to whom the message is delivered. The inner voice is captured first by the heart of the receiver, and then in a further step transfers from his heart to his brain, where he perceives this voice as though somebody is talking to him inside his mind. In this case, the inner voice is audible to one or a group of people related to each other, to whom it is propagated, even if they are within a crowd of non-related people.

by which they receive guidance from the invisible world and orient themselves and their followers to the straight path.

Furthermore, the Holy Books are introduced as revelations of sentences to the prophets, which were inspired in the manner of Vàhi by an invisible source. This invisible source can be an angel, Gabriel, or the soul of an advanced spiritual master, even after his death, to his disciple. This means that it is possible for an advanced master to teach the sentences of an existing book to his disciple and to send him on a mission purely by telepathy and telecommunication, or communication from a distance, to be more specific.

The fact that the mission of the prophethood includes the presence of a teacher or master amongst a group of people, a teacher who speaks the same language as those people and who lives amongst them and wishes to propagate his message, imposes the necessity of constant communication between him and the source of his information. He is an intermediary between the people and his own source. He receives questions from the people and trans-communicates them to his central source, and then receives the answer by telepathy, which he communicates back to his audience. One necessary aptitude in order to become a prophet is to have this developed inner ability of telecommunication. The seed of this ability or inner sense is innate in each individual, and can grow by employing a certain process of introspection. This is the method of Gnosticism. It is one of the reasons why, according to the description of the Holy Books, the majority of the prophets spent a period of time in seclusion and isolation, often in caves.[362]

Similar to the Quran's example of the bees, there are also certain passages mentioning bees amongst the manuscripts of the inhabitants of

---

[362] Such as Élie (hébreu: *ēliyahū*, 'Mon Dieu est Yahweh'; Syriaque: *īlyā*, إلياس *ilyās*) on the Carmel mountain, Moses on the Mountain of Tour of Sinai (طور سيناء), Jesus on the Olive Mountain (جبل الزيتون). The Qumran community were used to living in the hand-made caves in the mountainous region of the Dead Sea (بحرالميت).

Qumran. This is a perfect example of the solid continuity between the traditions of the spiritual masters to whom the lineage of Mohammad was related. The Quran and the scrolls of the Dead Sea do not specify how to care for bees or how to develop a colony of bees, but just refer to the inner sense of those insects. The reason for this is the fact that the people of the Qumran community were 'millenary people', and they expected the arrival of the Saviour. The manner in which they were expecting him was not passive, just waiting for his arrival, but rather active, by preparing the ground for him to appear. It was because of this fact that besides their trust in the certainty of his apparition, they also carried out intensive spiritual exercises and cultural researches in order to be ready to accomplish tasks as the soldiers of that eschatological Saviour in the moment of his appearance.

By studying the Quran, the influence and authority of a hidden master on the personality of Mohammad becomes clear. The mission of Mohammad does not consist of a series of confrontations between him and his contemporaries, because a third aspect perfectly dominates this equation. Instead, Mohammad was an intermediary between the invisible world and his people and had been trained to accomplish this mission from his childhood.

They are those that Allah guided, therefore (O Mohammad) follow their guidance[363]

أُولَٰئِكَ الَّذِينَ هَدَى اللَّهُ فَبِهُدَاهُمُ اقْتَدِهْ

Reporters such as ibn Husham, Tabari, ibn Eshagh and others believed that Mohammad received the first Vàhi at the age of forty. However, as we explained previously this hypothesis is incorrect and does not correspond with the verses of the Quran. As we explained before,

---

[363]- سورة الانعام الاية 90   The Quran, Surah al-An'âm. Verse 90

Mohammad received the first manifestations of invisible beings in his visions and dreams during his childhood,[364] and under this invisible guidance he started his cultural and spiritual education, first in Mecca under the teaching of the Honafa such as Abdul-Motalleb, Abu Talib, and Waraka ibn Nowfel, and then from the age of twelve years and onwards under the guidance of the Masters of the Bosra temple, known as Bahira (بحيراء). There is no doubt that according to the Quran, Mohammad knew more than one language and was able to read and write perfectly, and knew the content of a number of old scriptures by heart. He also knew the secret of exact recitation of the verses of the Holy Books. Yet he did not have the right to preach to people as he was still under the age of forty.

This is why we should distinguish two categories of the verses of the Quran related to the life of Mohammad. The first category refers to the verses that guided Mohammad to spiritual maturity, starting from his childhood to the age of forty. The second category refers to the verses that Mohammad received as an intermediary in order to communicate the teachings of the Book to the people. This distinction between the two periods of Mohammad's life, in relationship to the Quran, helps us to avoid the trap of an amalgam of misunderstanding.

During the first period, Mohammad learned the content of the old Holy Books such as Sohof and Zobor, memorising them perfectly, and he learned the art of preaching and reciting aloud. During the second period of his life after the age of forty, Mohammad, under the continuous orders that he received through Vàhi, started to preach gradually and step

---

[364] Ibn Husham. Ibid. Farsi version, vol. 1, p. 111. In his childhood, when Mohammad and some other children of his age were taking care of the goats, two men – dressed in white – took him and brought him out of the sight of the children. They opened his chest and cleaned his heart with white snow. Whilst performing this 'operation' they were talking to each other about Mohammad, and the immense weight of the prophethood-mission that he would carry on his shoulders. According to some reports, Mohammad was the only witness of this strange experience. This was the first meeting with the angels.

by step to the crowd. It was during this period that his invisible teacher ordered him to recite the report of Abraham to the people.[365] According to the Quran, it was not up to Mohammad to select a part of the Book that he knew and recite it to the people. Instead, he was following the guidance he received. Even a category of disbelievers who were amongst the daily audiences of Mohammad did not accuse him of inventing these tales himself. They did not have any doubt about the existence of a written scripture being the source of the speeches of Mohammad. Their position of denial was rather based on the idea that in their eyes the content of this written scripture was simply composed of old written tales (àsâtir), and not by divine guidance.[366]

They said: *'we heard (Mohammad reciting) and if we want to, we can do as he does, because he recites just the old written legends'*. In response to this Mohammad told them that the tales recited by him were extracted from the Holy Books. But these people considered the corresponding Holy Books that Mohammad referred to (such as the Bible), to be old written legends without any spiritual values.

The disbelievers who argued with Mohammad asked him from which written source he had gained the wisdom that made him consider himself as a messenger. Mohammad was reading, reciting, and introducing fragment by fragment the different sections of a Book, 'The Quran', and they kept asking him to show them the source of the validity of his information.[367]

---

[365] Surah as Sho'arâ verse 69   سورة الشعراء – الاية 69.

[366] Sàtàrà means writing text line by line, ketâb é màstour means a book written line by line, ostoureh means the text of a legend written line by line, and àsâtir is the plural of ostoureh.

[367] وَقَالَ الَّذِينَ كَفَرُوا لَوْلَا نُزِّلَ عَلَيْهِ الْقُرْآنُ جُمْلَةً وَاحِدَةً كَذَلِكَ لِنُثَبِّتَ بِهِ فُؤَادَكَ وَرَتَّلْنَاهُ تَرْتِيلًا / "الفرقان 32 -

214

The position of those who did not believe in the validity of the Quran

The monotheists of Mecca wanted to change the paradigms of the tribal traditions in Mecca and to create a different society based on human values.

People who were living in that region between Mecca and Medina were categorized by the Quran into two ranks: those 'of the Book' اهل الكتاب, and those who were called 'Ummi' امّی .

Say to the people of the Book اهل الكتاب, *and the Umiin did you convert to Islam? Surah 3, v: 20.*[368]

'People of the Book', (Ahl ol Ketab) is a global description to qualify the Christians, the Jews, and the followers of other monotheist religions such as Sabiean الصابئين and Majous المجوس. It does not mean that a person from the category of 'Ahl ol Ketab' is necessarily able to read the scriptures. It means that his world vision is based on the teachings of previous Holy Books. The second category named by the Quran is 'Ummi', which consists of those whose world vision is not related to the teachings of any previous book, but just on the sayings of their maternal tale tellers.

And among them are unlettered ones who do not know the Scripture except in wishful thinking, but they are only assuming. So woe to those who write the 'scripture' with their own hands, then say, 'This is from Allah,' in order to exchange it for a

---

small price. Woe to them for what their hands have written and woe to them for what they earn. Surah 2, v: 78, 79. [369]

And indeed, there is among them a party who alter the Scripture with their tongues so you may think it is from the Scripture, but it is not from the Scripture. And they say, 'This is from Allah,' but it is not from Allah. And they speak untruth about Allah while they know. Surah 3, v: 78. [370]

As we can see, according to the Quran, it was common during this period for certain literate people to fabricate false sentences by imitation, with their tongue or by pen, and attribute them to a divine source, namely Allah. Based on this logic, the disbelievers accused Mohammad of telling them things that were not even written in the frame of the Bible, and they asked him for information about his source. They said: 'maybe you want to change the paradigms of our tribe in order to become our chief, and you use Abraham's name as a pretext for your hidden plan.'

Those to whom We have given the previous Book recite يتلونه/ it (the Quran) with its true recital حق تلاوته. They are the ones who believe in it. And whoever disbelieves in it – it is they who are the losers. Surah 2, v: 121.

Indeed, those who have been given the Scripture well know that it (the Quran) is the truth from their Lord. And Allah is not unaware of what they do. Surah 2, v: 144.

Say, 'Then is it other than Allah I should seek as judge while it is He who has revealed to you the Book explained in detail?' And those to whom We previously gave the Scripture know that it (the Quran) is sent down from your Lord in truth, so never be among the doubters. Surah 6, v: 114.

---

[369] و منهم امیون لایعلمون الکتاب الا امانی و ان هم الا یظنون. فویل للذین یکتبون الکتاب بایدیهم ثم یقولون هذا من عندالله لیشتروا به ثمنا قلیلا فویل لهم مماکتبت ایدیهم و ویل لهم مما یکسبون سوره البقره الایات 78-79

[370] و ان منهم لفریقا یلون السنتهم بالکتاب لتحسبوه من الکتاب و ماهو من کتاب سوره آل عمران آیه 78

The disbelievers asked Mohammad to change the content of the Quran or to bring them another book, so that they could accept him as the Prophet and follow his guidance. They had a problem with the content of the Quran, because it contradicted the principles of their beliefs. For this reason they completely rejected the Quran.

And the Messenger has said, 'O my Lord, indeed my people have taken this Quran as a thing abandoned.' And thus have We made for every Prophet an enemy from among the criminals. But sufficient is your Lord as a guide and a helper. And those who disbelieve say, 'Why was the Quran not revealed to him all at once?' Thus it is that We may strengthen thereby your heart. And We have spaced it distinctly. Surah 25, v: 30 to 32.[371]

The disbelievers of Mecca doubted the origin of the Quran. A cited verse states: 'énnà Ghowmi' إنَّ قومى meaning 'my tribe', 'the people of my tribe'. The first people who Mohammad preached to were close members of his own family 'àshireh' عشيره.[372]

Therefore, the first verse by which Mohammad received the order to officialise his mission was to preach to his Ashireh; 'va Anzer àshiratakàl àghràbin' وَ أنذِر عَشيرَتَكَ الأقرَبين . So the closer members of Mohammad's family were the first people of his tribe to hear the appeal of Mohammad to change their paradigms, and the majority of his family rejected his call, as the verse stresses:

---

[371] و قال الرسول يا رب ان قومى اتخذوا هذا القرآن مهجورا . و كذلك جعلنا لكل نبى عدوا من المجرمين و كفى بريك هاديا و نصيرا . و قالا الذين كفروا لولا نزل عليه القرآن جمله واحده اكذلك لنثبت به فوادك و رتلناه ترتيلا .سوره الفرقان الايات 30تا 32

[372] Ashireh عشيره which can be considered the equivalent of 'family'. It is derived from the word 'àshàr, yà'shoro, oshr' عَشَرَ، يعشر، عُشر . The word àshàr عَشر means ten.

O my Lord, my people, the closer people of my tribe, of my land, abandon this Quran. [373] يارب ان قومى اتخذوا هذا القرآن مهجورا

The disbelievers of Mecca refuted any probable inner relationship between Mohammad and the invisible world. They rejected the words of Mohammad about Gabriel and the angel of revelation. They believed that the source of the Quran was a written text or scripture in a language different from Arabic that had been imported from other lands, based on the principle of anti-tribal rules; a strange manuscript from a foreign civilisation, to impose a new order upon the people of Mecca.

They say: 'What is this messenger that eats food and walks in the markets? Why was there not sent down to him an angel so he would be with him a warner?' Or why is not a treasure presented to him, or does he not have a garden from which he eats?' And the wrongdoers say, 'You follow not but a man affected by magic.' Look how they strike for you comparisons; but they have strayed, so they cannot find a way.' Surah 25, v: 7 - 9. [374]

And they say, 'Why has a sign not been sent down to him from his Lord?' Say, 'Indeed, Allah is Able to send down a sign, but most of them do not know.' Surah 6, v: 37. [375]

So in summary according to the Quran, the disbelievers said: Mohammad is just a man similar to others, eating and walking in the streets, and doing business in the markets. He does not have any special gifts; he doesn't even perform any miracles. How does he expect to be accepted by us as a prophet with his empty hands? His only difference to

---

[373] Surah 25 'al-Forghân', v: 30.

[374] و قالوا مالهذا الرسول ياكل الطعام و يمشى فى الاسواق لولا انزل اليه ملك فيكون معه نذيرا او يلقى اليه كنزا او نكون له جنه ياكل منها و قال الظالمون ان تتبعون الا رجلا مسحورا انظر كيف ضربوا لك الامثال فضلوا فلايستطيعون سبيلا. سورة الفرقان الايات 7-9

[375] و قالوا لولا نُزّل عليه آيه من ربه. قل " :ان الله قادر على ان يُنَزّل آيه ولكن اكثرهم لايعلمون "سوره انعام آيه 37

us is his faculty of inscribing. He is in fact a writer. He knows how to inscribe what is translated to him by his foreign companions. The disbelievers were certain that Mohammad was not alone in his activities. They suppose him to be the agent of a 'cultural invasion' against the Bedouin's ancestral principles. They accused him of being assisted by a team of non-Arabic اعجمى educated people. They believed that those people translated the sentences of the original scripture اساطير, one by one, and dictated them day and night to Mohammad, and that Mohammad in turn was carefully writing down the sentences and reciting them to the people of Quraysh.

And those who disbelieve say, 'This Quran is not except a falsehood he invented, and another people assisted him in it.' But they have committed an injustice and a lie (by doing this wrong accusation). And they say: 'written Legends of the former peoples which he has written down, and they are dictated to him morning and afternoon.' Say: O Mohammad, 'It has been revealed by He who knows every secret within the heavens and the earth. Indeed, He is ever Forgiving and Merciful.' Surah 25, v: 4 - 6.[376]*

And We certainly know that they say: 'It is only a human being who teaches the Prophet.' The language of the one they refer to is foreign, الاعجمى *and this Quran is in a clear Arabic language.* Surah 16, v: 103.[377]

The Bedouins thought that the acceptance of the Quran would be a violation of their tribal honour. This shows clearly that the majority of the companions of Mohammad in the first years at the beginning of his mission were non-regional people. The people of his own tribe were

---

[376] و قال الذين كفروا " :إن هذا الا افكٌ افتراه، و اعانه عليه قوم آخرون !"فقد جاٸوا ظلما و زورا و قالوا اساطير الاولين اكتتبها فهى ثملا عليه بكره و اصيلاً .قل انزله الذى يعلم السر فى السموات و الارض انه كان غفورا رحيما سوره الفرقان الايات 4- 6

[377] و لقد نعلم انهم يقولون انما يعلمه بشرٌ .لسان الذى يلحدون اليه اعجمى او هذا لسان عربى مبين سوره النحل آيه 103

mainly against him, while these people who were not part of any tribe supported him.

And when Our verses are recited to them as clear evidences, those who do not expect the meeting with Us say, 'Bring us a Quran other than this or change it.' Say, O Mohammad, 'It is not for me to change it on my own accord. I only follow what is revealed to me. Indeed I fear, if I should disobey my Lord, the punishment of a tremendous Day.' Say, 'If Allah had willed, I would not have recited it to you, nor would He have made it known to you, for I had remained among you a lifetime before it. Then will you not reason?' So who is more unjust than he who invents a lie about Allah or denies His signs? Indeed, the criminals will not succeed And they worship other than Allah that which neither harms them nor benefits them, and they say, 'These are our intercessors with Allah.' Say, 'Do you inform Allah of something He does not know in the heavens or on the earth?' Exalted is He and high above what they associate with Him. Surah 10, v: 15 - 18.[378]

In answer to them, Mohammad never denies his faculty for inscribing. Contrary to the wrong impression given by certain reporters who introduced Mohammad as an illiterate person, multiple verses of the Quran recognise his ability to read and write the scriptures. One aspect of Mohammad's life was the spiritual mission as a prophet that caused a cultural revolution, which consisted of encouraging the people of that region who had converted to Islam to learn to read and write. Mohammad was a good example for all Muslims,[379] as he knew this art before all of

---

378 ـ و اذا تُتلى عليهم آياتنا بينات قال الذين لايرجون لقاءنا " :أنتِ بقرآن غير هذا او بدّله !"قل" :مايكون لى أن ابدله من تلقاء نفسى إن اتبع الا ما يوحى الى انى اخاف أن عصيت ربى عذاب يوم عظيم ".قِل" :لو شاء الله ماتلوته عليكم و لا ادراكم به .فقد لبثت فيكم عمرا من قبله .افلا تعقلون؟ "فمن اظلم ممن افترى على الله كذبا اوكذّب بآياته انه لايُفلح المجرمون .ويعبدون من دون الله مالايضرهم و لاينفعهم و يقولون هولاء شفعائنا عند الله .قِل" :أ تنبئون الله بما لايعلم فى السموات و لا فى الارض سبحانه و تعالى عما يشركون "سوره يونس الايات 15-18

379 لقد كان لكم فى رسول الله اسوه حسنه   سورة الاحزاب. الآية 21

There exists a good example for you in the messenger of Allah   Surah al-Ahzâb, v: 21.

them. The Quran reminds Muslims of the necessity to become literate in order to be able to concretely trace their verbal promises and engagements.[380]

A point that has been stressed in the Quran is that the verses recited by Mohammad were all in a clear style in Arabic, while no book written in Arabic containing teachings similar to the content of the Quran existed in Mecca as a source during that Period of Ignorance. This argument confirms the position of the disbelievers who accused Mohammad of being a soldier of a cultural invasion from one of the civilisations in the neighbourhood of the Arabian Peninsula. However, Mohammad, without rejecting the idea of a cultural confrontation and war against the superstition of the Period of Ignorance, rejected the idea that he depended on any foreign political power and instead asserted the fact that he depended solely upon Allah and the invisible world, in continuity with the tradition of Abraham.

---

[380] *O you who have believed, when you contract a debt for a specified term, write it down. And let a scribe write it between you in justice. It is not allowed for a scribe to refuse to write as Allah has taught him. So let him write and let the one who has the obligation dictate. And let him fear Allah, his Lord, and not leave anything out of it. But if the one who has the obligation is of limited understanding or weak or unable to dictate himself, then let his guardian dictate in justice... And do not be too weary to write it, whether it is small or large, for its specified term. That is more just in the sight of Allah and stronger as evidence and more likely to prevent doubt between you, except when it is an immediate transaction which you conduct among yourselves. For [then] there is no blame upon you if you do not write it. And take witnesses when you conclude a contract. Let no scribe be harmed or any witness. For if you do so, indeed, it is [grave] disobedience in you. And fear Allah. And Allah teaches you. And Allah is Knowing of all things.* Surah 2, v: 282.

Section Four

Migration[381] to Medina 622 AD

Two versions of Islam in the same city

The predictions of Habakkuk about the apparition of an eschatological Saviour and the destruction of despotic systems and tyranny on one hand, and the renaissance of the path of Abraham on the other, were realised in the land of Pharan by the successful mission of Prophet Mohammad after his victorious peaceful conquest of Mecca, and the whole Arabian Peninsula in around 630 AD. Meanwhile, out of nowhere, an unexpected problem appeared in the capital of Islam, Medina, during the lifetime of Mohammad. Namely, the problem of the Monafeghin, (hypocritical, corrupted Muslims المنافقون) who were in opposition to Prophet Mohammad, and whose target and intention was to falsify the real teachings of the Quran by mixing them with their tribal behaviours.

And of the people are some who say: 'We believe in Allah and the Last Day,' but they are not believers. They [think to] deceive Allah and those who believe, but they deceive not except themselves and perceive [it] not. In their hearts is disease, so Allah has increased their disease; and for them is a painful punishment because they [habitually] used to lie. And when it is said to them: 'Do not cause corruption on the earth,' they say: 'We are but reformers.' Unquestionably, it is they who are the corrupters, but they perceive [it] not. And when it is said to them: 'Believe as the people have believed,' they say: 'Should we believe as the foolish have believed?' Unquestionably, it is they who are the foolish, but they know [it] not. And when they meet those who believe (to Mohammad), they say: 'We believe'; but when they are alone with their evil ones, they say: 'Indeed, we are with you; we were only

---

[381] Migration: الهجرة

mockers.' [But] Allah mocks them and prolongs them in their transgression [while] they wander blindly. Those are the ones who have purchased error [in exchange] for guidance, so their transaction has brought no profit, nor were they guided. Their example is that of one who kindled a fire, but when it illuminated what was around him, Allah took away their light and left them in darkness [so] they could not see. Deaf, dumb and blind – so they will not return [to the right path]. Or [it is] like a rainstorm from the sky within which is darkness, thunder and lightning. They put their fingers in their ears against the thunderclaps in dread of death. But Allah is encompassing of the disbelievers. The lightning almost snatches away their sight. Every time it lights [the way] for them, they walk therein; but when darkness comes over them, they stand [still]. And if Allah had willed, He could have taken away their hearing and their sight. Indeed, Allah is over all things competent. O mankind, worship your Lord, who created you and those before you, that you may become righteous. Surah 2, v: 8 - 21.[382]

From the first moments of the annunciation of his mission, Mohammad was opposed by the closest members of his tribe (Quraysh) قريش and an important part of his family, Banu Hashim بنوهاشم. This group was led by his own Uncle Abu Lahab ابو لهب, and his wife Ommé Jamil(ام جميل). An entire Surah, 'Màssàd', ' المَسَد ' was revealed in the Quran about these two adversaries.

> *May the hands of Abu Làhàb be ruined, and ruined is he.*
> *His wealth will not avail him or that which he gained.*
> *He will [enter to] burn in a Fire of [blazing] flame*
> *And his wife [as well] – the carrier of firewood.*
> *Around her neck is a rope of [twisted] fibre. Surah 111, v: 1 - 5.*[383]

---

382 - سورة البقرة 8-21

383سوره " المسد " الآيآت 1-5 "تبت يدا ابى لهب و تب ما اغنى عنه ماله و ما كسب سيصلى نارا ذات لهب وامراته حماله الحطب فى جيدها حبل من مسد"

The Migration to Medina (622 AD) and the conquest of Mecca (630 AD)

In 622 AD, a number of people such as Abu Jahl, Abu Sofian, Nazr ibn Haretheh, just to name a few, made a pact with each other to ban Mohammad from the Quraysh tribe, and then subsequently plotted to assassinate him at his home. When Mohammad, became aware of the plot, he left his home to hide from the plotters; and Ali entered Mohammad's house in his place, so as to give the illusion that Mohammad was still present in his home.

While the conspirators were waiting for the cover of the night, to attack Mohammad's home, Mohammad left Mecca and travelled in the direction of al-Yathrib اليثرب. On the way, he met Abu Bakr and they spent few hours inside of the cave called al-Thor غار الثور (about four kilometres from the centre of Mecca, in the mountains between Mecca and al-Yathrib)[384]. When the plotters couldn't find any trace of Mohammad in his house nor in the surrounding area, they returned back, and the Prophet managed to safely and peacefully reach his destination. After this important journey, which is named al- Hijrat الهجرة, the Prophet Mohammad changed the name of al-Yathrib to al-Medina المدينة, meaning the city or polis, as he wanted the city to become the foundation of a civilisation التمدّن, based on the humanity, brotherhood, chivalry, and tolerance[385].

384- ﴿إِلَّا تَنْصُرُوهُ فَقَدْ نَصَرَهُ اللَّهُ إِذْ أَخْرَجَهُ الَّذِينَ كَفَرُوا ثَانِيَ اثْنَيْنِ إِذْ هُمَا فِي الْغَارِ إِذْ يَقُولُ لِصَاحِبِهِ لَا تَحْزَنْ إِنَّ اللَّهَ مَعَنَا فَأَنْزَلَ اللَّهُ سَكِينَتَهُ عَلَيْهِ وَأَيَّدَهُ بِجُنُودٍ لَمْ تَرَوْهَا وَجَعَلَ كَلِمَةَ الَّذِينَ كَفَرُوا السُّفْلَى وَكَلِمَةُ اللَّهِ هِيَ الْعُلْيَا وَاللَّهُ عَزِيزٌ حَكِيمٌ﴾ سورة التوبة، آية: 40

قول أبو بكر: "لو أن أحدهم نظر إلى قدميه لأبصرنا تحت قدميه". فقال له النبي: ﴿يا أبا بكر ما ظنك باثنين الله ثالثهما﴾ رواه البخاري و مسلم فى صحيحيهما

385 Even in a modern western democratic society there are constitutional laws that allow those who are responsible for the safety and stability of the society, like the police, to investigate, prosecute and put stop to those groups who endanger the general safety and the stability of society. These laws are written by those responsible for the safety of the society, and regard exceptional cases. In a similar manner, the Prophet Mohammad, as the leader of his community, was faced with comparable situations and his actions against those who wanted to destabilise society, should be viewed with this perspective in mind,

This migration from Mecca to Medina was not just a short journey between two geographical points in the desert of Arabia, but was a historical evolution from the "Period of Ignorance" العصر الجاهلية towards a "Spiritual Civilisation التمدن الاسلامی. This was an opportunity for a new paradigm in the history of Islam. During this period, a large number of people originating from different countries (such as Byzantine, The Persian Empire, Yemen, Ethiopia) and the Muslims of Mecca and other Arabic regions joined the ranks of the followers of the Prophet Mohammad in Medina. From that moment onwards the plotters changed their tactics, and gathered their forces and decided to use their armies to invade Medina on multiple occasions and therefore, forced a number of bloody battles on Mohammad, his companions, and his community. The Muslims in Medina, by building strong defensive positions inside the city of Medina, resisted their attacks. Then in 628 AD, Mohammad and a group of about 1400 Muslims travelled peacefully to Mecca, for pilgrimage. During that journey they signed a peace treaty called al-Hudaybiyah (صلح الحديبية) with the inhabitants of Mecca, which included Mohammad's enemies, those who had attempted to invade Medina, and those who had plotted against Mohammad for nearly ten years. This treaty reduced the tension between the occupants of Mecca and Medina. Then in 630 AD, the Prophet Mohammad and his companions marched to Mecca during the month of Ramadan and took control of Mecca without any war, and emptied the house of Allah (Kabah) from all of the idols. During this victorious journey, almost all of the inhabitants of Mecca converted to Islam. Then finally, after a short stay in Mecca, Prophet Mohammad returned back to Medina.

---

and not viewed as example of preaching intolerance. The Prophet Mohammad's and Quran's views, as already stated in this book, on showing mercy and tolerance towards everyone are quiet clear. However, as the leader of his community, he could not show tolerance towards intolerance, because those who hold extremist views would have seen that as an opportunity. As for the extremists, this type of tolerance, is a void they can manipulate and fill with their own intolerant rhetoric.

However, it is important to remember that, the majority of those who converted to Islam, during the conquest of Mecca, did not truly believe in Islam. They had merely submitted and interrupted their outward hostility towards Islam. They had only superficially accepted to recognise Prophet Mohammad, as the head of Muslim community. However, in their hearts and mind they remained deeply attached to their tribal traditions.

The Bedouins say, "We have believed." Say, "You have not [yet] believed; but say [instead], 'We have submitted,' for faith has not yet entered your hearts. And if you obey Allah and His Messenger, He will not deprive you from your deeds of anything. Indeed, Allah is Forgiving and Merciful." Surah 49 v: 14[386]

Soon after their superficial submission, a part of this newly converted Muslims group made an alliance with the hypocrite Muslims in Medina, to oppose and weaken the leadership of the Prophet Mohammad upon the Muslim community.

Mohajerin and Ansâr

The most significant problem arose in Medina when a large number of people from the city of Mecca joined the ranks of the Muslims. They were part of those who were called Mohajerin.[387]

---

[386] قَالَتِ الْأَعْرَابُ آمَنَّا قُل لَّمْ تُؤْمِنُوا وَلَكِن قُولُوا أَسْلَمْنَا وَلَمَّا يَدْخُلِ الْإِيمَانُ فِي قُلُوبِكُمْ وَإِن تُطِيعُوا اللَّهَ وَرَسُولَهُ لَا يَلِتْكُم مِّنْ أَعْمَالِكُمْ شَيْئًا إِنَّ اللَّهَ غَفُورٌ رَّحِيمٌ . إِنَّمَا الْمُؤْمِنُونَ الَّذِينَ آمَنُوا بِاللَّهِ وَرَسُولِهِ ثُمَّ لَمْ يَرْتَابُوا وَجَاهَدُوا بِأَمْوَالِهِمْ وَأَنفُسِهِمْ فِي سَبِيلِ اللَّهِ أُولَئِكَ هُمُ الصَّادِقُونَ . قُلْ أَتُعَلِّمُونَ اللَّهَ بِدِينِكُمْ وَاللَّهُ يَعْلَمُ مَا فِي السَّمَاوَاتِ وَمَا فِي الْأَرْضِ وَاللَّهُ بِكُلِّ شَيْءٍ عَلِيمٌ . يَمُنُّونَ عَلَيْكَ أَنْ أَسْلَمُوا قُل لَّا تَمُنُّوا عَلَيَّ إِسْلَامَكُم بَلِ اللَّهُ يَمُنُّ عَلَيْكُمْ أَنْ هَدَاكُمْ لِلْإِيمَانِ إِن كُنتُمْ صَادِقِينَ . إِنَّ اللَّهَ يَعْلَمُ غَيْبَ السَّمَاوَاتِ وَالْأَرْضِ وَاللَّهُ بَصِيرٌ بِمَا تَعْمَلُونَ . سورة الحجرات. الآيات 14- 18

[387] والسابقون الاولون من المهاجرين و الانصار / التوبه .آيه 100 لقد تاب الله على النبى و المهاجرين و الانصار /. التوبه 117

Bukhari explains in his book Sahih that according to a revayat cited by Anas ibn Malik the words of Mohajerin and Ansar were used for the first time by the Quran. Bukhari. Sahih. Vol. IV, p. 221 In Surah 9 Towbeh, Repentance, in verses 100 and 117 these two terms are used. Ibn Athir. Al-Kâmil fit Tarikh. Vol. I, p.655. Ibn Husham. Ibid. Vol. II, p.292-293. Mohammad Jarir at-Tabari. History of people and kings. Vol. II, p.368-383. Ibn Sa'd.

Amongst the Muslim community in Medina (including Mohajerin and Ansâr), a category of people existed who submitted to Islam, however, according to their own interpretation of Islam. They tried to adapt the teachings of Mohammad to their own tribal traditions. Their chief was a man called Abdollah ibn é Obayy, ابّیّ بن عبدالله.[388] The difference between these new adversaries of Mohammad in Medina on one side, and his initial enemies from Mecca on the other, concerned the acceptance or negation of Islam. The Bedouins of Mecca stood up before Mohammad and rejected him and his appeal totally. They said to him: 'Bring another Quran, or at least change this one!'[389] But the adversaries of Mohammad from Medina were the people who had actually converted to Islam. They confronted Mohammad, the Quran, Islam, and the principle of monotheism from inside the community. They neither rejected the Quran openly, nor asked

---

at-Tàbàghât ol-Kobrâ. Vol. III, p. 136-151. Mughaddasi. Al-Ba' vàt-Târikh. Vol.V, p. 156-157. Jâhiz. Al-Bàyân vat-Tàbiin. Vol. II, p.219.

The Muslim migrants to Medina were called 'Mohajerin ', and the newly converted people to Islam of Medina were called Ansar. Abdollah ibn Obayy ibn Selloul, one of the chiefs of the Khazraj tribe in Medina, was surnamed 'Kabirol Monafeghon': the head of the hypocrites. The battle of Bani Mostalagh happened in year 6 after Hegira. Once Omar, one of the companions of Mohammad, told: 'O Prophet let me decapitate this hypocrite', but Mohammad said: 'No, people will say Mohammad kills his companions'.

388- عبد الله بن أبي بن سلول شخصية من شخصيات يثرب واحد قادة ورؤساء الخزرج ورد في سيرة النبي محمد صلى الله عليه و سلم كشخصية معادية للدين الإسلامي مهادنة ظاهرياً، يلقبه المسلمون بكبير المنافقين. قيل انه كان على وشك أن يكون سيد المدينة قبل أن يصلها الرسول صلى الله عليه و سلم. المكتبة الإسلامية ـ تفسير قوله تعالى " ولا تُصَلّ على أحد منهم مات أبدا ولا تقم على قبره"

The reporters such as ibn Husham share this opinion that the entire Surah of 'Monafeghon' is revealed to Mohammad in relation to Abdollah Obayy and his hypocrisy. He expected to be the head of Medina before the arrival of Prophet Mohammad. The presence of Mohammad and the Muslim community in Medina made him unhappy and over the years he took a number of opportunities to push Mohammad and the migrant Muslims out of Medina. Ibn Husham. Ibid. Farsi version, vol. 2, pp. 195 to 199.

89وَإِذَا تُتْلَى عَلَيْهِمْ آيَاتُنَا بَيِّنَاتٍ قَالَ الَّذِينَ لَا يَرْجُونَ لِقَاءَنَا: "ائْتِ بِقُرْآنٍ غَيْرِ هَذَاأَوْ بَدِّلْهُ "قُلْ: "مَا يَكُونُ لِي أَنْ أُبَدِّلَهُ مِن تِلْقَاءِ نَفْسِي إِنْ أَتَّبِعُ إِلَّا مَا يُوحَى إِلَيَّ إِنِّي أَخَافُ إِنْ عَصَيْتُ رَبِّي عَذَابَ يَوْمٍ عَظِيمٍ قُل لَّوْ شَاءَ اللَّهُ مَا تَلَوْتُهُ عَلَيْكُمْ وَلَا أَدْرَاكُم بِهِ فَقَدْ لَبِثْتُ فِيكُمْ عُمُرًا مِّن قَبْلِهِ أَفَلَا تَعْقِلُونَ. فَمَنْ أَظْلَمُ مِمَّنِ افْتَرَى عَلَى اللَّهِ كَذِبًا أَوْ كَذَّبَ بِآيَاتِهِ إِنَّهُ لَا يُفْلِحُ الْمُجْرِمُونَ سورة يونس. الآيات 15-17

Mohammad to change the content of his book, nor to replace his book by another Quran. Instead, they superficially accepted the Quran, and testified to the benefit of the mission of Mohammad as the Prophet and the messenger of Allah, but misled the people through deliberate misinterpretation of the verses of the Quran, skewed towards their own tribal traditions. This category of people was originally composed of disbelievers[390] who officially converted to Islam and joined the Muslim community, but for the sole purpose of diverting this newborn community to their own disbeliefs.

When the hypocrites come to you, [O Mohammad], they say: 'We testify that you are the Messenger of Allah.' And Allah knows that you are His Messenger, and Allah testifies that the hypocrites are liars. They have taken their oaths as a cover, so they averted [people] from the way of Allah. Indeed, it was evil that they were doing. That is because they believed, and then they disbelieved; so their hearts were sealed over, and they do not understand… And when it is said to them: 'Come, the Messenger of Allah will ask forgiveness for you,' they turn their heads aside and you see them evading while they are arrogant. It is all the same for them whether you ask forgiveness for them or do not ask forgiveness for them; never will Allah forgive them. Indeed, Allah does not guide the defiantly disobedient people. They are the ones who say: 'Do not spend on those who are with the Messenger of Allah until they disband.' And to Allah belongs the depositories of the skies and the earth, but the hypocrites do not understand. They say, 'If we return to al-Medina, the more honoured [for power] will surely expel there from the more humble.' And to Allah belongs [all] honour, and to His Messenger, and to the believers, but the hypocrites do not know. O you who have believed, let not your wealth and your children divert you from remembrance of Allah. And whoever does that – then those are the losers. And spend [in the way of Allah] from what We have provided you before

---

[390] Ibn Husham. Ibid Farsi version, vol. 1, pp. 348 to 357. Ibn Husham introduces many names of the Monafeghoun, their tribes and families.

229

death approaches one of you and he says: 'My Lord, if only You would delay me for a brief term so I would give charity and be among the righteous'. Surah 63, v: 1 - 10.[391]

The founders of this 'false Islam', which was based on lies, corruption, deviation, and hypocrisy, lived in the lifetime of Prophet Mohammad in the same city (Medina) as Mohammad. They created an 'anti-Islam' under the flag of Islam, and put a barrier in front of the newly converted Muslims. Confronting this type of enemy was not an easy matter. They were not obvious idol worshippers; on the contrary, they hid their disbelief in Islam, built mosques, prayed, read, and recited the verses of the Quran by heart, leading the prayers, and preaching to the worshippers of Allah. Their superficial respect towards the Quran made the new Muslims confused and the unity of the Muslim community was in danger.

It is not for the polytheists to maintain the mosques of Allah [while] witnessing against themselves with disbelief. [For] those, their deeds have become worthless, and in the Fire they will abide eternally. The mosques of Allah are only to be maintained by those who believe in Allah and the Last Day and establish prayer and give taxes - zakah/ الزكوة *and do not fear except Allah, for it is expected that those will be of the [rightly] guided.*[392]

And among them are those who made a covenant with Allah, saying, 'If He should give us from His bounty, we will surely spend in charity, and we will surely be among the

---

391ـ اذا جائك المنافقون قالوا" :نشهد إنك لرسول الله ."و الله يعلم إنك لرسولهُ و الله يشهدُ إن المنافقين لكاذبون اتخذوا أيمائهمجُنة فصدوا عن سبيل الله .إنهم ساء ماكانوا يعملون .ذلك بأنهم آمنوا ثم كفروا فطبع على قلوبهم فهم لايفقهون ... و إذا قيل لهم تعالوا يستغفر لكم رسولُ اللهِ لَوَّوارُوسَهم و رايتهم يصدون و هم مستكبرون .سواءٌ عليهم أستغفرتَ لهم ام لم تستغفر لهم لن يغفرَالله لهم إن اللهَ لايهدى القوم الفاسقين .هُم الذين يقولون لاتُنفقوا على من عند رسول الله حتى ينفضوا، ولله خزائنُ السموات و الارض ولكن المنافقون لايفقهون .يقولون لئن رجعنا الى المدينه لَيُخرجنَّ الاعزُّ منها الاذلة و لله العزه و لرسوله و للمومنين .ولكن المنافقين لا يعلمون .ياايها الذين آمنوا لا تُلهكُماموالُكُم و لا اولادكم عن ذكر الله و من يَفعل ذلك فاولئك هم الخاسرون .وَ أنفقوا من ما رزقناكم من قبل أن يأتيَ احدكُم الموتُ فيقول ربّ لولا أخرتنى إلى اجلٍ قريبٍ فأَصَّدَّقَ و أكن من الصالحين .سورة المنافقون - الايات 1 - 10

392 Surah 9, v: 17 - 18

righteous.' But when he gave them from His bounty, they were stingy with it and turned away while they refused. So He penalised them with hypocrisy in their hearts until the Day they will meet Him – because they failed Allah in what they promised Him and because they habitually used to lie. Did they not know that Allah knows their secrets and their private conversations and that Allah is the Knower of the unseen? Those who criticise the contributors among the believers concerning their charities and criticise the ones who find nothing to spend except their effort, so they ridicule them. Allah will ridicule them, and they will have a painful punishment.

Ask forgiveness for them, O Mohammad, or do not ask forgiveness for them. If you should ask forgiveness for them seventy times – never will Allah forgive them. That is because they disbelieved in Allah and His Messenger, and Allah does not guide the defiantly disobedient people. And when a Surah was revealed enjoining them to believe in Allah and to fight with His Messenger, those of wealth among them asked your permission to stay back and said. 'Leave us to be with them who sit at home.' They were satisfied to be with those who stay behind, and their hearts were sealed over, so they do not understand. But the Messenger and those who believed with him fought with their wealth and their lives. Those will have all that is good, and it is those who are the successful. They swear to you so that you might be satisfied with them. But if you should be satisfied with them – indeed, Allah is not satisfied with a defiantly disobedient people.

The Bedouins of the tribes of the Peninsula of Arabia àl-à'râb are stronger in disbelief and hypocrisy and more likely not to know the limits of what laws Allah has revealed to His Messenger. And Allah is Knowing and Wise. And among the Bedouins of the tribes of the Peninsula of Arabia àl-à'râb are some who consider what they spend as a loss and await for you turns of misfortune. Upon them will be a misfortune of evil. And Allah is Hearing and Knowing. But among the Bedouins of the tribes of the Peninsula of Arabia àl-à'râb are some who believe in Allah and the Last Day and consider what they spend as means of nearness to Allah and of [obtaining] invocations of the Messenger. Unquestionably, it is a means of nearness for them. Allah will admit them to His mercy.

Indeed, Allah is Forgiving and Merciful. And the first forerunners [in the faith] among the Mohajerin المهاجرين and the Ansâr الانصار and those who followed them with good conduct – Allah is pleased with them and they are pleased with Him, and He has prepared for them gardens beneath which rivers flow, wherein they will abide forever. That is the great attainment. And among those around you of the Bedouins of the tribes of the Peninsula of Arabia àl-à'ràb are hypocrites, and [also] from the people of Medina. They have become accustomed to hypocrisy. You, O Mohammad, do not know them, but We know them. We will punish them twice in this world; then they will be returned to a great punishment. And there are others who have acknowledged their sins. They had mixed a righteous deed with another that was bad. Perhaps Allah will turn to them in forgiveness. Indeed, Allah is Forgiving and Merciful. Take, O, Mohammad, from their wealth a charity by which you purify them and cause them increase, and invoke Allah's blessings upon them. Indeed, your invocations are reassurance for them. And Allah is Hearing and Knowing.

Do they not know that it is Allah who accepts repentance from His servants and receives charities and that it is Allah who is the Accepting of repentance, the Merciful? And say: 'Do as you will, for Allah will see your deeds, and so, will His Messenger and the believers. And you will be returned to the Knower of the unseen and the witnessed, and He will inform you of what you used to do.' And there are others deferred until the command of Allah – whether He will punish them or whether He will forgive them. And Allah is Knowing and Wise. And there are those hypocrites who took for themselves a mosque for causing harm and disbelief and division among the believers and as a station for whoever had warred against Allah and His Messenger before. And they will surely swear, 'We intended only the best.' And Allah testifies that indeed they are liars. Do not stand for prayer within it (this mosque) – ever. A mosque founded on righteousness from the first day is more worthy for you to stand in. Within it are men who love to purify themselves; and Allah loves those who purify themselves. Then is one who laid the foundation of his building on righteousness with respect for Allah and seeking His approval better or one who laid the foundation of his building on the edge of a bank about to collapse, so it collapsed with him into the fire of Hell? And Allah does not guide the wrongdoing people. Their building which they built will not cease to be a cause of scepticism in their hearts until their hearts are stopped. And Allah is Knowing and Wise. Indeed,

Allah has purchased from the believers their lives and their properties in exchange for that they will have Paradise...

So rejoice in your transaction, which you have contracted. And it is that which is the great attainment. Such believers are the repentant, the worshippers, the praisers of Allah, the travellers for His cause, those who bow and prostrate in prayer, those who enjoin what is right and forbid what is wrong, and those who observe the limits set by Allah. And give good tidings to the believers…

And whenever a Surah is revealed, there are among the hypocrites those who say: 'Which of you has this increased faith?' As for those who believed, it has increased them in faith, while they are rejoicing. But as for those in whose hearts is disease, it has only increased them in evil in addition to their evil. And they will have died while they are disbelievers. Do they not see that they are tried every year once or twice but then they do not repent nor do they remember? And whenever a Surah is revealed, they look at each other, saying, 'Does anyone see you?' and then they dismiss themselves. Allah has dismissed their hearts because they are a people who do not understand. There has certainly come to you a Messenger from among yourselves. Grievous to him is what you suffer; [he is] concerned over you and to the believers is kind and merciful.[393]

And of the people are some who say: 'We believe in Allah,' but when one of them is harmed for the cause of Allah, they consider the trial of the people as if it were the punishment of Allah. But if victory comes from your Lord, they say: 'Indeed, We were with you.' Is not Allah most knowing of what is within the breasts of all creatures? And Allah will surely make evident those who believe, and He will surely make evident the hypocrites. And those who disbelieve say to those who believe, 'Follow our way, and we will carry your sins.' But they will not carry anything of their sins. Indeed, they are liars. But they will surely carry their own burdens and other burdens along with their burdens, and they will surely be questioned on the Day of Resurrection about what they used to invent.[394]

---

[393] Surah 9, v: 75 - 128.

[394] Surah 29, v: 10-13.

Remember when the hypocrites and those in whose hearts was disease said: 'Their religion has deluded those Muslims.' But whoever relies upon Allah – then indeed, Allah is Exalted in Might and Wise. And if you could but see when the angels take the souls of those who disbelieved... They are striking their faces and their backs and saying, 'Taste the punishment of the Burning Fire.'[395] *The hypocrites are apprehensive lest a Surah be revealed about them, informing them of what is in their hearts. Say: 'Mock as you wish; indeed, Allah will expose that which you fear.' And if you ask them, they will surely say: 'We were only conversing and playing.' Say: 'Is it Allah and His verses and His Messenger that you were mocking?' Make no excuse; you have disbelieved after your belief. If We pardon one faction of you – We will punish another faction because they were criminals. The hypocrite men and hypocrite women are of one another. They enjoin what is wrong and forbid what is right and close their hands. They have forgotten Allah, so He has forgotten them accordingly. Indeed, the hypocrites – it is they who are the defiantly disobedient. Allah has promised the hypocrite men and hypocrite women and the disbelievers the fire of Hell, wherein they will abide eternally. It is sufficient for them. And Allah has cursed them, and for them is an enduring punishment.*[396]

And remember when the hypocrites and those in whose hearts is disease said: 'Allah and His Messenger did not promise us except delusion,' And when a faction of them said: 'O people of Yathrib البثرب, there is no stability for you here, so return home.' And a party of them asked permission of the Prophet, saying: 'Indeed, our houses are unprotected,' while they were not exposed. They did not intend except to flee. And if they had been entered upon from all its surrounding regions and fitnah [sedition] الفتنة had been demanded of them, they would have done it and not hesitated over it except briefly. And they had already promised Allah before not to turn their backs and flee. And ever is the promise to Allah that about which one will be questioned. Say: O Mohammad, 'Never will fleeing benefit you if you should flee from death or killing; and then if you did, you would not be given enjoyment of life except for a little.'Surah 33, v: 12-16

---

[395] Surah 8, v: 49-50

[396] Surah 9, v: 64-68.

That Allah may reward the truthful for their truth and punish the hypocrites if He wills or accept their repentance. Indeed, Allah is ever Forgiving and Merciful. 'Surah 33, v: 24

And do not obey the disbelievers and the hypocrites but do not harm them, and rely upon Allah. And sufficient is Allah as Disposer of affairs. 'Surah 33, v: 48

If the hypocrites and those in whose hearts is disease and those who spread rumours in al-Medina do not cease, We will surely incite you against them; then they will not remain your neighbours therein except for a little. 'Surah 33, v: 60

It was so that Allah may punish the hypocrite men and hypocrite women and the men and women who associate others with Him and that Allah may accept repentance from the believing men and believing women. And ever is Allah Forgiving and Merciful.[397]

How the Quran describes the 'false Muslims'

O you who have believed, obey Allah and obey the Messenger and those in authority among you. And if you disagree over anything, refer it to Allah and the Messenger, if you should believe in Allah and the Last Day. That is the best [way] and best in result. Surah 4, v: 59 [398]

The Quran guides real Muslims to be obedient only towards Allah, His messenger, and the commandants among the community and not to bring their affairs to the opinions of the Taghut الطاغوت (Anti- Allah, Monafegh, Kafir).

Have you not seen those who claim to have believed in what was revealed to you, [O Mohammad], and what was revealed before you? They wish to refer legislation to Taghut, while they were commanded to reject it; and Satan wishes to lead them far astray. And when it is said to them, 'Come to what Allah has revealed and to the Messenger,' you

---

[397] Surah 33, v: 12 - 16; v: 24; v: 48; v: 60; v: 73.

[398] ـ يَاۤ أَيُّهَاالَّذِينَ آمَنُوۤا أَطِيعُوا اللَّهَ وَأَطِيعُوا الرَّسُولَ وَأُوْلِي الأمْرِ مِنْكُمْ فَإِنْ تَنَازَعْتُمْ فِي شَيْءٍ فَرُدُّوهُ إِلَى اللَّهِ وَالرَّسُولِ إِنْ كُنْتُمْ تُؤْمِنُونَ بِاللَّهِ وَالْيَوْمِ الآخِرِ ذَلِكَ خَيْرٌ وَأَحْسَنُ تَأْوِيلا سورة النساء. الآية 59

235

see the hypocrites turning away from you in aversion. So how [will it be] when disaster strikes them because of what their hands have put forth and then they come to you swearing by Allah, 'We intended nothing but good conduct and accommodation.' Those are the ones of whom Allah knows what is in their hearts, so turn away from them but admonish them and speak to them a far-reaching word. And We did not send any messenger except to be obeyed by permission of Allah. And if, when they wronged themselves, they had come to you, [O Mohammad], and asked forgiveness of Allah and the Messenger had asked forgiveness for them, they would have found Allah Accepting of repentance and Merciful.[399]

O you who have believed, believe in Allah and His Messenger and the Book that He sent down upon His Messenger and the Scripture which He sent down before. And whoever disbelieves in Allah, His angels, His books, His messengers, and the Last Day has certainly gone far astray. Indeed, those who have believed then disbelieved, then believed, then disbelieved, and then increased in disbelief – never will Allah forgive them, nor will He guide them to a way. Give tidings to the **hypocrites** *that there is for them a painful punishment. Those who take disbelievers as allies instead of the believers. Do they seek with them honour [through power]? But indeed, honour belongs to Allah entirely. And it has already come down to you in the Book that when you hear the verses of Allah [recited], they are denied [by them] and ridiculed; so do not sit with them until they enter into another conversation. Indeed, you would then be like them. Indeed Allah will gather* **the hypocrites and disbelievers** *in Hell all together. Those who wait [and watch] you. Then if you gain a victory from Allah, they say: 'Were we not with you?' But if the disbelievers have a success, they say [to them], 'Did we not gain the advantage over you, but we protected you from the believers?' Allah will judge between [all of] you on the Day of Resurrection, and never will Allah give the disbelievers over the believers a way [to overcome them].* **Indeed, the hypocrites [think to] deceive Allah, but He is deceiving them. And when they stand for prayer, they stand lazily, showing [themselves to] the people and not remembering Allah** *except a little, Wavering between them, [belonging] neither to*

---

[399] Surah 4, v: 59 - 64

the believers nor to the disbelievers. And whoever Allah leaves astray - never will you find for him a way. O you who have believed, do not take the disbelievers as allies instead of the believers. Do you wish to give Allah against yourselves a clear case? Indeed, **the hypocrites will be in the lowest depths of the Fire – and never will you find for them a helper** *– Except for those who repent, correct themselves, hold fast to Allah, and are sincere in their religion for Allah, for those will be with the believers. And Allah is going to give the believers a great reward. What would Allah do with your punishment if you are grateful and believe? And ever is Allah Appreciative and Knowing.*

Allah does not like the public mention of evil except by one who has been wronged. And ever is Allah Hearing and Knowing. If [instead] you show [some] good or conceal it or pardon an offense – indeed, Allah is ever Pardoning and Competent. **Indeed, those who disbelieve in Allah and His messengers and wish to discriminate between Allah and His messengers and say: 'We believe in some and disbelieve in others,' and wish to adopt a way in between – Those are the disbelievers, truly.** *And We have prepared for the disbelievers a humiliating punishment. But they who believe in Allah and His messengers and do not discriminate between any of them – to those He is going to give their rewards. And ever is Allah Forgiving and Merciful. The People of the Scripture ask you to bring down to them a book from the sky. But they had asked of Moses [even] greater than that and said, 'Show us Allah outright,' so the thunderbolt struck them for their wrongdoing. Then they took the calf [for worship] after clear evidences had come to them, and We pardoned that. And We gave Moses a clear authority.*[400]

In the sentences reproduced above, the Quran put the hypocrites and the disbelievers in the same category of people in this world and in the world of Hereafter. These people are those who would like to bring together their own beliefs with the principles of monotheism, explained by the Quran, to find a parallel way inside the Muslim community. They

---

[400] Surah 4, v: 136 - 153.

perform prayers out of hypocrisy. The Quran forbids the Muslim community, in a radical way, to follow the leadership of 'the false Muslim', as it forbids them to accept the hegemony and supremacy of the disbelievers. Taghut, or anti-Allah, personifies the main world vision of the hypocrites and disbelievers. According to the Quran, Muslims should follow the guidance of Allah, his messengers, and the authorities that come from monotheist values. This principle was to guarantee the immunity and health of the Muslim community in the time of Mohammad, and after his death.

The word 'Taghut' الطاغوت is derived from Taghâ طغى , meaning overlapping the borders, like a flood of water over-passes the borders of the river, breaking all barriers and causing immense damage. In the jargon of the Quran, the term Taghut indicates the personality of those whose powerful ego takes over the territory of their being and metamorphoses them into dictators-despots-tyrants, who manipulate the religious beliefs of people and canalise their energy to establish a dictatorial system upon society, in order to violate human rights and the rights of the citizens in the name of Allah and monotheism, and to reduce free born individuals to slaves. One of the examples of Taghut given by the Quran is the Egyptian Pharaoh. Allah gave a mission to Moses, in the company of his brother Aaron, to go and change the mind of the Pharaoh, because he was violating, transgressing, overlapping the borders. *'Go to Pharaoh, he is violating.'* Surah 20, v: 24.[401]

Taghut, or anti-Allah, misleads people. According to the Quran, Allah is 'Wali' (guide) of those who believe in Him only, and conducts them from darkness to light, and on the contrary those who are disbelieving (in Allah) are under the supremacy of Taghuts, who conduct them from light to

---

401 اذهب الى فرعون انه طغى سورة طه الاية 24

darkness.⁴⁰² In this situation, the best guarantee to avoid being under 'welayat', authority of Taghut, is not to acknowledge their hegemony at all.

*O Prophet, fight against the disbelievers and the hypocrites and be harsh upon them.... He penalised them with hypocrisy in their hearts until the Day they will meet Him – because they failed Allah in what they promised Him and because they [habitually] used to lie.*⁴⁰³

The Quran mentions the case of 'yowm ol Honayn' يوم الحنين in which Mohammad went to confront the invading tribes and encouraged the Muslims to go with him, but the hypocrites refused to follow his appeal and discouraged others as well, under the pretext of bad weather!

Those who remained behind rejoiced in their staying [at home] after [the departure of] the Messenger of Allah and disliked to strive with their wealth and their lives in the cause of Allah and said: 'Do not go forth in the heat.' Say: 'The fire of Hell is more intensive in heat' – if they would but understand. So let them laugh a little and [then] weep much as recompense for what they used to earn. If Allah should return you to a faction of them [after the expedition] and then they ask your permission to go out [to battle], say: 'You will not go out with me, ever, and you will never fight with me an enemy. Indeed, you were satisfied with sitting [at home] the first time, so sit [now] with those who stay behind.' And do not pray [the funeral prayer, O Mohammad], over any of them who has died – ever – or stand at his grave. Indeed, they disbelieved in Allah and His Messenger and died while they were defiantly disobedient. And let not their wealth and their children impress you. Allah only intends to punish them through them in this world and that their souls should depart [at death] while they are disbelievers. And when a Surah was revealed [enjoining them] to believe in Allah and to fight with

---

⁴⁰² Surah 2, v: 257.

⁴⁰³ Surah 9, v: 73 and 77.

His Messenger, those of wealth among them asked your permission [to stay back] and said, 'Leave us to be with them who sit [at home].'

They were satisfied to be with those who stayed behind, and their hearts were sealed, so they do not understand. But the Messenger and those who believed with him fought with their wealth and their lives.

Those will have [all that is] good, and it is those who are the successful. Allah has prepared for them gardens beneath which rivers flow, wherein they will abide eternally. That is the great attainment. And those with excuses among the Bedouins of the tribes of the Peninsula of Arabia came to be permitted [to remain], and they who had lied to Allah and His Messenger sat [at home]. There will strike those who disbelieved among them a painful punishment. There is not upon the weak or upon the ill or upon those who do not find anything to spend any discomfort when they are sincere to Allah and His Messenger. There is not upon the doers of good any cause [for blame]. And Allah is Forgiving and Merciful. Nor [is there blame] upon those who, when they came to you that you might give them mounts, you said: 'I can find nothing for you to ride upon.' They turned back while their eyes overflowed with tears out of grief that they could not find something to spend [for the cause of Allah]. The cause [for blame] is only upon those who ask permission of you while they are rich. They are satisfied to be with those who stay behind, and Allah has sealed over their hearts, so they do not know. They will make excuses to you when you have returned to them. Say: 'Make no excuse – never will we believe you. Allah has already informed us of your news. And Allah will observe your deeds, and [so will] His Messenger; then you will be taken back to the Knower of the unseen and the witnessed, and He will inform you of what you used to do.' They will swear by Allah to you when you return to them that you would leave them alone. So leave them alone; indeed they are evil; and their refuge is Hell as recompense for what they had been earning. They swear to you so that you might be satisfied with them. But if you should be satisfied with them – indeed, Allah is not satisfied with a defiantly disobedient people.

The Bedouins of the tribes of the Peninsula of Arabia are stronger in disbelief and hypocrisy and more likely not to know the limits of what [laws] Allah has revealed to His Messenger. And Allah is Knowing and Wise. And among the A'râbs/ Bedouins of the tribes of the Peninsula of Arabia are some who consider what they spend as a loss and await for you turns of misfortune. Upon them will be a misfortune of evil. And Allah is Hearing and Knowing. But among the A'râbs/Bedouins of the tribes of the Peninsula of Arabia are some who believe in Allah and the Last Day and consider what they spend as a means of nearness to Allah and of obtaining invocations of the Messenger. Unquestionably, it is a means of nearness for them. Allah will admit them to His mercy. Indeed, Allah is Forgiving and Merciful. And the first forerunners in the faith among the Mohajerin , [المهاجرين] those who migrated from Mecca to Medina to join Mohammad and the Ansar, [الانصار], the inhabitants of Medina who had converted to Islam and gave refugee to the migrated companions – and those who followed them with good conduct – Allah is pleased with them and they are pleased with Him, and He has prepared for them gardens beneath which rivers flow, wherein they will abide forever. That is the great attainment. And among those around you of the A'râbs/Bedouins of the tribes of the Peninsula of Arabia are hypocrites, and also from the people of Medina. They have become accustomed to hypocrisy.

You, O Mohammad, do not know them, but We know them. We will punish them twice in this world; then they will be returned to a great punishment. And there are others who have acknowledged their sins. They had mixed a righteous deed with another that was bad. Perhaps Allah will turn to them in forgiveness. Indeed, Allah is Forgiving and Merciful. Take, O, Mohammad, from their wealth a charity by which you purify them and cause them increase, and invoke Allah's blessings upon them. Indeed, your invocations are reassurance for them. And Allah is Hearing and Knowing. Do they not know that it is Allah who accepts repentance from His servants and receives charities and that it is Allah who is the Accepting of repentance, the Merciful? And say: 'Do as you will, for Allah will see your deeds, and so will His Messenger and the believers. And you will be returned to the Knower of the unseen and the witnessed, and He will inform you of what you used to do.' And there are others deferred until the command of Allah

– whether He will punish them or whether He will forgive them. And Allah is Knowing and Wise. Surah 9, v. 81 - 106.[404]

Mosques built and used by the hypocrites

One of the very important traces of the hypocrites at the beginning of the history of Islam, and the newborn Muslim community in Medina concerns the misuse of the Islamic worshipping place or mosque. The following is a description of the building of a mosque, and its destruction by Mohammad. It is the case of the mosque of Dirar (مسجدالضرار).[405]

And [there are those hypocrites] who took for themselves a mosque for causing harm and disbelief and division among the believers and as a station for whoever had warred against Allah and His Messenger before. And they will surely swear, 'We intended only the best.' And Allah testifies that indeed they are liars. Do not stand for prayer within it – ever. A mosque founded on righteousness from the first day is more worthy for you to stand in. Within it are men who love to purify themselves; and Allah loves those who purify themselves. Then is one who laid the foundation of his building on righteousness with respect towards Allah and seeking His approval better or one who laid the foundation of his building on the edge of a bank about to collapse, so it collapsed with him into the fire of Hell? And Allah does not guide the wrongdoing people. Their building, which they built, will not cease to be a cause of scepticism in their hearts until their hearts are stopped. And Allah is Knowing and Wise. Indeed, Allah has purchased from the believers their lives and their properties in exchange for that they will have Paradise.[406]

---

404 وَمِمَّنْ حَوْلَكُم مِّنَ الْأَعْرَابِ مُنَافِقُونَ وَمِنْ أَهْلِ الْمَدِينَةِ مَرَدُواْ عَلَى الدِّفَاقِ لاَ تَعْلَمُهُمْ نَحْنُ نَعْلَمُهُمْ سَنُعَذِّبُهُم مَّرَّتَيْنِ ثُمَّ يُرَدُّونَ إِلَى عَذَابٍ عَظِيمٍ. وَآخَرُونَ اعْتَرَفُواْ بِذُنُوبِهِمْ خَلَطُواْ عَمَلاً صَالِحًا وَآخَرَ سَيِّئًا عَسَى اللّهُ أَن يَتُوبَ عَلَيْهِمْ إِنَّ اللّهَ غَفُورٌ رَّحِيمٌ . سورة التّوبه ـ الايات 101و 102

405 Ibn Husham. Ibid. Farsi version. Vol. 2, p. 334.

406 Surah 9, v: 107 - 111.

Conclusion

A short overview of the life of Prophet Mohammad

As we mentioned previously, from 500 AD a small group of monotheist people (named Honàfà) appeared in Mecca. Some of them were literate, educated, and multilingual people related to the community of the righteous people of Syria, and expecting the arrival of the promised Saviour of Allah, according to the prediction of the Pesher of Habakkuk. The most famous amongst them was Waraka ibn Nowfel.[407] His father Nowfel was the brother of Hashem, and he was the father of Abdul-Motalleb. They ran a spiritual-cultural school المدرسة in Mecca, where they translated the content of the old Holy Books and manuscripts of the Qumran community, alongside other scriptures, into Arabic and inscribed them using a particular style of writing رسم الخط named Hijazi الحجازى . This style was born from the process of the evolution of the Syriac alphabet السريانى to the Musnad alphabet المسندand to the Jazm alphabet الجزم. From those translations they created texts, inscribed on pages made from the skin of goats and other animals.

They also made different books out of those pages. Waraka and his companions used to take those books and walk amongst the visitors to and pilgrims of Mecca to preach to them and try to lead them from the superstition of the Period of Ignorance towards monotheism التوحيد and to belief in the unique Creator of the universe. This group of monotheists الموحّدون was related to the temple of Bosra in Syria. Prophet Mohammad

---

[407]روى البخارى في صحيحه بخصوص ورقة بن نوفل : '' كان امرأ تتصر في الجاهلية، وكان يكتب الكتاب العبراني، فيكتب من الإنجيل بالعبرانية ما شاء الله أن يكتب، وكان شيخا كبيرا قد عمى '' صحيح البخارى : 3/1

243

was born and educated by his grandfather Abdul-Motalleb and his uncle Abu Talib in this atmosphere. At the age of twelve he went to Bosra البُصرى and met Bahira who revealed to him and to his uncle that the "Sun" of the expected Saviour of the end of time المنجى الموعود فى الآخر الزمان was reflected in the mirror of his heart, and that therefore he was the manifestation of the predicted Namus (Saviour).

From this period onwards, the life of Mohammad was consecrated to his historical divine mission. He began regular journeys to Syria. From the age of twenty onwards, he became a manager for a very important trader, a monotheist woman named Khadijeh, خديجة cousin of Waraka, who was a notable person of the Hanif community of Mecca. He often travelled as a trading director to Syria, staying weeks and months in that region. When Mohammad was twenty-five years old he married Khadijeh. From the age of thirty-five to forty Mohammad took time to practise periods of retreat and seclusion and, at the age of forty, he publicly announced his mission to the people of his tribe. He stayed in Mecca until the age of fifty-three before making his historical migration from Mecca الهجرة. It was in 622 AD that Mohammad went to Medina and stayed there for about ten years. During this period of his life he experienced a number of military confrontations with the pagans of Mecca.[408] He led his community in resistance and defence, through sieges, raids, diplomacy, alliances, and peace, until the final victory when the conquest of Mecca took place.

---

[408] *Permission to fight is given to those who are being attacked and assaulted because they have been wronged. Truly Allah has the power to support them. Those who were expelled from their homes without any right, merely for saying 'our Lord is Allah'.* Surah 22, v: 39, 40.

The "farewell pilgrimage" (حَجّة الوداع)

During February 632 AD (Zol Hajjah), the Prophet Mohammad travelled to Mecca to lead the Hajj pilgrimage. This journey is also known as the "farewell pilgrimage" (حَجّة الوداع) as it was Mohammad's last trip to Mecca.

A few months after this pilgrimage, and after the last public speech that Prophet Mohammad gave in a place called Ghadir é Khom, Prophet Mohammad passed away (632 AD) and left the Quran and Islam as his legacy.

In reality, from the first moment of the annunciation of his mission, the Bedouins, who were the majority of the inhabitants of Mecca and the region surrounding it, refused to recognise him as a prophet. But the 'righteous people' and the people originating from other lands and cultures believed him and his mission.

The first military action was named the battle of Badr. It ended with the victory of Mohammad's camp. Returning to Medina, Mohammad said to his companions: 'We have returned from "Jihad Asghar" الجهاد الاصغر (lesser battle) to face "Jihad Akbar" الجهاد الاكبر (greater battle), which is fighting our own Nafs, egoistic drives.'[409]

---

[409]حديث رواه البيهقي: "رجعنا من الجهاد الأصغر إلي الجهاد الأكبر" قالوا : "وما الجهاد الأكبر؟ قال : جهاد القلب" ورواه الخطيب البغدادي بلفظ : "رجعنا من الجهاد الأصغر إلي الجهاد الأكبر ، قالوا : وما الجهاد الأكبر ؟ قال : مجاهدة العبد هواه"

الدرة اليتيمة في تخريج أحاديث التحفة الكريمة

This is a saying (Hadith) cited by Beyhaghy and quoted by Rumi in his famous book Mathnavi. For the commentary of this Hadith in Mathnavi of Rumi please see Appendix.

Islam after the death of its founder

After the death of Prophet Mohammad, and the end of the period of his four successors – Râshidoun Caliphate الخلافة الراشدون (632- 661 AD) – a long period of religious despotism, under the name of Islam, appeared in the world: the non-Râshidoun Caliphate غير الراشد , including the Omayyad dynasty بنو الامّية (661-750 AD) and the Abbasid dynast بنو العباس (750 - 1517 AD).

The founder of the Omayyad dynasty was Mo'âvieh ibn Abou Sofian معاوية ابن ابى سفيان (602 AD in Mecca - 680 AD in Damascus). His father was Abu Sofian ibn Harb ابوسفيان ابن حرب ابن امية ibn Omayyeh (560 AD in Mecca- 650 AD in Medina) — one of the richest and most famous chiefs of the Quraysh tribe, who was an adversary of Mohammad, and kept a strong attachment to all the tribal traditions of the Bedouins of the Peninsula of Arabia and his opposition to the appeal of Mohammad in Mecca and in Medina. He financially supported several assassination plans and wars in an attempt to get rid of Mohammad and his close companions. The mother of Mo'âvieh was Hind bint Utba عتبة هند بنت. She was against Mohammad and participated in the numerous wars, particularly the battle of Ohod غزوة الاحد where she paid a man called Vahshi وحشى to murder Hamza ibn Abdul-Motalleb عبدالمطلب حمزة ابن the uncle of Mohammad. She cut open the chest of Hamzeh ibn Abdul-Motalleb's body, took out his liver, and devoured it with her teeth to quieten her anger towards Mohammad and her hate towards Islam.[410]

The aunt of Mo'avieh, sister of Abu Sofian, was called 'Umm é Jamil أمّ جميل, who was the wife of an uncle of Mohammad called Abdul

---

[410] And she cut the nose and ears off the uncle of Mohammad, and the others who were killed in that battle, and made out of them a necklace which she wore around her neck. Ibn Husham. Farsi version, vol. 2, p.115.

Ozza ibn Abdul-Motalleb عبدالعّزى ابن عبدالمطلب, also known as Abu Lahab ابولَهَب (who had been born in Mecca and died there in 624 AD).

During the migration period of the Muslim community from Mecca to Medina, Abu Lahab and Umm é Jamil tried several methods of psychological warfare against Mohammad in an attempt to quell his persistence in his mission to alter the tribal behaviour of the inhabitants of Mecca to the Islamic ethics. An entire Surah, Massad, is revealed against this family in the Quran.[411] Both of them passed away before the conquest of Mecca. But the group of Abu Sofian, Hind, Mo'âvieh, and Vahshi converted to Islam on the day of the peaceful conquest of the city of Mecca by the Muslim community under the leadership of Mohammad (a few years before his death) when they heard that Allah would forgive the crimes of those who converted to Islam on that day (of the conquest of Mecca). They felt that they had been forced, rather than had converted out of inner conviction.

Later, the third Caliph Othman declared Mo'avieh ibn abi Sofian the 'Emir' of the territory of Syria and sent him to Damascus. He refused to obey the hegemony of the fourth Caliph, Ali ibn abi Talib, and

---

[411] Ismail ibn Omar ibn Kathir al Qarashi Ad Dameshghi (700-774 H.) The commentary of the Quran edition Dar ot Tayyebeh, 2002, p. 514:

"Mohammad went to a region named Bathâ' and claimed the hill. There he appealed to the inhabitants of Mecca by saying "Yâ Sàbâ hâh". The people of Quraysh came and gathered around the hill. He told them: "If now I announce that the enemy is coming to invade your houses, do you believe me?" They replied him "yes, we do." He told them "so now I warn you about a very hard punishment." Abu Lahab –between people – told: "did you appeal us to come to hear this kind of words? Wishing you to be cut!" And Allah revealed this Surah to Mohammad in reply to Abu Lahab: "May the hands of Abu Lahab be ruined, and ruined is he. His wealth will not avail him or that which he gained. He will [enter to] burn in a Fire of [blazing] flame, and his wife [as well] – the carrier of firewood. Around her neck is a rope of [twisted] fibre."

قال البخاري :حدثنا محمد بن سلام ، حدثنا أبو معاوية ، حدثنا الأعمش ، عن عمرو بن مرة ، عن سعيد بن جبير ، عن ابن عباس : أن النبي صلى الله عليه وسلم خرج إلى البطحاء ، فصعد الجبل فنادى " يا صباحاه " . "فاجتمعت إليه قريش ، فقال " :أرأيتم إن حدثتكم أن العدو مصبحكم أو ممسيكم ، أكنتم تصدقوني ؟ . "قالوا :نعم قال " : فإني نذير لكم بين يدي عذاب شديد . " فقال أبو لهب : ألهذا جمعتنا ؟ تبا لك .فأنزل الله : تبت يدا ابى لهب و تب ما أغنى عنه ماله و ما كسب سيصلى نارا ذات لهب و امراته حماله الحطب فى جيدها حبل من مسد

managed to organize a large army to fight him. When Ali was assassinated by Abd or Rahman e Muljam عبدالرحمن ابن ملجم مرادى , one of the members of the group of fundamentalist Muslims called Khavarij الخوارج, Mo'avieh automatically proclaimed himself as 'Amir ol Mo'menin' الامير المومنين (The chief of the Muslim community and Caliph) and founded, by force, the illegitimate despotic religious Omayyad dynasty. He imposed a treaty of 'obligatory peace' upon Hassan ibn Ali (the oldest son of Ali ibn abi Talib) to push him out of the field of political activities. Mo'avieh's successor was his son Yazid ibn Mo'avieh ibn abi Sofian, يزيد بن معاوية بن ابى سفيان who sent an army to Kerbela الكربلا in Iraq to fight Hussein ibn Ali ibn abi Talib (the second son of Ali ibn abi Talib) and Fatimah bint Mohammad (daughter of Prophet Mohammad), to decapitate him with his seventy-two companions, and capture the women including Zeynab bint Ali-Fatimah (granddaughter of Prophet Mohammad) in company of their children, and bring them as **their slaves** from Iraq to Syria.

This newborn empire, the 'Omayyad', spread from the borders of China far into Africa. The warriors (Jihadists) of this dynasty occupied a very important part of Europe, Asia, and Africa.

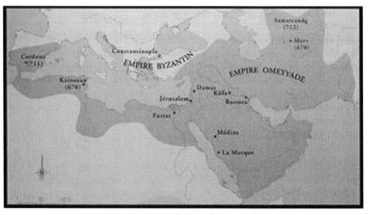

Figure 18 - A map of The Omayyad Empire

During this period a multitude of Bedouin tribal traditions, originating from the tribes of the Arabian Peninsula, were exported to the conquered nations and imposed by the numerous tyrannical successors upon the people of the conquered territories in the name of Islam. These included stoning, circumcision of girls, imposed veil, application of brutal violence, and so forth. The rulers applied these hard, strict, and violent tribal traditions to Muslim societies under the flag of Islam, which had nothing to do with the teachings of the Quran.

The Quran, which guides the faithful towards tolerance, brotherhood, equality, and justice, became a forgotten scripture, whereas a category of theologians (Motekalemin المتكلمين), closely connected to the religious state of the Caliphate, created a social system based on violence, religious supremacy, and strictness towards people in the name of the religion of Mohammad, thereby replacing unity and love. This system never had any respect for humanity, human rights, or the rights of citizens. On the contrary, it reduced the place of 'the vicar of Allah on earth' خليفة الله فى الارض to a blind obedient creature, following the orders of the clergy.

Before concluding this final chapter, we once again remind readers to take note of the source of inspiration for this book, the Quran, and the verses revealed in Medina, which clearly and openly uncover the false version of Islam, which is an invention (bed'àt) of the Monafeghon, the hypocrites. In these verses, the Quran urgently warns people not to fall naively into the trap of those whose objective is to disorient the believers of Islam towards religious superstitions originating from pre-Islamic tribal traditions.

O mankind يا ايها الناس *, have respect for your Lord, who created you all from one soul and created from it its mate and dispersed from both of them many men and women. Surah4, v: 1*[412]

The Islam ol Bàdàwi and the Islam ol Màdàni

According to the Quran **"human being"** الانسان is bearer of the divine burden of Trust الامانة :

Indeed, we exposed the Trust الامانة *to the heavens and the earth and the mountains, and they declined to bear it and feared it; but* **man** الانسان *[undertook to] bear it…… Surah 33, v: 72*[413].

Because of the **"respect for human being"** *(bearer of the divine Burden)* the Quran does not advise stoning, polygamy, hanging or killing other humans because of difference in opinions, but all this is performed under the name of Islam, based on fabricated sayings (False Revayat الروايات) that were attributed deliberately and wrongly to the founder of Islam (Prophet Mohammad).

In fact during Mohammad's lifetime, two religions seemed to have been born, under the same name and in the same time. That's why in the Quran there are verses that criticise the false Muslims or "Monafeghoun". These false Muslims were followers of their ancestral tribal traditions which were full of superstitions, and had nothing to do with the spiritual-cultural teachings of Prophet Mohammad.

These false Muslims believed in their pre-Islamic ancestral superstitions and idolatry, and had merely verbally converted to the

---

412- يا ايها الناس اتقوا ربكم الذى خلقكم من نفس واحدة و جعلمنها زوجها و بثّ منهما رجالا كثيرا و نساءً. سورة النساء الايه1]

413- إنّا عَرَضْنَا الأمَانَةَ عَلَى السّمَاوَاتِ والأَرْضِ والجِبَالِفَأَبَيْنَأَن يَحْمِلْنَهَاوَأَشْفَقَنَ مِنْهَا وَحَمَلَهَا الإنسَانُ إِنّهُ كَانَ ظَلُومًا جَهُولًا . سورة الاحزاب. الاية 72

appeal of Mohammad, but still remained attached to their tribal beliefs, and therefore they created a group of false Muslims within the new-born Muslim community in Mecca.

These false Muslims pretended to convert to the religion of Islam, by confessing verbally (Shàhâdàt ol Léssânnieh, شهادة اللسانية) about the Unity of Allah and the prophethood of Mohammad, without believing in their heart. Once they were integrated into the Muslim community, they built mosques to pray and to preach in the name of Allah, but according to their own version and interpretations, in order to mislead people from the spiritual teachings of the Quran. They did not directly oppose Islam, but instead attempted to undermine Mohammad's teachings by infiltrating the ranks of the Muslim community, in order to skip over Mohammad and his guidance, and to take control of the leadership of the Muslim community. In reality, these false Muslims did not believe in Islam which was in concordance with the Quran's teachings. This false community of "Muslims" appeared in Medina during the life-time of the Prophet Mohammad. So in other words, since 622 AD (after the migration of the founder of Islam and his companions from Mecca to Medina), the history of humanity witnessed the birth of two opposing versions of a religion, both under the name of Islam (Islam- ol-Movahedin, and Islam-ol-Monâfeghin).

There are enormous differences between these two versions of Islam, the Islam of the superstitious Bedouins, and the Islam of the citizenship (**al-Islam ol Màdàni**: in Medina). The Quran guided the people towards the building of civilised societies based on justice, equality, fraternity, tolerance, chivalry, education, and respect for citizenship. The Quran introduces the kingdom of David and Solomon as examples of the spiritual culture and social society.

The Quran regards each individual as a representative of God on earth. On the contrary, the Nomads or Bedouins who led a nomadic life, didn't have a permanent residence and were against civilisation. Their vision of the world didn't comply with the values and achievements of civilisation. They survived, by conquering the properties and goods of others. They were a destructive force against civilisation. All throughout history these two versions have co-existed. The nomadic vision of life and its values is not only absent in the Quran, but it is against the Quran. Instead of the verses of the Quran, certain sayings were spread by number of clerics throughout history which became popular amongst those who were unable to read and write. These invented sayings are known as "False Revayats" and are attributed to Prophet Mohammad. These invented sayings or False Revayats are those that do not correspond with the teachings of Quran, and are different to Revayats that agree directly with the Quranic verses (legitimate Revayats). However, for those who wish to follow the path of spirituality led by Mohammad, it is important for us to understand and to know the Quran, and not to be distracted by the comments and interpretations of others.

The Quran has two aspects: The most important is the teaching that shows how each individual can learn to develop his or her substance, which is possible for each and every individual. The other part contains laws and principles that shows how a social society can be organised, which has an evolutionary aspect and should be adapted to the circumstances of time and place. The Quran states that everyone is equal and should have equal opportunity. The only difference between individuals arises from their grade of closeness to God and their development in perfection. And it is only God who knows this. Therefore, everyone should be considered to be equal.

O mankind, *indeed We have created you from male and female and made you peoples and tribes that you may know one another. Indeed, the most noble of you* *in the sight of Allah is the most righteous of you. Indeed, Allah is Knowing and Acquainted.* Surah 49, v: 13[414]

This world view based on equality of human beings, had never existed before within the Arabic Peninsula nor in its surrounding regions, and is implied by the teaching of the Quran. The Quran states, that each human individual is potentially a representative of God, and this is not dependant on skin colour, race, language, culture etc.

O mankind, *there has to come to you instruction from your Lord and* **healing for what is in the breasts** شفاءٌ لِمَافِى الصدور *and guidance and mercy for the believers.* Surah 10, v: 57[415]

In many verses the Quran does not even discuss Muslims and non-Muslims, but instead talks about the children of Adam "Bani Adam آدَم بَنِي".

O children of Adam, *let not Satan tempt you as he removed your parents from Paradise* Surah 7, v: 27 [416] **O children of Adam,** *if there come to you messengers from among you relating to you My verses, then whoever fears Allah and reforms - there will be no fear concerning them, nor will they grieve.* Surah 7, v: 35 [417]

414- يا أيها الناس إنا خلقناكم من ذكر وأنثى وجعلناكم شعوبا وقبائل لتعارفوا إن أكرمكم عند الله أتقاكم إن الله عليم خبير. سورة الحجرات. الآية 13

415- ياايهاالناس قدجانتكم موعظة من ربكم و شفاء لما فى الصدور وهدىً و رحمةٌللمومنين. سورة اليونس. الايه 57

416- يا بنى آدم لا يفتننّكم الشيطان كم اخرج ابويكم من الجنة سورة الاعراف. الاية 27

417- يَٰبَنِى ءَادَمَ إِمَّا يَأْتِيَنَّكُمْ رُسُلٌ مِّنكُمْ يَقُصُّونَ عَلَيْكُمْ ءَايَٰتِى فَمَنِ ٱتَّقَىٰ وَأَصْلَحَ فَلَا خَوْفٌ عَلَيْهِمْ وَلَا هُمْ يَحْزَنُونَ سورة الاعراف الايه 35

The historical evolution of society and the Quranic principle of Naskh (abrogation) النسخ.

The Quran guides "Man", and the society towards the gradual steps of the substantial evolution. The method of education according to the chronological teachings of the Quran applies the principle of "annulment". It is stated in the Quran:

"*O Man, you are walking towards your Lord and will meet Him*". Surah 84, v: 6; [418]

And in another verse the Quran states: "*Indeed, the most noble of you in the sight of Allah is the most righteous of you.*" Surah 49, v: 13 [419]

The principle of Naskh, approves the nullification of an older verse by a new verse. Naskh means "abrogation, obliteration, cancellation, transfer, suppression, suspension". The structure of the principle of Naskh is introduced in different verses of the Quran such as Surah 7-v: 154, Surah 45-v: 29, Surah 22-v: 52, Surah 2-v: 106, and the Surah 16-v: 101. These verses of the Quran are known as the "verses of abrogation".

"*None of Our revelations do We abrogate or cause to be forgotten, without substituting something better or similar.*" Surah 2, v:106

ما ننسخ من آية أو ننسها نأت بخير منها أو مثلها ألم تعلم أن الله على كل شيء قدير . سورة البقرة. الاية 106

"*When We substitute one revelation for another, – and Allah knows best what He reveals (in stages),– they say, "You are but a falsifier": but most of them do not understand.*" Surah 16, v: 101

وإذا بدلنا آية مكان آية والله أعلم بما ينزل قالوا إنما أنت مفتر. سورة النحل. الاية 101

418ـ يَـٰٓأَيُّهَا ٱلْإِنسَـٰنُ إِنَّكَ كَادِحٌ إِلَىٰ رَبِّكَ كَدْحًا فَمُلَـٰقِيهِ . سورة الانشقاق. الاية 6

419 ان اكرمكم عندالله اتقيكم. سورة الاحزاب. الاية 13

These verses clearly define the principle of abrogation of an older verse and its substitution with a newer one. According to this principle the annulled verse (Mansoukh) gains a lower level of credence in comparison to the new verse (nasekh) which is given a higher authority. In the path of substantial evolution, a newly converted person to Islam starts to learn the stages of the inner seeking in order to improve his or her soul's qualities, in a step by step manner. If a novice commits a mistake he or she is forgiven, however, it is forbidden for an advanced seeker to commit the same mistake as the novice.

The historical evolution of humanity, started with the formation of small groups of men, women and children who were living together in different corners of the earth according to the lifestyle of the primitive communal Stone Age period. After more than hundred thousand years, these primitive groups evolved and took a new historical step and formed the first states-cities, in places like Mesopotamia, and later on the first flourishing civilisations appeared such as the Sumerian, Babylonian, Assyrian, Persian, Greco- Roman civilisations one after another. Centuries later, the old civilisations gave place to the modern societies. Therefore, human civilisation over time has undergone a step by step evolution, from slavery based societies to democratic civilisations that respect human rights.

The historical records confirm that during the 6th century AD in the neighbourhood of two important civilisations of Persia and Byzantine, the lifestyle of the nomadic Bedouins of the peninsula of Arabia had not yet experience this historical evolution, because the Bedouins of Arabia were strongly attached to their ancestral beliefs and tribal superstitious traditions.

The teachings of the Quran contain multiple aspects, in order to start a spiritual- cultural- social revolution in that region. During the twenty three years that the Quran's teachings were revealed to Mohammad, the educational verses of the Quran also perfectly implemented a stepwise method of evolution. Quran's step by step evolution is based on a method of education that endeavours to advance the daily lifestyle of the people in the Arabian Peninsula from their ignorant idol worshipers state towards becoming Muslims (believers), then to reach the Mo'mens (trustful Muslim) state, next evolve towards the Mottaghi (the pious Muslim) step, and then to arrive at the Seddigh (righteous Muslims) stage, and finally to attain the Abd (A Monotheist who has knowledge of the Unity of Existence) level.

In parallel with the instructions for gaining spiritual evolution and wisdom, the Quran also stresses the importance of learning to read and the studying of books[420]. One of the first orders given by Prophet Mohammad to the migrant Muslims in Medina, was to go to the Jewish schools in order to become literate. Prophet Mohammad's spiritual teachings were intertwined with teachings that helped to evolve human values in society. This is because he realised that spiritual evolution was not enough in order to stand up against despotism and superstitions, and for creating a peaceful democratic civilisation.

O Prophet, fear Allah and **do not obey the disbelievers and the hypocrites.** *Indeed, Allah is ever Knowing and Wise.* **And follow that which is revealed to you from your Lord.** *Indeed Allah is ever, with what you do, Acquainted.* **And rely upon Allah;** *and sufficient is Allah as Disposer of affairs. Surah 33, v: 1 - 3*

---

[420] *Certainly did Allah confer [great] favour upon the believers when He sent among them a Messenger from themselves, reciting to them His verses and purifying them and teaching them the Book and wisdom, although they had been before in manifest error.* Surah 3, v: 164

لَقَد مَنَّ اللّهُ عَلَى المُؤمِنينَ إِذ بَعَثَ فيهِم رَسولًا مِن أَنفُسِهِم يَتلو عَلَيهِم آياتِهِ وَيُزَكّيهِم وَيُعَلِّمُهُمُ الكِتابَ وَالحِكمَةَ وَإِن كانوا مِن قَبلُ لَفي ضَلالٍ مُبين سورة آل عمران الآيه ١٦٤

يا أَيُّهَا النَّبِيُّ اتَّقِ اللَّهَ وَلَا تُطِعِ الْكَافِرِينَ وَالْمُنَافِقِينَ إِنَّ اللَّهَ كَانَ عَلِيمًا حَكِيمًا. وَاتَّبِعْ مَا يُوحَى إِلَيْكَ مِن رَّبِّكَ إِنَّ اللَّهَ كَانَ بِمَا تَعْمَلُونَ خَبِيرًا. وَتَوَكَّلْ عَلَى اللَّهِ وَكَفَى بِاللَّهِ وَكِيلًا سورة الاحزاب. الايات 1-3

Glossary

àémméh = a'imma = ائمة = means leaders; it is the plural form of émâm

ahl = اهل =inhabitants: ahl ol Beyt(ar Rasoul) اهل البيت الرسول الله = those who live in the house[421] of Mohammad, إنما يريد الله ليذهب عنكم الرجس أهل البيت ويطهركم تطهيرا . احزاب/33 . Ahl ol Beyt means those who are closely associated to Mohammad such as Ali, Fatima, Hossein, Hassan. The expression Ahl ol Beyt even surpasses the bloodline, as it is said in the Quran regarding Noah, 'Your son is not a member of your company; He did the wrong acts.'

قال يا نوح إنه ليس من أهلك إنه عمل غير صالح سوره هودـ آيه 46 .

âl = آل = people

àl-à'râb = al-ʿarab = الاعراب = the Arab tribes و من الاعراب من يومن بالله و اليوم الأخر / سوره التوبةـ الايه 99 .

Amir ol Mo'menin = amīr al-muʾminīn = امير المؤمنين = head of the Muslim community

àshàr = aʿšar = عَشَر = ten

421ـ ر . ك . القاموس المحيط مجد الدين فيروزآبادي ج 1 ص 331 مادة أهل مؤسسة الرسالة بيروت ـ

لسان العرب ابن منظور ج 11 ص 28 – 29 مادة أهل أدب الحوزة قم ـ مفردات الراغب ص 29 ماده أهل المكتبة المرتضوية

ر . ك . القاموس المحيط مجد الدين فيروزآبادي ج 1 ص 331 مادة أهل مؤسسة الرسالة بيروت ـ

لسان العرب ابن منظور ج 11 ص 28 – 29 مادة أهل أدب الحوزة قم ـ مفردات الراغب ص 29 ماده أهل المكتبة المرتضوية

ashireh = ʿašīra = عشيرة = the close family members within a tribe وأنذر عشيرتک الاقربين / الشعراء 214, for example Bani Soufian or Bani Hâshem in Quraysh

àslèm = أسلِم = find your peace, establish the health of your heart. It is used in the sense of prescription of a doctor to someone who is ill

àslàmto = àslàmtu = أسلمتُ = I do establish my health (Abraham answers 'Aslam-to' = I will establish health, اذقال له ربه اسلِم قال أسلّمتُ لرب العالمين / البقرة- الاية 131 he does not answer 'sàllàmto' = I will submit or be obedient)

bàlàd = بلد = city

bàyân = *bayān* = بيان = the art of speech or speaking about a matter in detail

Dar ol Asnam = dār al-aṣnām = دار الأصنام = house of idolatry

éghrà' = aqra' = اقراء = read aloud

émâm = imām = امام = leader

Eslam, Islam = Islam = اسلام = the process or path to establish the health of the heart

Fotowwat = fotūwa = فتوة = chivalry

fozoul = fuḍūl = فضول = circle of spiritual chevaliers in Mecca

ghabileh = qabīla = قبيلة = tribe, for example Quraysh

ghesseh, qesseh = qiṣṣa = قصة = tale, legend, story

hâfezoun = ḥāfiẓūn = حافظون = those who memorise texts by heart

hejâbàt = ḥiǧāba = حجابة = covering the Kabah once per year

Honafa = ḥunafa' (pl)/ Hanif= ḥanīf, (si) = حنيف، ج: حنفاء = believers to only one God ijma = iğmāʿ = اجماع = unanimous opinion of the high religious authorities – doctors in the Islamic law

jàzm = ğazm = جزم = Arabic writing style

jihâd akbar = ğihād akbar = جهاد اكبر = great battle/fight

jihàd asghar = ğihād aṣrar = جهاد اصغر = lesser battle/fight

Kà'bàh = kàʾbà = كعبة = the house of God in Mecca, the Kabah.

ketâb = kitāb = كتاب = book

ketâb é màstour = ketāb mastūr = كتاب مسطور = a book written line by line

khalafa = ḫalāfa = Caliphate = خلافة = following after a preceding person, taking a place of someone who has carried a responsibility

khàttà, yàkhotto, khat = ḫatta, yaḫuttu, ḫatt = خط ، يخط، خط = to inscribe a text with a pen on paper

Khàvârij = ḫawāriğ = خوارج = group of fundamentalist Muslims

kotob = kutub = كتب = books

Quran = Qur'an= Coran= Qur'aan=Koran- قرآن

lowh = lawḥ = لوح = stone tablet; metal plate; timber panel; or clay tablet

màdreseh = màdràsà = مدرسة = school

modàrres = mudàrris = مدرس = teacher

mostà'rébeh = mustaʿraba = مستعربة = one of the category of the inhabitants of the Arabian Peninsula, not originating from that land

motekalemin = mutakallimīn = متكلمين = theologians. A category of the theologians were closely connected to the religious state. They created a social system based on violence, religious supremacy, and strictness towards people under the name of the religion of Mohammad

musnàd = مسند = Arabic writing style

nafs = نفس = egotistic drives

nâmous ol akbar = nāmūs al-akbar = ناموس الأكبر = the promised eschatological Saviour

noun = nūn = نون = ink cup

ostoureh = ustūra = اسطورة = written text line by line (written tale, written legend)

qàlàm = قلم = pen

qàrâtis = qrâtīs = قراطيس = scrolls

qasideh = qasīda = قصيدة = long poetry

revâyat = riwāya = رواية = reports about the events concerning Islam from the time of the Prophet

saghifeh = saqīfa = سقيفة = place with a roof top, i.e. gathering place

sahifeh = ṣaḥīfa = صحيفة = written page

sàllém = sàllim= سَلِّم = 'Submit!' 'Be obedient!' or 'ask the salutation of a person'

sàlâm = سلام health, peace, salutation. The inhabitants of heaven send their salutations upon you ونادوا اصحاب الجنة أن سلام عليكم . الاعراف. الاية 46 And our messengers met Abraham with happiness and said to him 'Sàlâm.' He replied 'Salam.' ولقدجائت رسلنا ابراهيم بالبشرى قالوا سلاما. قال سلام. هود. الاية 69 . Dar os Sàlâm = دار السلام = heaven, paradise. Allah invites you to heaven الله يدعوا الى دار السلام يونس. الايه 25 . Sàlâm is also one of the names of Allah. Surah 59, v: 23 - 23 الايه . الحشر السلام القدوس الملك الاهو لااله الذى هوالله

sâlem = healthy وكانوا يدعون الى السجود و هم سالمون القلم. الايه 43

sàlim = سَليم = healthy, vaccinated اذجاء ربه بقلب سليم. و ان من شيعته لابراهيم.
. الصافات. الايه 83-84

sàlslà tol jàràs = salsala al-ǧaras = سلسلة الجرس = vibrating/sounding of a bell

sàtàrà = saṭara = سطرة = writing text line by line

sedânat = the task of keeping the key of the Kabah and taking care of it

seghâyat = seqāya = سقاية = the task of serving water to the pilgrims

sélm = سِلم = health of the heart, peace

shâ'er = šāʿir = شاعِر = poet

she'r = šiʿr = شِعر = poetry

sho'àrâ' = šuʿara' = شُعراء = poets

soghm = suqm = سُقم = illness of the heart

sohof = suḥuf = صحف = written pages

Sohof el Oulâ = suḥuf al-'ūlā = الصحف الأولى = a part of the Quran that was taught by Mohammad as an already written book and that existed before the complete Quran

Tàdris = تدريس = to teach

tàlâwàt = talawāt = تلاوت = reading loudly, reciting from a written text

tànzil = تنزيل = what is given or sent downward or revealed gradually

towghifi = tawfiqī = توقيفى = something which is fixed according to the will of the Prophet, and not decided by the people themselves

tàsleem = taslīm = تسليم = submission (osàllém = I submit)

vàhi = waḥī = وحى = revelation, inner hearing of a message from a spiritual being yaktoboun = yaktubūn = يكتبون = redacting books, contracts and letters

yastoroun = yasṭurūn = يسطرون = writing texts line by line

youhoun = yūḥūn = يوحون = to do the revelation

yozakkihem = yazakkīhum = يُزَكِّيهِم = to clean the disciples from the darkness of Ignorance

'Zadokites' Hebrew language = Sadougin = a synonym in the Quran Seddyghoun, صدّيقون

Zobor é Oula= Old psalms

Index of Names

Aaron

In the Hebrew Bible and the Quran, Aaron هارون was the older brother of Moses (Exodus 6:16-20, 7:7 Quran 28:34) and a prophet of God. Aaron is also mentioned in the New Testament of the Bible. Unlike Moses, who grew up in the Egyptian royal court, Aaron and his elder sister Miriam remained with their kinsmen in the eastern border-land of Egypt (Goshen). When Moses first confronted the Egyptian king about the Israelites, Aaron served as his brother's spokesman ('prophet') to Pharaoh. (Exodus 7:1)

واجعل لى وزيرا من اهلى. ʻهارونʼ اخى. اشدد به ازرى. واشركه فى امرى. كى نسبحك كثيرا و نذكرك كثيرا. انك كنت بنا بصيرا. طه. 35-29

And appoint for me a minister from my family. Aaron, my brother. Increase through him my strength, and let him share my task. That we may exalt You much, and remember You much. Indeed, You are of us ever Seeing. Surah 20, v: 29-35.

Abdollah ibn Amr ibn al-As عبدالله ابن عمرو بن العاص

'Abd Allah ibn 'Amr ibn al-'As (died 684 AD/65 AH, the son of 'Amr ibn al-'As) was a companion of Prophet Mohammad. He was the author of *Al-Sahifah al-Sadiqah* (*The Truthful Script*, الصحيفة الصادقة), a Hadith compilation document which recorded about one thousand of Mohammad's narrations.

He embraced Islam in the year 7 AH, a year before his father did, Amr ibn al-'As. Prophet Mohammad showed preference to Abd Allah ibn 'Amr because of his knowledge. He was one of the first companions to write down the Hadith, after receiving permission from Prophet Mohammad to do so. Abu Huraira used to say that Abd Allah ibn 'Amr was more knowledgeable than himself.

His work Al-Sahifah al-Sadiqah remained in his family and was used by his grandson 'Amr ibn Suhayb. Ahmad ibn Hanbal incorporated the whole of the work of Abd Allah ibn 'Amr in his voluminous book *Musnad Ahmad ibn Hanbal*, thereby covering up for the missing Al-Sahifah al-Sadiqah which was written in the days of Prophet Mohammad.

Abdollah ibn é Obayy ibn Selloul عبدالله بن ابی ابن سلول

Abd-Allah ibn Obayy عبد الله بن أبي بن سلول, died 631AD, also called ibn Salul in reference to his mother, was a chief of the Arab tribe Banu Khazraj and one of the leading men of Medina (then known as Yathrib). Upon the arrival of Mohammad, ibn Obayy became a Muslim, though the sincerity of that conversion is disputed. Because of repeated conflicts with Mohammad, Islamic tradition has labelled him a *Monafegh* (hypocrite) and 'leader of the Monafeghin'.

Abdor Rahman ibn Muljam al-Muradi عبدالرحمن بن ملجم المرادي was the Kharijite الخوارج assassin of Ali ibn abi Talib, the first cousin and son-in-law of Mohammad.

A number of the Kharijites met in Mecca and remembered the Battle of Nahrawan (that was fought in 659AD by the Caliphate under Ali) with the Kharijites in Baghdad which resulted in Khariji defeat. One of the Kharijis said 'If we just bought ourselves revenge for the honour of our deceased brothers'. They agreed to assassinate three of the leaders of Islam: ibn Muljam was to kill Ali, Alhujjaj Al Tamimi was to kill Muawiya, and Amr ibn Bakr Al Tamimi was to kill 'Amr ibn al-'Aas. The assassination attempts were to occur simultaneously as the three leaders came to lead the Morning Prayer (Faj'r) in their respective cities of Damascus, Fustat, and Kufah. The plan was to come out of the prayer ranks and strike the targets with a sword dipped in poison. Only the assassination of Ali was successful while the other two assassinations failed.

Abraham   ابراهيم

وماكان ابراهيم يهوديا و لانصرانيا ولكن كان حنيفا. (آل عمران. الاية 67) ابراهيم

'Abraham was neither Jewish, nor Christian, but Hanif.' Surah 3, v: 67. Abraham is recorded in the Torah as the ancestor of the Israelites through his son Isaac, born to Sarah through a promise made in Genesis.

The sacred text of Christianity is the Christian Bible, the first part of which, the Old Testament, is derived from the Jewish Bible, leading to similar ancestry claims as above, though most Christians are gentiles who consider themselves grafted into the family tree under the New Covenant; see significance of Abraham for Christians for details.

It is the Islamic tradition that Mohammad, as an Arab, is descended from Abraham's son Ishmael. .(و اوحينا الى ابراهيم و اسماعيل و اسحاق و يعقوب). (النساء- 163). Surah 4, v: 163. Jewish tradition also equates the descendants of Ishmael, Ishmaelites, with Arabs, just as the descendants of Isaac by Jacob, who was also later known as Israel, are the Israelites.

Other terms sometimes used include Abrahamic faiths, Abrahamic traditions, religions of Abraham, Abrahamic monotheistic religions, Semitic religions, Semitic monotheistic religions, and Semitic one god religions.

Abraheh   ابر هه

Abraha, the Christian ruler of Yemen, which was subject to the Kingdom of Aksum of Ethiopia, marched upon the Kaaba with a large army, which included one or more war elephants, intending to demolish it. The Year of the Elephant عام الفيل, ʿĀmu l-Fīl is the name in Islamic history for the year approximately equating to 570 AD. According to Islamic tradition, it was in this year that Mohammad was born. The name is derived from an event said to have occurred at Mecca. However, the elephant in front of the army, called Mahmud, is said to have stopped at the boundary around Mecca, and refused to enter. It has been theorised that an epidemic such as by smallpox could have caused such a failed invasion of Mecca. The year came to be known as the Year of the Elephant, beginning a trend for reckoning the years in the Arabian Peninsula which was used until it was replaced with the Islamic calendar during the rule of Omar.

Recent discoveries in southern Arabia suggest that Year of the Elephant may have been 569 or 568AD, as the Sassanian Empire overthrew the Axumite- and Byzantine-affiliated regimes in Yemen around 570 AD. However, historians today believe that this event occurred at least a decade prior to the birth of Mohammad. The year is also recorded as that of the birth of Ammar ibn Yasir.

Abu Bakr ابو بكر الصديق

Abdollah ibn abi Quhaafah عبد الله بن أبي قحافة, transliteration: *'Abd Allāh ibn Abī Quhāfah*. 573 AD–23 August 634 AD, popularly known by his nickname Abu Bakr (Arabic: أبو بكر), was a senior companion (*Sahabi*) and the father-in-law of Mohammad. He ruled over the Rashidun Caliphate from 632 to 634 AD, when he became the first Muslim Caliph following Mohammad's death. As Caliph, Abu Bakr succeeded to the political and administrative functions previously exercised by Mohammad. He was also commonly known as The Truthful (Arabic: الصديق *Al-Siddiq*).

Abu Hurairah ابو هريرة

Abd ar-Raḥmān ibn Ṣakhr ad-Dawsī al-Azdī عبد الرحمن بن صخر الدوسي الأزدي; 603–681AD, born 'Abd ash-Shams عبد الشمس, but better known by the *kunyah* Abu Hurairah أبو هريرة, *Abū Hurayrah*, 'Father of the Kitten', was a companion of Mohammad and the most prolific narrator of Hadith in Sunni Hadith compilations. Abu Hurairah spent two years in the company of Mohammad and went on expeditions and journeys with him. It is estimated that he narrated around 5,375 Hadith. Abu Hurairah has been described as having a photographic memory.

Abdollah ibn Mas'ud عبدالله بن مسعود, Abdollāh ibn mas'ūd, was a ṣaḥābī or companion of the Islamic prophet Mohammad, and an early convert to Islam after Mohammad started preaching in Mecca. He became qāḍī of Kufa in about 642 AD.

Abu Jahl ابوجهل

He was son of Hisham the chief of Banû-makhzum. At first he was known as Abul Hakam meaning the father of wisdom and justice. Because he was a wise man in the Quraysh Tribe. But later the Muslims named him Abu Jahl meaning the father of ignorance.

Abu Lahab ابولهب

Abū Lahab أبو لهب 549–624AD was Muḥammad's paternal uncle. Because of his open opposition to Islam, he is condemned by name in the Quran in *sura* al-Masad.

Abu Lo'lo' ابو لوءلوء

Pīrūz Nahāvandi پیروز نهاوندی- Firuzan or Piruzān also known in Arabic as *Abu-Lu'lu'ah al-Majusi* أبو لؤلؤ المجوسي was a Sassanian soldier who served under the commander Rostam Farrokhzad, but was captured in the Battle of al-Qādisiyyah in 636 AD when the Sassanians were defeated by the Muslim army of Caliph `Omar ibn al-Khattāb on the western bank of the Euphrates River. After he was brought to Arabia as a slave, he managed to assassinate Omar in 644–645 AD.

Abu Sofian ابو سفيان

Sakhr ibn Harb صخر بن حرب, more commonly known as Abu Sufyan (560–650AD), was the leader of the Quraysh tribe of Mecca. He was a staunch opponent of the Islamic prophet Mohammad before accepting Islam and becoming a Muslim warrior later in his life. His mother, Safia, is the paternal aunt of Maymuna bint al-Harith.

Ali ibn abi Talib على بن ابيطالب son of Abu Tâleb, cousin of Mohammad, fourth Caliph, Ali ibn abi Talib علي بن أبي طالب 600–661AD was the cousin and son-in-law of the prophet Mohammad, the fourth Sunni Caliph, the first Shia Imam, and well known for his general knowledge, wisdom, and eloquence as an orator and a poet. Most of the Sufi orders of Islam claim their descent from Ali.

Asad ibn Abd-al-Uzza اسد ابن عبدالعزى Mohammad's matrilineal great-great grandfather

Barrah bint Abdul Uzza برة بنت عبد العزى ibn Othman ibn Abd-al-Dar ibn Qusay ibn Kolab was the maternal grandmother of Mohammad (mother of his mother Aminah bint Wahb), and wife of Wahb ibn 'Abd Manaf, his maternal grandfather.

Bahira بحيرا, 'Sergius the Monk', was a Syriac or Arab Gnostic Manichean Nasorean or Nestorian Christian (or Arian) monk who, according to tradition, foretold to the adolescent Mohammad his future prophetic career. His name derives from the Syriac *bhīrā*, meaning 'tested (by God) and approved'.

Ghadir é Khumm. The event of Ghadir Khumm

After the ceremony of the "farewell pilgrimage" (حَجّة الوداع), on the 18th of Dhu al-Hajjah and during the return journey to Medina, Mohammad received a revelation of a verse of the Quran and ordered all the pilgrims (which numbered around 10,000 men and women) to stop and gather in a place called "al-Ghadir" so that he could address them. The verse which was revealed to him is as follows:

O Messenger! Proclaim the (message) which has been sent to You from your Lord. If you did not, you would not have fulfilled your mission. And Allah will preserve you from (the hostility of) people. For Allah guide not those who reject Faith (Surah 5, v: 67)[422].

During this long speech, خطبة الغديرProphet Mohammad stated: "Whomever I am his Mowla (Master) Ali is also his/her Mowla (Master)[423]."

After he had addressed the crowd, Mohammad, his companions and the Muslim community returned to Medina. Whilst in Medina, the Prophet received another revelation:

This day have those who reject faith given up all hope of your religion: yet fear them not but fear Me. This day have I perfected your religion for you, completed My favour upon you, and have chosen for you Islam as your religion (Surah5, v: 3)[424].

---

[422]يأيها الرسول بلغ ما أنزل إليك من ربك وإن لم تفعل فما بلغت رسالته والله يعصمك من الناس إن الله لا يهدي القوم الكافرين. سورة المائده. الاية 67

[423]من كنت مولاه فهذا على مولاه

[424]اليَوْمَ أَكْمَلْتُ لَكُمْ دِينَكُمْ وَأَتْمَمْتُ عَلَيْكُمْ نِعْمَتِي وَرَضِيتُلَكُمُ الإِسْلامَ دِينًا. سورة المائده. الاية 3

Rumi in the 6th volume of his Mathnavi refers to this historical event by the following lines of poetry:

نام خود و آن على مولا نهاد   زین سبب پیغمبر با اجتهاد

بند رقیت ز پایت بركند   كیست مولا؟ آن كه آزادت كند

Ḥafsah bint Omar حفصة بنت عمر (605–665AD) was a wife of Mohammad Ṣalla llāhu ʿalay-hi wa-alehe-wa-sallam صلى الله عليه و آله وسلم and therefore a *Mother of the Believers.*

Hafsah was the daughter of Omar ibn al-Khattab and Zeynab bint Mazoon. She was born 'when Quraysh were building the House *Kaba*h, five years before the Prophet was sent,' i.e., in 605AD. She was married to Khunais ibn Hudhaifa but became a widow in August 624AD.

Halimeh Sa'dieh the wet nurse of Mohammad.

بن عبد الله بن الحارث بن شجنة بن جابر بن رزام بن ناصرة بن فصية بن حليمة بنت أبي ذؤيب نزار بن مضر بن عيلان بن قيس بن منصور بن عكرمة بن خصفة بن هوازن بن بكر بن سعد نصر بن عدنان بن معد بن

Hamza ibn ʿAbdul-Motalleb حمزة بن عبد المطلب 566–625AD was a companion and paternal uncle of Mohammad. His *kunyas* were Abu Omara (أَبُو عُمَارَة) and Abu Yaala (أَبُويَعْلَى). He had the by-names *Lion of God* (أسد الله) and the *Lion of Paradise* (أسد الجنة), and Mohammad gave him the posthumous title *Sayyid-ush-Shuhda* ('Chief of the Martyrs').

Hassan ibn Ali حسن بن على بن ابيطالب

Hassan ibn ʿAli ibn abi Talib الحسن بن علي بن أبي طالب, also Hasan (625–670 AD), commonly called Hasan, was the second Shiite Imam, succeeding his father Ali and preceding his younger brother Husayn ibn Ali. He was the elder son of Ali and Mohammad's daughter, Fatimah. Muslims respect him as the grandson of Mohammad and a member of Ahl al-Bayt and Ahl al-Kisa. After the death of his father, Hasan also succeeded him as Rashidun Caliph. He abdicated after six or seven months, and Mo'avieh, who became the first Omayyad Caliph, succeeded him. For the rest of his life, Hasan lived in Medina in seclusion until he died at the age of forty-five or forty-six, and was buried in the Al-Baqi' cemetery in Medina. His wife, Ja'da bint al-Ash'at is commonly accused of having poisoned him at the instigation of Mo'avieh.

Husayn ibn 'Alī ibn Abī Tālib الحسين بن علي بن أبي طالب; (08 January 626 AD–10 October 680 AD) (third/fourth Sha'aban 4AH – tenth Muharram 61 AH), sometimes spelled Hussein or Hossein, was the son of Ali ibn abi Ṭalib and Fatimah Zahra (daughter of Mohammad) and the younger brother of Hasan ibn Ali. Husayn is an important figure in Islam, as he is a member of the Ahl al-Bayt (the household of Mohammad) and Ahl al-Kisa, as well as being the third Shia Imam.

Husayn is highly regarded by Shiite Muslims because he refused to pledge allegiance to Yazid I, the Omayyad Caliph, because he considered the rule of the Omayyads unjust. As a consequence, he left Medina, his home town, and travelled to Mecca. There, the people of Kufa sent letters to him, asking his help and pledging their allegiance to him. So he travelled towards Kufa. At Karbala his caravan was intercepted by Yazid's army. He was killed and beheaded in the Battle of Karbala in 680 (61 AH) by Shimr ibn Thil-Jawshan, along with most of his family and companions. The annual memorial for him, his family, his children and his companions is called *Ashura* (tenth day of Muharram) and is a day of mourning for Shiite Muslims. The killings at Kerbella fuelled the later Shiite movements. Anger at Husayn's death was turned into a rallying cry that helped undermine and ultimately overthrow the Omayyad Caliphate.

Jesus عيسى بن مريم also referred to as Jesus of Nazareth, is the central figure of Christianity, whom the teachings of most Christian denominations hold to be the Son of God. Christianity regards Jesus as the awaited Messiah (or 'Christ') of the Old Testament and refers to him as Jesus Christ, a name that is also used in non-Christian contexts.

Khadijeh or Khadīja bint Khuwaylid خديجة بنت خويلد or Khadīja al-Kubra (Khadijeh the great) (555AD or 567–620 AD) was the first wife of Mohammad. She is commonly regarded by Muslims as the 'Mother of the Believers' i.e. Muslims. She was the first person to convert to Islam.

Mani مار مانى حيّا ابن فاتک البابلى(216–274 AD), of Iranian origin, was the prophet and the founder of Manichaeism, a Gnostic religion of late antiquity which was once widespread but is now extinct. Mani was born in or near Seleucia-Ctesiphon in Parthian Babylonia (Iraq), at the time still part of the Parthian Empire. Six of his major works were written in Syriac-Aramaic, and the seventh, dedicated to the Sassanid shahanshah, Shapur I, was written in Middle Persian, his native language. He died in Gundeshapur, under the Sassanid Empire.

Mo'avieh ibn abi Sofian معاوية بن ابى سفيان

Mo'avieh I *Mu'āwiyah ibn 'Abī Sufyān*; (معاوية ابن أبي سفيان 602 AD–April 29 or May 1, 680 AD) established the Omayyad Dynasty of the Caliphate, and was the second Caliph from the Omayyad clan, the first being Othman ibn Affan. Mo'avieh was politically adept in dealing with the eastern Roman Empire and was therefore made a secretary by Mohammad. During the first and second caliphates of Abu Bakr and Omar (Omar ibn al-Khattab), he fought with the Muslims against the Byzantines in Syria.

To curtail Byzantine harassment from the sea, Mo'avieh developed a navy in the Levant and used it to confront the Byzantine Empire in the Aegean Sea and the Sea of Marmara. The Caliphate conquered several territories including Cyzicus which were subsequently used as naval bases.

Mohammad محمد ابن عبدالله; c. 570 – 8 June 632 AD, full name Abū al-Qāsim Muḥammad ibn ʿAbd Allāh ibn ʿAbdul Motalleb ibn Hāshim, المطلب ابن هاشم ابو القاسم محمد ابن عبد الله ابن عبد Father of Qasim Mohammad son of Abd Allah son of Abdul Motalleb son of Hashim, from Mecca, unified Arabia into a single religious polity under Islam. Believed by Muslims and Bahá'ís to be a prophet and messenger of God, Mohammad is almost universally considered by Muslims as the last prophet sent by God to mankind. While non-Muslims generally regard Mohammad as the founder of Islam, Muslims consider him to have restored the unaltered original monotheistic faith of Adam, Abraham, Moses, Jesus, and other prophets in Islam.

Moses موسى in both the Septuagint and the New Testament) is a prophet in Abrahamic religions. According to the Hebrew Bible, he was a former Egyptian prince who later in life became a religious leader and lawgiver, to whom the authorship of the Torah is traditionally attributed. Also called *Moshe Rabbenu* in Hebrew ('Moses our Teacher'), he is the most important prophet in Judaism. He is also an important prophet in Christianity and Islam, as well as a number of other faiths.

Musaylimah مسيلمة or Musaylimah bin Ḥabīb مسيلمة بن حبيب was one of a series of people (including his future wife) who claimed prophethood in sixth century Arabia, which included the Islamic prophet Mohammad. He is considered by Muslims to be a false prophet, and is always referred to as 'the Liar' الكذّاب *al-Kaḏḏāb*. His followers were also very devout.

Musaylimah's name was *ibn Habib al-Hanifi*, which indicates that he was the son of Habib, of the tribe Banu Hanifa, one of the largest tribes of Arabia that inhabited the region of Najd. Banu Hanifa was a Christian branch of Banu Bakr and led an independent existence prior to Islam. His teachings were almost lost but a neutral review of them does exist in Dabestan-e Mazaheb. He prohibited pigs and wine, taught three daily prayers to God, facing whatever side, Ramadan fasting at night, and no circumcision.

Musaylimah shared verses purporting them to have been revelations from God and told the crowd that Mohammad had shared power with him. Musaylimah even referred to himself as Rahman, which suggests that he may have attributed some divinity to himself. Thereafter, some of the people accepted him as a prophet alongside Mohammad. Gradually the influence and authority of Musaylimah increased with the people of his tribe. He also took to addressing gatherings as a messenger of Allah just like Mohammad, and would compose verses and offer them as Quranic revelations. Most of his verses extolled the superiority of his tribe, the Bani Hanifa, over the Quraysh.

Musaylimah also proposed the sharing of power over Arabia with Mohammad. Then one day, in late 10 Hijri, he wrote to Mohammad:

'From Musaylimah, Messenger of God, to Mohammad, Messenger of God. Salutations to you. I have been given a share with you in this matter. Half the earth belongs to us and half to the Quraysh. But the Quraysh are people who transgress.'

Mohammad, however, replied:

'From Mohammad, the Messenger of God, to Musaylimah, the arch-liar. Peace be upon him who follows (God's) guidance. Now then, surely the earth belongs to God, who bequeaths it to whom He will amongst his servants. The ultimate issue is to the God-fearing.'

During the apostasy movement which emerged following the death of Mohammad, Sajah bint al-Harith ibn Suaeed declared she was a prophetess after learning that Musaylimah and Tulayha had declared prophethood. Four thousand people gathered around her to march on Medina. Others joined her against Medina. However, her planned attack on Medina was called off after she learned that the army of Khalid ibn al-Walid had defeated Tulayha al-Asadi (another self-proclaimed prophet). Thereafter, she sought cooperation with Musaylimah to oppose the threat of Khalid. A mutual understanding was initially reached with Musaylimah. Later, the two married and she accepted his self-declared prophethood. Khalid then crushed the remaining rebellious elements around Sajah, and then moved on to crush Musaylimah. Musaylimah fought and was killed in the Battle of Yamama by Wahshi ibn Harb, the same man who killed Mohammad's uncle Hamza in the battle of Uhud before his conversion to Islam. After Musaylimah was killed, Sajah converted to Islam.[425]

Nadr ibn al-Harith نضر بن الحارثة was an Arab Pagan at the time of Mohammad.

Obayy ibn Ka'b ابی بن کعب (died 649 AD), also known as Abu Mundhir (the father of Mundhir), was a companion of Mohammad and a person of high esteem in the early Muslim community.

Omar, also spelled Umar (عمر بن الخطاب, transliteration: `Omar ibn al-Khattāb, Omar Son of al-Khattab*, born 577 AD, died 3 November 644 AD), was one of the most powerful and influential Muslim caliphs (successors) in history. He was a senior Sahaba of Mohammad. He succeeded Abu Bakr (632–634AD) as the second caliph of the Rashidun Caliphate on 23 August 634 AD. He was an expert Islamic jurist known for his pious and just nature, which earned him the epithet Al-Farooq الفاروق ('the one who distinguishes between right and wrong'). He is sometimes referred to as Omar I by historians of Islam, since a later Omayyad caliph, Omar II, also bore that name. According to Sunnis, Omar is the second greatest of the Sahaba after Abu Bakr.

Othman ibn Affan عثمان بن عفان, also spelled *Uthmān ibn 'Affān* (577–17 June 656AD) was a companion of Mohammad, and the third of the Muslims *Rashidun* or 'rightly guided caliphs'. Born into a prominent Meccan clan of the Quraysh tribe, he played a major role in early Islamic history, succeeding Omar ibn al-Khattab as caliph at age sixty-five. He was also the Prophet's son-in-law twice, being married to two of his daughters, Ruqayyah and Umm Kulthum.

---

[425] This article incorporates text from a publication now in the public domain: Wood, James, ed. (1907). *The Nuttall Encyclopaedia*. London and New York: Frederick Warne. Article extracted from Wikipedia, the free encyclopaedia.

Under the leadership of Othman, the empire expanded into Fars in 650 AD (present day Iran), some areas of Khorasan (present day Afghanistan) in 651 AD and the conquest of Armenia was begun in the 640 AD.

Omru'ol Qays or Imra' ul Qais – kings and poets of the family of Omru'ol Qays in al-Hira.

Imra' ul Qais bin Hujr al-Kindi إمرؤ القيس ابن حجر الكندي / ALA-LC: *Imrū' al-Qays ibn Ḥujr al-Kindī*) was an Arabian poet in the sixth century AD, and also the son of one of the last Kindite kings. He is sometimes considered the father of Arabic poetry. His qaseeda, or long poem, 'Let us stop and weep' قفا نبك is one of the seven Mu'allaqat poems prized as the best examples of pre-Islamic Arabian verse. Imru' al-Qais was born in the Najd region of northern Arabia some time in the early sixth century AD. His father was said to be Hujr bin al-Harith حجر ابن الحارث / *Ḥujr ibn al-Ḥārith*, the Kindah monarchy's regent over the tribes of Asad and Ghatfan, and it is believed that Imru' al Qais was born in the territory of Asad. His mother was said to be Fatimah bint Rabi'ah al-Taghlibi فاطمة بنت ربيعة التغلبي / *Fāṭimah bint Rabī'ah al-Taghlibī*.

Legend has it that Omru' al-Qais was the youngest of his father's sons, and began composing poetry while he was still a child. His father strongly disapproved of this habit in his son, believing poetry to be an unseemly pastime for the son of a king. His father also disapproved of Imru' al-Qais' scandalous lifestyle of drinking and chasing women, and eventually banished him from his kingdom, or so the legend goes. Later, when the tribe of Asad rebelled and assassinated his father, Omru' al-Qais was the only one of his brothers to take responsibility for avenging his death. Renouncing wine and women, he fought the tribe of Asad until he had exacted revenge in blood, and spent the remainder of his life trying to regain his father's kingdom.

Qusay ibn Kolab ibn Murrah, also known as Qusayy or Kusayy, كلاب بن مُرة قصي بن;(400–480AD) was the great-grandfather of Shaiba ibn Hashim (Abdul-Motalleb), thus the great-great-great-grandfather of Mohammad.

Saʿd ibn Abī Waqqās سعد بن أبي وقاص was an early convert to Islam in 610–11 AD and one of the most important companions of Mohammad. Sa'd was the seventeenth person to embrace Islam at the age of seventeen. He is mainly known for his commandership in the conquest of Persia in 636, governorship over it, and diplomatic sojourns to China in 616 and 651 AD.

Waraka (or Waraqah) ibn Nawfal ibn Asad ibn Abd-al-Uzza ibn Qusay al-Qurashi (Arabic ورقه بن نوفل بن أسد بن عبد العزّى بن قصي القرشي) was the paternal first cousin of Khadijeh, the first wife of the Islamic prophet Mohammad.

Waraka and Khadijeh were also the first cousins twice removed of Mohammad: their paternal grandfather Asad ibn Abd-al-Uzza was Mohammad's matrilineal great-great-grandfather. By another reckoning, Waraka was Mohammad's third cousin once removed: Asad ibn Abd-al-Uzza was a grandson of Mohammad's patrilineal great-great-great-grandfather Qusay ibn Kolab.

Waraka was a Nestorian priest and is revered in Islamic tradition for being one of the first monotheists to believe in the prophecy of Mohammad.

Zacharias, spelled also Zakhary or Zechariah, was a character in the Hebrew Bible and traditionally considered the author of the Book of Zechariah, the eleventh of the Twelve Minor Prophets. He was a prophet of the two-tribe Kingdom of Judah, and, like the prophet Ezekiel, was of priestly extraction. www.wikipedia.org

Zeyd ibn Haritheh

Zeyd ibn Harithah زيد بن حارثة or Zeyd mawla Mohammad (581–629 AD) was a companion of Mohammad who was at one stage regarded as his (adoptive) son. He is the only companion whose name appears in the Quran (33:37).

Zeyd ibn Thâbit, (seventh century AD) was an Ansâr, and worked as a scribe for Mohammad. He was twelve years old when Mohammad left Mecca. He took part in the battles for the new religion since his age permitted him to do and thus was part of the army at the battle of Ohud and all subsequent battles. During the battle of Al-Yamâmah against Musaylima around 1,200 Muslims lost their lives. Between those killed were thirty-nine of Mohammad's closest companions and seventy master reciters of the Quran. This made the Caliph Abu Bakr think that the Quran might vanish from the memory of the followers and thus entrusted Zeyd to compile a book.

Zeynab bint Ali

Zeynab bint Ali زينب بنت علي Also: Zainab, Zeinab, or with the title *Sayyeda/Sayyidah* was one of the daughters of the Rashid Caliph and first Shia Imam, Ali and his first wife Fatimah. Mohammad the Islamic prophet was her maternal grandfather and thus she is a member of *ahl al-bayt* (the household of Mohammad) and is therefore often revered not only for her admirable characteristics and actions but also for her membership in and continuation of the biological line of Mohammad. Like other members of her family she became a great figure of sacrifice, strength, and piety in Islam – in the Sunni and Shia sect of the religion. Zeynab married Abdollah Jafar and had three sons and two daughters. When her brother Husayn rebelled against Caliph Yazid I in 680 AD (61 AH), Zeynab accompanied his army, which was defeated by government forces at the Battle of Karbala. Zeynab played an important in protecting the live of her nephew Ali ibn Al Husayn and, because of her sacrifice and heroism, she became known as the 'Hero of Karbala'. Zeynab died in 681 AD, and her shrine is located in Damascus, Syria.

Bibliography

Abegg, Jr. G Martin, Peter Flint, and <u>Eugene Ulrich</u>. **The Dead Sea Scrolls Bible**. The Oldest Known Bible Translated for the First Time into English, San Francisco: Harper, 2002.

Abi Ya'ghoub ibn Vazeh Ya'ghoubi. Ahmad **'Tarikh é Yaghoubi'** Farsi translation. M.E. Ayati. Edition: Entesharaté Elmi va Farhanghi. Tehran 1366. 198.

Abu Reyhan al-Biruni. (390 H. 1000 AD) **Athar-ul- Bakiya ànél Ghoroun él Khalià**./ **'Vestige of the Past'**. English version translated from the Arabic Text by Edward Sachau. **The Chronology of Ancient Nations**. London, 1879. New publication Minerva Verlag, 1984. Acta Iranica 9. Leiden./Tehran./Liège. 1975. Manichean Middle Persian and Parthian: Texts with notes. Introduction of the text of al-Biruni. Abu Reyhan. (390 H. 1000 AD) about body and soul according to the teachings of Mâni. Qw2.

Abuhaiba. Ibrahim S. I. **A Discrete Arabic Script for Better Automatic Document Understanding**. **The Arabian Journal of Science and Engineering**. 2003. 28:1B.

Al Baghavi Hoseyin ibn Mas'oud. **Mà'âlim ot Tanzil fi Tafsir ol Qur'an**. At Tafsir ol Bàghàvi. Edition: Dar ot Taybah. Beyrout. Dâr ol Ehyâ ot Torâth ol Aràbi.1997.

Al Balazuri Abul Hassan Ahmad ibn Yahia ibn Jaber ibn Davoud al-Baghdadi al-Balazuri. **Ansabul-Ashraf**. كتاب جمل من أنساب الأشراف Dar ol Fekr. Sohil Zarkâr, Ryaz Zarkoli. 1417 H. **Fotuh ol Buldan**. كتاب فتوح البلدان

Al-Dàméshghi, Esmail ibn Omar ibn Dàméshghi al-Qorashi. **Al-Bédâyàt vàn-Nahaiàt**. Dâr ol Alàm ol Kotob, 2003.

Allberry R.C. Charles. **A Manichean Psalm**. Translated in Farsi by Abul Gâsim Ebrâhimpoor. **Zabur é Mâni**. Téhran. Ostoureh,1388:2009.

Almogadasi Abu Nasr ibn Mottahar ibn Taher. al **Bad' vat Tarikh** و البدء التاريخ

Al-'Asqalani Ahmad ibn Ali ibn Mohammad.Ibn Hajar .**Fat hol-Bâri.** معرفة البارى فى شرح صحيح البخارى - Dar ol Ma'refat. Beyrout. 2010 .

Al-Muaikel, Khalil. **Pre-Islamic Arabic Inscriptions from Sakaka, Saudi Arabia**. Studies on Arabia in honour of Professor G. Rex Smith. Journal of Semitic Studies. Oxford University Press. 2002.

Al-Nadim, ibn. **The Fihrest of al-Nadim**. Bayard Dodge, editor and translator. New York. Columbia University Press, 1970.

Al-Saggār, Moḥammad Sa`īd. **Introduction à l'Etude de l'évolution de la Calligraphie Arabe** – traduit de l'Arabe par Rayya Saggar. Saggar. www.Saggar.com. Abjadiyyat al-Saggar: **al-Mashru` wa-al-Miḥnah**. Damascus. Dar al-Mada, 1998.

Al-Said, Said F. Weninger, Stefan. Eine **Unvollendete Sabäische Urkunde**. *Arabian Archaeology and Epigraphy*, 2004. http://onlinelibrary.wiley.com/doi/10.1111/j.1600-0471.2004.00024.x/abstract. Article first published online: 10th May 2004.

Al Soyouti. Jalal od Din Abdor Rahman ibn Kamal abi Bakr ibn Mohammad Sabegh ed Din al Khozayri. **Al-Etghan fi Olum el- Quran**.

Al-Theeb, S.A. **Two New Dated Nabataean Inscriptions from al-Jawf. Journal of Semitic Studies**. 1994.

Asmussen. J.P. **Manichean Literature**. Persian heritage series 22. Delmar. N.Y. 1975.

Baigent Michael & Leigh Richard. **The Dead Sea Scrolls Deception**, Great Britain: Corgi Books. 1992.

Baigent. Michael Richard Leigh: **The Complete Dead Sea Scrolls in English**: Seventh Edition (Penguin Classics). 2012

Bellamy, James A. **The new Reading of al-Namarah Inscription. Journal of the American Oriental Society**. 1985. **Two Pre-Islamic Arabic Inscriptions Revisited. Journal of the American Oriental Society**, 1988.

Black, Matthew. **The Scrolls and Christianity**, London: S.P.C.K ,1969.

Boyce. M. A **Catalogue of the Iranian Manuscripts in Manichean Script in the German Turfan Collection**. Berlin, Institut Fur orientforcung, 1960.

Burrows, Millar. **The Dead Sea scrolls**, American School of Oriental Research, 1951.

Campebell Johnathan. **Dead Sea Scrolls, the Complete Story.** Berkeley. Ulysses Press Berke, 1998.

Collins J. John. **Seers Sibyls and Sages in Hellenistic-Roman Judaism**, The Netherlands, Leiden. 1997.

Christiansen Arthur. **Iran in the Sassanid Period.** Encyclopédie Iranica. Cambridge.1939. Translated in Farsi by: Yasami Rashid. Tehran. Amir Kabir. 1988.

Clark Larry. **The Book of Giants [Ketâb Goulân]** is titled Kawan as well. 1982 cited from the collection of the treatise called: **'Emerging from darkness'** studies in the recovery of Manichean sources edited by Paul Mirecki and Jason BeDuhn, edition Brill. 1996.

Coughlan Sean. **Oldest Quran fragments found in Birmingham University.** Online at: http://www.bbc.co.uk/news/business-33436021 (accessed 22-7-15).

Cross, F. L. **The Oxford Dictionary of the Christian church.** New York: Oxford University Press, 2005.

Desroches François. Claude. Louis. **Les manuscrits du Coran : Aux origines de la calligraphie coranique.** - 1985. **Les manuscrits du Coran: Du Maghreb à l'Insulinde.** - 1996. **The Abbasid tradition, Qur'âns of the 8th to the 10th centuries.**- 1996. **Les manuscrits du Coran en caractères higâzî, Position du problème et éléments préliminaires pour une enquête.** - 1998. **Le manuscrit arabe 328 (a) de la Bibliothèque nationale de France (en coll.).** - 1999. **Buchkunst zur Ehre Allâhs, Der PrachtQuran im Museum für Islamische Kunst** (en coll.). - 2000. **Manuel de codicologie des manuscrits en écriture arabe** (en coll.). - 2001. **Le manuscrit Or. 2165** (f. 1 à 61) de la British Library (en coll.). - 2004. **Le livre manuscrit arabe, Préludes à une histoire.** - 2006. **Le Coran.** - 2009. **La transmission écrite du Coran dans les débuts d'Islam. Le Coran.** Que sais-je? PUF. Paris. 2005- **Catalogue des manuscrits arabes,** fascicules 1 et 2, Bibliothèque nationale (France), département des manuscrits, Bibliothèque nationale. Paris 1983.

Ebrahim Ahmad al Moghafi. **Al-Mo'jam ol-Modon vàl Ghabâél ol-Yàmàniieh.** Edition: al-Mànshourat Dâr ol-Hekmat. Sàn'â. 1985

Ehsan Yarshater, Cambridge. **History of Iran, The Seleucid, Parthian and Sasanian.** Cambridge, 1983.

Eisenman Robert. **The Sectarian Torah and the Teacher of Righteousness**.

Encyclopedia of Islam. **The foundation of the Muslim world**. The article about Hafseh bint Omar ibn Khattab.

Goldziher Ignas. **Le dogme et la loi de l'Islam**. Paris 1920. Farsi translation by Ali Naghi Monzavi. Kamanghir. 2nd eds., 1357:1978.

Graham. A William. **Beyond the Written Word: Oral aspects of scripture in the history of religion**. Cambridge, University of Cambridge Press. 1987.

Graystone Geoffrey. **The Dead Sea Scrolls and the originality of Christ**. New York: Sheed & Ward.

Guillaume, A. **The Life of Mohammad. Translation by Sirat Rasul Allah**. Mohammad ibn Eshaq. Oxford. Oxford University Press. 1955.

Haloun, G. Henning. W.B. **The Compendium of the Doctrines and styles of the Teachings of Mâni, the Budha of Light.** Asia Major 3. Hidemi Takahashi, 1953.

Hashtroudi, Fatemeh. **The Scrolls of the Dead Sea. History and Opinions**. (Farsi) The University of the Religions and Denominations. Qom/ Iran, 2011.

Hamidullah M. **Some Arabic inscriptions of Madinah of the early years of Hijrah**. Islamic Culture, 1939.

Healey, John F. **The Nabataean Tomb Inscriptions of Mada'in Salih**. Journal of Semitic Studies. Supplement 1. Oxford. Oxford University Press, 1993.

Healey, John F. and Drijvers, Han J.W. **The Old Syriac Inscriptions of Edessa and Osrhoene**. Leiden, Brill, 1999.

Hussein, Mohamed A. **Origins of the Book: From Papyrus to Codex**. New York Graphics Society Ltd. Greenwich, Connecticut. 1970.

Ibn Husham. Abu Mohammad Abdul ibn Husham al Basri. **As Sirat-on Nabavyieh**. 2. Vols. Beyrout. An Nour lil Màtbou'ât, 2004. Farsi translation, Tehran Eslamieh. 1364:1985.

Ibn Kathir. Ismail ibn Omar ibn Kathir al- Qorashi al-Dameshqi. **The Commentary of ibn Kathir**. Dar Tayyebeh.1420: 1999. New publication 2002.

Ibn Nadim Mohammad, ibn Eshagh. **Al-Fihrest/ al-Fihrest ol Uloum**. The Fihrest of al-Nadim. Bayard Dodge, editor and translator, New York Columbia University Press, 1970.

Ibn Sa'd Mohammad. **Tabaqat ol Kobra**. Translated by Haq, S. M. ibn Sa'd's Ketab al-Tabaqat al-Kabir, Delhi: Ketab Bhavan. Encyclopaedia of Islam.

Ibn Salim Seyed Abdul Aziz. **At-Târikh ol Arab fil-Asr el-Jâhelieh**. Edition: Dâr ol-Nehzat el-Arabiyah.1978. **Al-Hey'at ol-Ammeh les-Syahat val-Athir- Athâr ol-Oxodus**. Edition: al-Esdâr ol Héy'àt ol-Ammeh lel-Athâr. 2007.

Jull, A. J. T. Et Al '**Radiocarbon Dating of scrolls and Linen Fragments from the Judean Desert**', 1995.

Online at:
https://journals.uair.arizona.edu/index.php/radiocarbon/article/viewFile/1642/1646

Kasser Rodolphe, Marvin M. Meyer, Gregor Wurst. 'The Gospel of Judas' - From Codex Tchakos The Gospel of Judas. 2006 online at: www.nationalgeographic.com/lostgospel/_pdf/GospelofJudas.pdf. (Accessed. 21-7-15)

Khan, Gabriel Mandel. **Arabic Script: Styles, Variants, and, Calligraphic** Adaptations. Abbeville Press Publishers. New York. 2001.

Khan, Majeed. **The Origin and Evolution of Ancient Arabian Scripts**. Ministry of Education and Department of Antiquities and Museums. Riyadh. 1993.

Koenen. L. '**Manichean Apocalypticism at the crossroads of Iranian, Egyptian, Jewish and Christian thought**' - in Codex Manichaeicus Coloniensis. Ed: L. Cirillo and A. Roselli. Cosenza 1986

Licht, Jacob & Feredrick Fyvie Bruce '**Dead Sea Scrolls**', in: The Encyclopaedia Judaica, vol. 5. 1971

Mādūn, Muḥammad `Alī. **Khatt al-Jazm ibn al-Khatt al-Musnad**. Dar Ṭlās lil-Dirāsāt wa al-Terjamah wa al-Nashr. Damascus. First Edition. 1989.

McGuire, Gibson. Nippur. The Oriental Institute of the University of Chicago. 2001-2002 Annual Report.

http://oi.uchicago.edu/research/pubs/ar/01-02/nippur.html
MacKenzie. D.N, '**Mâni's Shabuhragan I**'. Bosas 1979 II. 1980.

Majlessi. Molla Mohammad bagher. **Bihâr ol Anwar**- Qom.

Mâne'Mohammad Mânè. **Al Àmâken ol Atharieh fi Shebh é Jazirà tol Arabieh**. Ed: Vekalat Béenajat Lila'lam. Arabis. 1987.

Mani ibn Patak.

Shaburragan.http://www.iranicaonline.org/articles/sabuhragan

Miles, G. C. **Early Islamic Inscriptions Near Ta'if in the Hijaz.** Journal of Near Eastern Studies. 1948.

MM. ED. Chavannes et P. Pelliot. **Traité Manichée retrouvé en Chine.** Journal Asiatique. March - April 1913.

Moghafi. Ebrahim Ahmad. **al Al-Mo'jam ol-Modon vàl Ghabâél ol-Yàmàniieh.** Edition: al-Mànshourat Dâr ol-Hekmat. Sàn'â. 1985.

Moore Cross Jr., Frank. **The Ancient Library of Qumran and Modern Biblical Studies.** Doubleday, Garden City. 1958.

Mohammad ibn Ahmad al Ansari al Qardabi (from Cordoba) **Al Jami' li Ahkam él Qor'an (The commentary of the Qur'an)** by Qartabi. Dar ol Fekr./ Moassesseh al Risalat. 1427H. -2006.

Omniglot. **Writing Systems and Languages of the World.** Avestan. http://www.omniglot.com.

Polotsky and Böhlig, **Coptic homily 'Of the Great War'** 1934, cf. Stroumsa, 1981.

Rokn od Din Homayun Farrokh, **History of Book and the Imperial Libraries of Iran.** Ministry of Art and Culture. Tehran. 1963.

Ramiar Mahmoud. **History of the Qur'an.** Tehran. 1346 new publication. 1362- 1983.

Robin Christian Julien. **Langues et écritures.** Published in p. 127, p.131 'Routes d'Arabie. Archéologie et histoire du Royaume d'Arabie Saoudite'. Edition Louvre. Paris 2010.

Rostovtzeff, M. I. The **Caravan Gods of Palmyra**. The Journal of Roman Studies. Part 1: Papers Dedicated to Sir George MacDonald. 1932.

Rowley, H. H. **The Dead Sea Scrolls and The New Testament**, London: S.P.C.K. 1964.

Safadi, Y. H. **Islamic Calligraphy**. Shambhala Publications, Inc. Boulder. 1997.

Sahih Bukhari. (البخارى. صحيح كتاب)Ketab ol Fazael. Chapter of Fazâél ol Ansar. Vol.6 p.106, and his book Ketab ot Tafsir. Chapter about the companions of the Prophet.

Saifulla, M. S. M.; Ghuniem, Mohammad; Zaman, Shibli. From Alphonse Mengana to Christoph Luxenberg. **Arabic script and the alleged Syriac Origins of the Qur'an**.

Saad D. Abulhab Baruch College, CUNY. **Roots of Modern Arabic Script: From Musnad to Jazm**. Online at: http://arabetics.com/public/html/more/History%20of%20the%20Arabic%20Script_article.htm (accessed 15-7-15).

Segal, J. B. **Four Syriac Inscriptions**. Bulletin of the school of Oriental and African Study. University of London. Fiftieth Anniversary Volume.1967. Some Syriac Inscriptions fron the 2nd - 3rd Century A. D. **Bulletin of the school of Oriental and African Study**. University of London. 1954.

Schiffman Lawrence. **Reclaiming the Dead Sea Scrolls: their True Meaning for Judaism and Christianity**, Anchor Bible Reference Library, Doubleday, 1995.

Schiffman, Lawrence H. (2005), **'Dead Sea Scrolls'**, in: The Encyclopaedia of Religion, Mirca Eliade 2nd eds., MacMillan Publ, vol. 4.

Sheridan, Susan Guise, Ph.D. University of Notre Dame. Department of Anthropology. **Pictures from a trip to Petra**. Online at: http://www.nd.edu/%7Esheridan/Jordan%202000/Jordan%202000.html. (Accessed 24-8-2015)

Shirazi. A. Afshar. **Motoun é Arabi va Farsi dar bâryé Mâni và Mânàviyat**. Tehran 1335 -1956.

Smithsonian. National Museum of Natural History. Written in Stone: **Inscriptions from the National Museum of Saudi Arabia**. Online at: http://www.mnh.si.edu/epigraphy/ (accessed at-24-08-15)

Starcky, Jean. The Nabataean: A Historical Sketch. **The Biblical Archaeologist**. December 1955.

Sommer, A. Dupont. **The Dead Sea Scrolls**. tr. E. Margaret Rowley, Basil Blackwell Publ. 1952.

Tabari Mohammad Jarir. **Jami'ol Bayan fi Tafsir él Qor'an / commentary of the Qur'an**/ Egypte. Al-Amiriah. **History of people and kings.** 1325. - 1946.

Taher Ashour Mohammad 'Tafsir ot Tahrir vat Tanvir' /-Tunisia- Dar ot Tunesieh linashr. 2008.

Thiering Barbara. **Jesus & the Riddle of the Dead Sea Scrolls**. Article published by the Sidney University about the struggle between the righteous teacher and the man of lie. **Jesus the Wicked Priest**. Schism Paperback – March 27, 2008. The **'Letter of the teacher of Righteousness to the Wicked priest' found in the cave 'QMMT4'**. Decoding the Real Story of Jesus and Mary Magdalene. 2006.

Ben Zion Wacholder. **The Dawn of Qumran.**

http://www.researchgate.net/publication/249593524_Ben_Zion_WACH
OLDER_The_Dawn_of_Qumran._The_Sectarian_Torah_and_the_Teac
her_of_Righteousness_(Monographs_of_the_Hebrew_Union_College_N
umber_8)_Hebrew_Union_College_Press_Cincinnati_1983_xviii_and_31
0_pp._cloth__25_

Willian A. Graham. **Beyond the Written Word: Oral aspects of scripture in the history of religion**. Cambridge, University of Cambridge, 1987.

Wherry, Rev. E. M. **A Comprehensive Commentary on the Quran comprising Sale's translation and Preliminary Discourse**. London, Trubner & Co., 1882-1886/ London. K. Paul, Trench, Boston: Houghton, Mifflin and Company, 1896.

Ya'ghoubi ibn Vazeh Ahmad abi Ya'ghoub. **'Tarikh é Yaghoubi'** Farsi translation. M.E. Ayati. Edition: Entesharaté Elmi va Farhanghi. Tehran 1366.'

Yaghoub Ahmad ibn abi; àt-Tarikh Ya'ghoubi ; Farsi translation by Mohammad Ibrahim Ayati. Entesharat Elmi-Farhangi. 5th publication; Tehran- 1987.

تاریخ یعقوبی. احمدبن ابی یعقوب. ترجمه فارسی عبدالحمید آیتی. انتشارات علمی۔ فرهنگی۔ چاپ پنجم. 1987

Other web references:

Ancient Hebrew Research Centre. Museum of Hebrew Script. Alphabet. http://www.ancient-hebrew.org

Ancient Scripts. Pahlavi. http://www.ancientscripts.com/pahlavi.html

Arab Calligraphy: Portrait of Magnificence, Majesty, and Grace. *Areen: Arabcin's Monthly Magazine.* 2001. 25.
http://www.arabcin.net/areen/areen_english/25/cover1.htm

http://www.birmingham.ac.uk/news/latest/2015/07/quran-manuscript-22-07-15.aspx

https://www.ccel.org/bible/phillips/CN711NTinOT.htm

http://www.christnotes.org/bible.php?ver=kjv

Forum Ancient Coins. Nabataean Numerals and Number Words.
http://www.forumancientcoins.com

The Catholic Encyclopaedia. Petra.
http://www.newadvent.org/cathen/11777b.htm

http://www.quran.com/

Following books in PDF: مكتبة الاسلامية Maktabat ol Islamieh

http://www.unituebingen.de/en/13002?tx_ttnews%5Btt_news%5D=23132

Islamic Civilisation. http://www.cyberistan.org/islamic/letters.html

http://arabetics.com/public/html/more/History%20of%20the%20Arabic%20Script_article.htm

http://idb.ub.uni-tuebingen.de/diglit/MaVI165

Inscription in Nabatean alphabet. South of Syria- Bosra. Louvre Museum

Altar. Inscription to the god Dushara. Mid-1st century AD. British Museum.

http://www.catholic.org/bible/book.php?id=42&bible_chapter=3 1 A prayer of the prophet Habakkuk; tone as for dirges.

http://arabetics.com/public/html/more/History%20of%20the%20Arabic%20Script_article.htm

مناقب آل ابیطالب. ابو عبدالله محمد بن علی بن شهر آشوب سَروی مازندرانی ـ ۴۸۸/۹ ـ ۵۸۸ ق ـ معروف به ابن شهر آشوب و ملقب به « رشیدالدین » «و » « عزّالدین ». ناشر العربی ـ المکتبة الحیدریة. 1376 القمری. ناشر الفارسی: علامه. قم. 1379 القمری

Encyclopaedia of Islam, Online Ed.

'السنن' ابی داود سلیمان بن الأشعث السجستانی. المکتبة العصریة، صیدا ـ بیروت

'السنن' ابن ماجه. أبو عبد الله محمد بن یزید بن ماجه . تحقیق محمد فؤاد عبد الباقی ـ دار الحدیث ـ القاهرة

کتاب الغدیر. علامه امینی.

'تفسیر القرآن' ابن کثیر إسماعیل بن عمر بن کثیر القرشی الدمشقی. 2008

'تفسیر القرآن' القرطبی الجامع لأحکام القرآن الإمام أبو عبد الله محمد بن أحمد الأنصاری القرطبی . 2015

'تفسیر البغوی' الحسین بن مسعود *البغوی* أبو محمد . دار طیبة

فتح الباری فی شرح صحیح البخاری. احمد ابن حجر العسقلانی. دارالریان للتراث. 1986

السنن. سنان بن علی بن شعیب بن احمد النسائی. مکتب النشر سنة الاسلامیه المطبوعات. 1994

المسند. امام احمد حنبل. النشر العربی التراث. 1993

صحیح. ابوعبدالله حافظ بخاری ـ البخاری. نسخه الکترونیکی. شعبان 1433

مباحث فی علوم القرآن. مناع قطان. مکتبة وهبة. القاهره.2000

مناهل العرفان فی علوم القرآن. محمدبن عبدالعظیم الزرقانی. دارالکتاب العربی. بیروت. 2008

مجمع البیان فی تفسیرالقرآن. ابوعلی حسن بن فضل الطبرسی. ترجمه فارسی/ سی مجلد.تفسیر مجمع البیان جوان ـ برگرفته از **تفسیر مجمع البیان طبرسی / تالیف محمد** بیستونی.قم : بیان جوان؛ مشهد: آستان قدس رضوی، شرکت به نشر ، 1390 .

طبقات الكبرى. اِلطبقات الكبرى ''و ''الطبقات الصحابه و التابعين''محمدبن سعد منيع كاتب واقدى البغدادى. بيروت لبنان. 1960

Encyclopaedia Britannica Online Academic Edition'.

Global.britannica.com. Retrieved July 2014.

Encyclopaedia of Islam. The foundation of the Muslim world. The article about Hafsah bint Omar ibn Khattab. 6314

الخصائص، ابن جنّى، ابوالفتح عثمان، تحقيق محمد على النجّار، قاهره: الهيئه المصريه. (1446ق)

الايضاح فى شرح المفصّل، ابن الحاجب النّحوى، تحقيق الدكتور موسى نباى العليلى، بغداد: المطبعه العانى. (1976 م

مقدمه ابن خلدون، ابن خلدون، عبد الرحمن، قاهره(1348 ق

كتاب الملاحن، تحقيق عبد الاله نبهان، بيروت: مكتبه لبنان ناشرون. ابن دريد، ابوبكر محمد الأزدى، (1996) م

شرح المقرّب، ابن عصفور الاشبيلى الاندلسى، قاهره: مطبعه السعاده(1990 م

الممتّع فى التّصريف، تحقيق الدكتور فخر الدّين قباوه، بيروت: دارالمعرفه1987

انباه الرّواه على انباه النّهاه، تحقيق محمد ابوالفضل ابراهيم، قاهره: دارالفكر عربى ابن القفطى، جمال الدّين، (1406 ق

تسهيل الفوائد و تكميل المقاصد، ابن مالك اندلسى، تحقيق محمّد كامل، قاهره. (1967 م

لسان العرب، بيروت: دار صادر. ابن منظور، (1388 ق

الصّاحبى، تحقيق السيد احمد صقر، قاهره: مطبعه عيسى البابى الحلبى ابوالحسين احمد بن فارس بن زكريا، 1977 م

الزّينه فى الكلمات الأسلاميه العربيه، تحقيق حسين الهمدانى، قاهره. ابوحاتم رازى، (1957 م

شرح شافيه ابن الحاجب، به تحثيث محمّد نور الحسين و ...، بيروت: دارالكتب العلميّه. رضى الدّين محمّد استرآبادى المفصّل فى النّحو، النّحوى، (1395 ق

اخبار النّحويين البصريّين، السّيرافى، ابوسعيد، (1374 ق قاهره: شركه المصطفى البابى الحلبى.

الايضاح فى علل النَحو، قاهره1967

شرح شواهد المغنى جلال الدِن عبد الرَحمن السَيوطى/ محمّد محمود التلاميد التركزى السَنقيطى، لجنه التراث العربى .

الاشباء و النظائر فى النَحو م)، ، تحقيق عبد الاله، دمشق: مجمعاللّغه العربيه1985 .

ضياء السالک الى اوضح المسالک، قاهره: المطبعه السَعاده .محمّد عبد العزيز النَجار، (1393 ق

مثنوى معنوى، به اهتمام رينولد نيکلسون مولوى بلخى، مولانا جلال الدَين، (1933 م

کشف الأسرار و عدَه الأبرار .ميبدى، رشيد الدَين، به اهتمام على اصغر حکمت، تهران . 1325

معجم الادباء، ياقوت الحموى، ابو عبدالله، (1355)،

تفسير التحرير والتنوير .محمد الطاهر بن عاشور .الناشر: الدار التونسية للنشر.2008.

The commentary of the Quran by Qartabi. Mohammad ibn Ahmad ah Ansari al Qardabi (from Cordoba) - Dar ol Fekr.

Appendix

تفسیر 'رَجَعنَا مِن الجَهادِالاصغَر اِلَی الجَهادِ الاکبَرِ'

ای شهان ! گشتیم ما خصم برون   ماند خصمی زو بتر در اندرو

کشتن این، کار عقل و هوش نیست   شیر باطنسخرهٔ خرگوش نیست

دوزخست این نفس و دوزخ اژدهاست   کو به دریا نگردد کم و کاست

هفت دریا را در آشامد هنوز   کم نگردد سوزش آن خلقسوز

سنگ ها و کافران سنگدل   اندر آیند اندرو زار و خجل

هم نگردد ساکن از چندین غذا   تا ز حق آید مرورا این ندا

سیر گشتی؟ سیر؟ گوید: نه هنوز'   اینت آتش اینت تابش اینت سوز

عالَمی را لقمه کرد و در کشید   معدهاش نعره زنان هل من مزید

حق، قدم بر وی نهد از لامکان   آنگه او ساکن شود از کن فکان

چونک جزو دوزخست این نفس ما   طبع کل دارد همیشه جزوها

این قدم، حق را بُوَد کو را گُشد   غیر حق خود کی کمان او کشد

در کمان، ننهند الا تیر راست   این کمان را باژگون کژ تیرهاست

راست شو چون تیر و وارَه از کمان   کز کمان هر راست بجهد بیگمان

چونکه وا گشتم ز پیکار برون   روی آوردم به پیگار درون

'قد رَجَعنَا مِن جَهادِ الاصغَر' یم   با نبی اندر جهاد اکبریم

قوّت از حق خواهم و توفیق و لاف   تا به سوزن بر کنم این کوه قاف

سهل شیری دان که صف ها بشکند   شیر آنست آن که خود را بشکند

مثنوی مولانا جلال الدین رومی- دفتر اول

/http://ganjoor.net/moulavi/masnavi/daftar1/sh76

The Truth about Jihad

The word *jihad*, nowadays is used incorrectly, often with a very negative, even terrifying, connotation: as the basis of "Islamic" terrorism and suicide attacks.

However, one must take seriously the dangers caused by arbitrary commentaries of sacred texts. Anyone can read the Quran, the Bible, and the Torah, but not anyone can interpret them, because each person projects his own state of mind into his interpretation. People who are ignorant are ruled by the impulses of their ego; they live in the era of ignorance, even if we are in the twenty-first century. Their interpretations of the sacred texts - the Bible, Gospel, and the Quran - correspond to the low, materialistic level of their comprehension and imagination. You cannot blame the book if the interpretation is false.

"*Jihad*" means "supreme effort." The root of the word is *jihad*, which means "effort." The one who makes considerable effort to reach an important goal is a mojahid. The word jihad and all derivatives belong to Quranic vocabulary and occur forty-one times in the Quran. Jihad is one of the pillars of Islam. According to the Sunnis, there are five religious obligations: salat (daily prayer), zakat (two religious taxes), som (fasting), haj (pilgrimage to Mecca), and jihad (all efforts are for God). While according to the Shiites, there are eight pillars: salat, som, khoms and zakat, haj, jihad, amr bil ma'rouf (the mind is instructed in doing good deeds) nahi menal monkar (the ego is prevented from acting badly).

The Quran describes the believers as people who regularly pray, pay their religious taxes, and make sincere efforts to forego material goods, and suppress their egos on the way to God. In other words, to be a good Muslim, you must respect the importance of *jihad*. But contrary to popular belief nowadays, the religious obligation of *jihad* is outside of any connotation of war. The words designating war in the Quran are harb and ghetal, with their derivatives:

a) **Harb** is a war declared by one person or a group against moral or physical enemies. For example, in in the second surah (set of verses) of the Quran, the 275th verse of surah of bakara, strictly condemns usury:

God allowed selling, but not usury (Surah 2, v: 275). *O you believers! Respect the will of God and renounce – if you are true believers- what remains, as profit from usury.*

But if you do not renounce, be prepared for the war (harb) that God and his prophet consider against you (Surah 2, v: 278-279).

In another verse:
Every time the enemies -try to provoke the fire of war (harb), God puts it out (Surah 5, v: 64).

b) **Ghetal** means to "engage in war" Ghetal can be negative if it aims at scorning justice oppressing the liberty of people. It has a positive connotation when it is meant to legitimise defence of life, dignity; goods and another's houses against an invading aggressive enemy. God has allowed Muslims to make war in case of "legitimate defence." This happened when the prophet and his companions were forced to leave Mecca for no justified reason, and in fear of their lives. They were attacked many times by their enemies. The 39th verse of surah "Haj" reports this historical event, using the word ghetal and not jihad.

"Authorisation was given to those who resist militarily (yo-ghteloun) since they have been oppressed and God can grant them victory." (Surah 22, v: 39)

David and Goliath

In various verses the Quran refers to the military confrontation between the companions of prophets, in a defensive position, and their invading adversaries with the word guetal. One example is the story of the confrontation between, the Israelites, under the leadership of David, and their enemies, headed by Goliath (Surah 2, v: 245-251):

Have you not seen the Ancients among the people of Israel after Moses? They told the prophet, "Give us a king, we will fight (Ghatala) in the way of God." It is impossible for us not to fight (ghatala) in the way of God, because we have been chased from our houses and separated from our families." Their prophet answered: "God has sent you

Saul as king." They said: "We are not capable today of resisting Goliath and his army."
But those among them who believed in meeting God answered: "How many times has a
small group of men won over a large army with the permission of God. God is on the side
of those who are patient." With the permission of God, their enemy had to flee and David
killed Goliath. God gave David the kingdom and wisdom; he taught him what he
wanted.

Just after these verses, the Quran makes the following deduction:

If God did not push back certain people using other people, the earth would be filled
with corruption (Surah 2, v: 251). And it is added:
Fight (ghatelou) on the way to God and learn that God learn that hears and knows
everything (Surah 2, v: 244).

Following the logic of the Quran, we may deduce that resistance
against injustice, invasion and barbarity is legitimate. Still, it must be
emphasised that in these verses the word jihad is not used; rather, ghetal or
mokateleh are used. In other words, jihad does not correspond at all with a
military action, neither offensive nor defensive.

The word jihad means a very important effort and corresponds to an
inner, individual action that each believer is invited to undertake to come
gradually closer to the final goal of esoteric ascension towards Allah. On
this subject, the Quran states:

Those who use their efforts on us (jahadou), we will guide them on our ways (Surah
29, v: 69).

And in the same surah, this verse completes the explanation:

The one who does jihad does it for his own good or the one who fights, fights to train
his nafs. (Man jahada faennama youiahid le nafseh) (Surah 29, v: 6).

Thus, *jihad* is a war that each believer declares upon his inner-self against his most primitive impulses and instinctive pressures. During this fierce-and pitiless fight, the believer tries to develop in himself ever more humane and chivalrous attributes, such as friendship, love, generosity, while repressing negative characteristics such as jealousy, hard feelings, and meanness.

The goal of jihad is to fight the nafs (ego). In fact, nafs does not truly mean "soul," but "ego." It is a part of ourselves that carries instinctive impulses causing barbarity, obscurantism and ignorance. Nafs is the most primitive aspect of the human race, corresponding to the reptilian part of the brain. It is under the pressure of the nafs that humanity remains, in general, in the domain of the law of the jungle. Nafs is in complete contradiction with everything concerning the divine spirit.

Attar, a mystical Persian poet of the 6th century of the Hegira, compares the nafs and its characteristics to a jungle dominated by various animals such as the wild wolf, the cunning fox, the bear of sexuality the tiger of aggressiveness, the snake, the bat, the scorpion, etc. The believer's duty is to fight all these animals in himself to turn the jungle of his personality into a garden of flowers and fragrances. Mowlana of Balkh compares the nafs to a dragon with seven hundred heads, all of them set against the sky. God has sent the prophets to awaken us from the sleep of egotism and to distinguish the source of danger hidden in our inner-selves. The Quran states:

I do not acquit my nafs, because my nafs orders me permanently unhealthy actions (Surah 12, v: 53). Also, Moses gives this explicit message to the believers: O you people, come back to your Lord and kill your nafs (Surah 2, v: 54).

To fight against "the nafs, commander of bad actions," (ammara bissou) is a necessary condition for the evolution of the soul towards the superior values of humanity, unity and divinity. By suppressing this first obstacle, the person can progressively become himself, conforming to the image of God; and at the end of a long and difficult journey, he can become

God's vicar. That is why the believer will never be able to part with his sword of piety and never renounce this inner fight. The mystics explain that, with the help of *jihad*, the human being can overcome these successive steps to realise and, actualise, in the end, the image of God in himself; it is the only guarantee the traveller has against the vicissitudes of his nafs.

The first appeal of the prophets to their disciples is *jihad*, because this supreme effort opens the door to perfection. Thus a *jihad* against our own ego, because our most powerful enemy is our own nafs, and as long as we do not manage to control our nafs, we will not be able to develop our latent capacities.

The Distinction between Jihads

In the Muslim tradition, the sunna (Muslim tradition), the foghaha, or doctors of Islamic law, have distinguished three kinds of jihad: the great jihad (jihad al-akbar), jihad against the inner-enemy ; (jihad al-asgar), the lesser jihad, jihad against an external enemy to defend the religion; and the noblest of all, the jihad al-afdal, which means "saying the truth in the face of an oppressor" (hadith quoted by Muslim and Bokhari).

One event of the first wars of Islam shows the importance of the evolving and spiritual meaning of jihad. One day the prophet and his companions were attacked by the army of a pagan tribe. The Muslims maintained their defensive positions and won the battel. After the enemy's retreat, the prophet found the Muslims very satisfied with their own efforts and their victory. He said to them: "We go back now from this little battle to the great battle and engage now in the greatest jihad (Farajena menal jihad alasgar ela aljihad alakbar)" (hadith quoted by Muslim and Bokhari and also quoted by Mowlana in the Masnavi volume I).

The Muslims, shocked by these words, answered: "But this was the worst enemy that we have ever defeated." And, Muhammad answered: "No. your greatest enemy lives in each of you; each one must fight against his own ego (a 'da adovokom alnafs allati baina djanbeikom)." On this subject, Mowlana of Balkh makes this remark[426]:

"Consider as little valiant a lion who rushes in the row of enemies. Consider as a real lion the one who overcomes, himself."

A short overview of the Bible

The Bible, including the Old and New Testaments, is an old book that consists of about 1,800 pages. The content of this Holy Book is written in a hermeneutical language full of expressions, parables, symbols, and mysteries that are not easy to comprehend. The Torah, otherwise known as the Old Testament, contains 1,338 pages and begins with the Sefer of Genesis and ends with the book of Sahifeh Melaky Nabi. In Hebrew, the word 'Torah' means 'to guide', 'to teach', 'doctrine', 'instruction' and 'law'.[427] The term 'Torah' is furthermore used in a very general practical sense to include both written and oral law, including the Mishnah, the Talmud, and the Midrash.

The Pentateuch, also known as the Five Books of Moses or the Written Torah, makes up the first part of the Hebrew Bible. It consists of: Genesis (origin), Exodus (going out), Leviticus (relating to the Levites), Numbers (numbering of the Israelites), and Deuteronomy (second law). In addition to the five books of the 'Asfar é khamseh' (The Pentateuch) we find in the frame of the Old Testament an ensemble of books (Ketab) and manuscripts (Sohof) which are:

Nevi'im (The prophets), which is composed of Yehoshua (Joshua); Shoftim (Judges); Shmuel (I & II Samuel); Melakhim (I & II Kings); Yeshayah (Isaiah); Yirmyah (Jeremiah); Yechezqel (Ezekiel).

The Twelve (treated as one book) which are composed of Hoshea (Hosea); Yoel (Joel); Amos; Ovadyah (Obadiah); Yonah (Jonah); Mikhah

---

[426] Masnawi/volume I/ p.38 Translated from Masnavi Mirkhani (Tehran, 1953)
[427] Lev 10:11

(Micah); Nachum; Chavaqquq (Habbakkuk); Tzefanyah (Zephaniah); Chaggai; Zekharyah (Zechariah); Malakhi.

Kethuvim (The Writings) which are composed of Tehillim (Psalms); Mishlei (Proverbs); Iyov (Job); Shir Ha-Shirim (Song of Songs); Ruth; Eikhah (Lamentations); Qoheleth (the author's name) (Ecclesiastes); Esther; Daniel; Ezra and Nechemyah (Nehemiah) (treated as one book); Divrei Ha-Yamim (The words of the days) (Chronicles).

The New Testament is the second major part of the Christian Biblical canon, the first part being the Old Testament (above). Christians hold different views about the Old Testament from those of the Jews, in that they regard both, the Old and New Testaments, as sacred scripture. The New Testament is an anthology, a collection of Christian works, written at different times by various writers, who were early Jewish disciples of Jesus of Nazareth, in the common Greek language of the first century. In almost all Christian traditions today, the New Testament consists of twenty-seven books. The original texts that were written in the first and perhaps the second centuries of the Christian era are generally believed to be in Koine Greek, which was the common language of the eastern Mediterranean from the time of the conquests of Alexander the Great (335–323 BC) until the evolution of the Byzantine Greek Empire (600 AD). All the works, which were eventually incorporated into the New Testament, seemed to have been written no later than around 150 AD. Collections of related texts such as letters of the Apostle Paul (a major collection, which must have already been formulated by the early second century) and the canonical Gospels of Matthew, Mark, Luke, and John (asserted by Irenaeus of Lyon in the late second century as *the* Four Gospels) were gradually joined with the other collections and single works in various combinations in order to form the various Christian canons of the scripture. In summary, the New Testament consists of:

- four narratives of the life, teaching, death, and resurrection of Jesus, called 'Gospels' or 'good news';

- a narrative of the Apostles' ministries in the early church, called the 'Acts of the Apostles', and probably written by the same writer as the Gospel of Luke, and continuing it;

- twenty-one letters, often called 'epistles' in the Biblical context, written by various authors, and consisting of Christian doctrine, counsel, instruction, and conflict resolution;

- an Apocalypse, the Book of Revelation, which is a book of prophecy, containing some instructions to seven local congregations of Asia Minor, but mostly containing prophetical symbology, about the end of time.

Some scriptural evidences on rocks and stones

Figure 19 - Examples of Alphabets used in Asia Minor and the Middle East

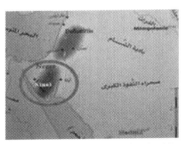

Figure 20 - Carved on rock. Arabic writings with petroglyphs

Figure 21 - Region of Negev Sinai in which the Arabic writings were made

a very old example of Arabic alphabet written on the stone

Figure 22 - Old Arabic on a stone

Figure 23 - Old Arabic on a bone

Figure 24 - Old scriptures in multiple alphabets on Mountain in Negev and Sinai. In Greek, Aramaic, Safaitic, Nabataean, early Arabic. During pre-Islamic period.

Figure 25 - Greek scripture. Harran, South of Syria AD.[428]

Figure 26 - Aramaic language and alphabet North-west of Arabia[429]
Fifth century BC.

Figure 27 - Bosra, Syria. Nabataean scriptures[430]

Figure 28 - Nabataean Script, Umm al-Jamal, Jordan[431].

---

[428] Louvre Museum, France.

[429] Louvre Museum, France.

[430] Inscription in the Nabatean alphabet. South of Syria – Bosra. Louvre Museum

[431] Altar. Inscription to the god Dushara. Mid-first century AD. British Museum.

Figure 29 - Syriac inscription of Edessa – Osrhoene[432]..

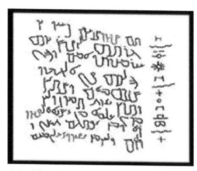

Figure 30 - Text in Nabataean, Pre-Islamic Period.

Figure 31 - Greek text in Negev; Sinai.

---

[432] Healey, John F. and Drijvers, Han J.W. The Old Syriac Inscriptions of Edessa and Osrhoene. 1999. Brill.

Figure 32 - Yemen - The Sabean Language and alphabet, first century AD.
On a bronze plaque.

Figure 33 - Carved stone in Nabataean language and alphabet, Jordan, 36 AD[433].

---

[433] Louvre Museum, France.

Figure 34 - Safaitic alphabet, on a carved stone. South-west of Syria. First century AD.[434]

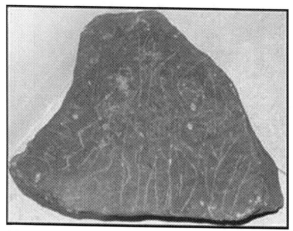

Figure 35 - Safaitic alphabet, South-west of Syria - First century AD[435].

---

[434] Louvre Museum, France.

[435] Louvre Museum, France.

Figure 36 - A multilingual inscription including Greek, Syriac, and Arabic. Zabad. Northern Syria. The third line is in Arabic script, in the Musnad style. 512 AD. [436]

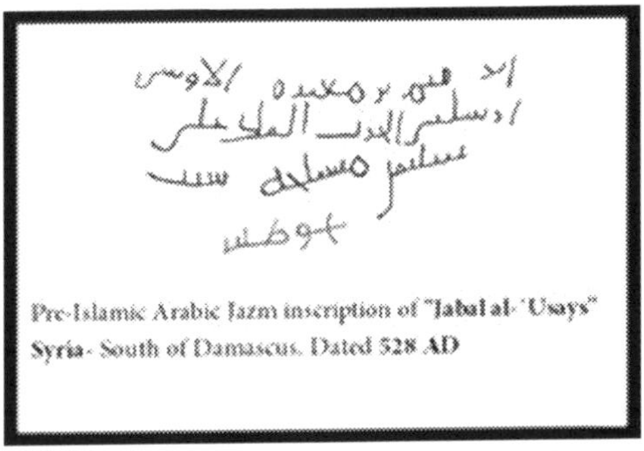

Pre-Islamic Arabic Jazm inscription of "Jabal al-'Usays"
Syria- South of Damascus. Dated 528 AD

Figure 37 - Musnad style Arabic writing

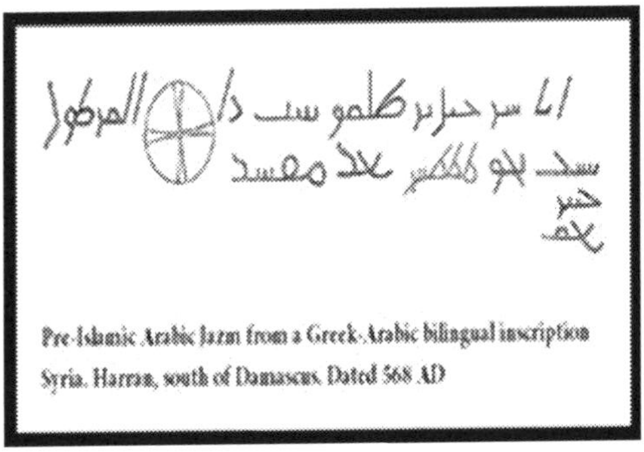

Pre-Islamic Arabic Jazm from a Greek-Arabic bilingual inscription
Syria. Harran, south of Damascus. Dated 568 AD

Figure 38 - Arabic scripture - Jazm style, 568 AD.[437]

---

[436] Pre-Islamic trilingual inscription of Zabad found near Aleppo, Syria, including Syriac (top left), Greek (top right) and Arabic (bottom) scripts. Dated 512 AD. Arabic text is isolated below and traced for clarity.

[437] http://arabetics.com/public/html/more/History%20of%20the%20Arabic%20Script_article.htm

Figure 39 - Arabic language – Nabataean alphabet.
About King Umru'ol Qays, 560 AD.[438]

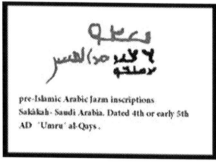

pre-Islamic Arabic Jazm inscriptions
Sakākah- Saudi Arabia. Dated 4th or early 5th
AD 'Umru' al-Qays.

Figure 40 - Arabic language and alphabet.
Sakaka. Saudi Arabia, sixth century AD[439]

Article de Christian Julien Robin. Langues et écritures. Ibid. P.127.

[438] A carved stone about Umru'ol Qays, King of Hira, who died in AD 560. Nabataean alphabet. Arabic language. Louvre Museum.

[439] One of two pre-Islamic Arabic Jazm inscriptions found in Sakākah, Saudi Arabia. Actually Umru'ol Qays was one the most famous kings of the Lakhmid dynasty in the kingdom of Hirah. This kingdom was a marvellous little Arabic civilisation and ally of the Sassanid dynasty. The courageous kings of this kingdom often received the princes of the Sassanid dynasty to teach them literature, poetry, travel in the desert, hunting, riding etc.

Figure 41 - A wooden tablet, al-Lowh, with
Arabic script, Surah 107 from the Quran. West Africa.[440]

24 .AH

سنه اربع و عشرين

زحير

Figure 42 - Arabic stone scripture – Saudi Arabia.Twenty-four after Hegira.
Dated by its scribe signed Zohayr Traditional period between Jazm and old Kufi style
(Yahoudieh-style).

---

[440] British Museum, United Kingdom.

Figure 42 - Kufi petroglyph scriptures with painting441

Figure 43 - The shrine of 'Imamzadeh Ebrahim' on a mountain top.
In the west of present day Iran, in the region of Nahavand, not far from the city of Joudi, is this peculiarly shaped mountain. An old temple existed there which was dedicated to 'Ebrahim'.

---

441 This inscription calls upon God to accept the prayers and fasting of Abd al-Ala Sa'id. It includes an image of a horse and rider with a lance. Found in Wadi Shireh, Jordan. It is dated to the month of Ramadan AH 109/ 727-8 AD. Photo: Robert Hoyland. British Museum.

Figure 44 - Abu Qubays Mountain, in Mecca, just behind the Kabah.
On one of the four walls of the Kabah a black stone named 'Hajar ol Aswad' (Black Stone) is placed. Beside it there is a pillar named Magam-e Ebrahim (Station of Ebrahim). According to an old legend it is said that at the foot of the mountain of Abu Qubays, there existed the tombs of Seth (a son of Adam) and Sem (a son of Noah). Close to these tombs there was a temple, which was restored by Abraham and Esmail to celebrate the memory of the fathers of humanity.

Figure 45 - Dr Seyed Mostafa Azmayesh next to a tomb with Kufi inscription.

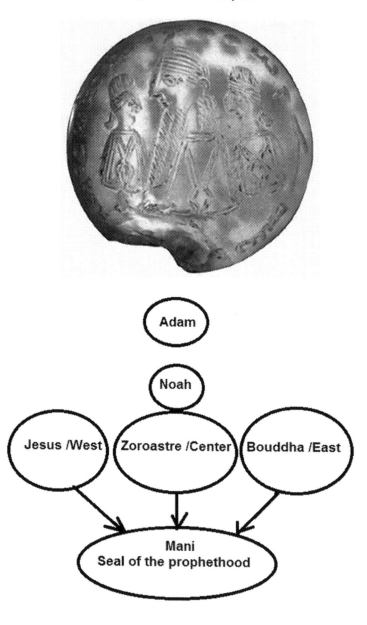

Figure 46 – The Seal of Prophecy of Mani - Bibliothèque nationale de France

List of Figures and Illustrations

Printed in the United States
By Bookmasters